do it for le$$!

The how-to cookbook
and guide to catering
your own party for
12 to 75 guests without
breaking the bank.

parties

Tricks of the trade from a professional caterer's kitchen.

Denise Vivaldo with Cindie Flannigan,
Martha Hopkins, and Andy Sheen-Turner

TERRACE

do it for less!

parties

The how-to cookbook and guide to catering your own party for 12 to 75 guests without breaking the bank.

Tricks of the trade from a professional caterer's kitchen.

Denise Vivaldo with Cindie Flannigan, Martha Hopkins, and Andy Sheen-Turner

TERRACE

Published by Food Fanatics, Inc.
Packaged by Terrace Publishing
Distributed by Terrace Publishing through IPG
Copyright © 2005 Denise Vivaldo, Cindie Flannigan,
Martha Hopkins, and Andrew Sheen-Turner

Editorial and design: Martha Hopkins and Randall Lockridge
Editorial assistant: Kristen Green
Illustrations (pages 1-113): Cindie Flannigan
Menu illustrations and lettering: Lee Newton
Cover photographs: Susan Goldman
Interior photographs (pages 21,33,37,38,48,66, 191, 221): Victor Boghossian
Photograph (page 47): Eric Futran/PictureArts/FoodPix

Printed in China
First Edition
ISBN: 0-9653275-1-5
Library of Congress Control Number: 2004109564

**For wholesale orders to the
book trade, contact**

IPG: Independent Publishers Group
814 North Franklin St.
Chicago, IL 60610
312.337.0747
312.337.5985 fax
800.888.4741 orders only
orders@ipgbook.com
www.ipgbook.com

**For retail orders, review copies,
or interview requests, contact**

Terrace Publishing
2309 Colcord
Waco, TX 76707
254.753.2843
254.753.5350 fax
800.372.2311 toll-free
martha@terracepartners.com
www.terracepublishing.com

To learn more about *Do It for Less! Parties*,
visit www.DIFLParties.com.

10 9 8 7 6 5 4 3 2 1

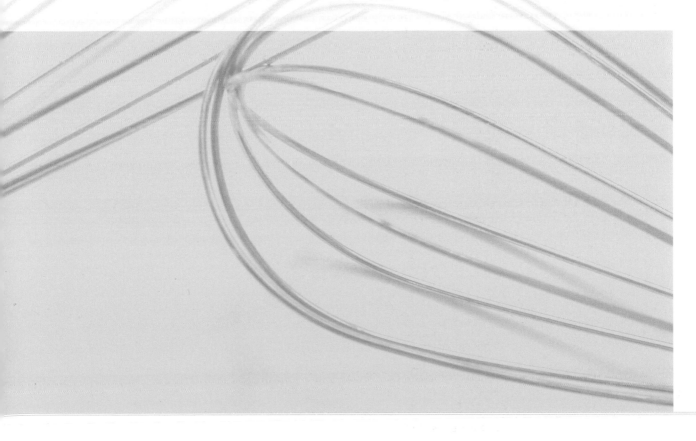

I dedicate my love to the best husband I've ever had, Ken Meyer. –Denise Vivaldo

table of contents

preface

After 20 years as a professional chef and caterer, I've learned how to organize spectacular parties on short notice, cook delicious food on a budget, minimize stress on everyone involved, and still enjoy myself. But I realized through my teaching and cooking demonstrations that not all cooks felt as confident about hosting their own parties.

Everywhere I went, people asked me questions about entertaining. How much time would it take? How much money would they have to spend? How could they cook for more than eight guests? Is any party really worth all the effort?

Of course it's worth it! Parties are the gift of celebrating life's grand moments, both big and small. Whether you want to host a baby shower, a second wedding, or have the in-laws over for your first Thanksgiving, you'll find memorable meals of all sorts in *Do It For Less! Parties*.

I know most people are just plain scared to entertain, and rightly so, if they've had little experience in entertaining. For years I've wanted to write a book that bridged the gap between the professional caterer and the home entertainer. Now, I'm thrilled to finally be able to share with people the hundreds of tips I have gathered and tucked away through my years of experience about recipes, party favors, and décor planning. (It's amazing what you learn after producing 10,000 parties and events.)

With *Do It For Less! Parties*, we've worked hard to make entertaining a manageable affair for everyone, from beginners to seasoned entertainers. The first half of the book gives you the tools you'll need to plan your own party, and the second half gives you twice-tested, dependable recipes that take all the guesswork out of quantity cooking. This book will show you how to apply the same professional party techniques to your own event that helped me manage a successful catering business, and teach you how to save time, money, and energy in the process.

So, let me introduce you to this terrific book and also to Cindie Flannigan and Martha Hopkins. Had Cindie and Martha not devoted their time and research to this book, it would never have happened. It took a village of chefs—and illustrators, photographers, designers, and editors—to capture it all in one carefully crafted volume, and I know you will enjoy the organization and ease it brings to your next party. Please e-mail us your successful entertaining stories at info@diflparties.com. We want to hear from you!

Denise Vivaldo

let's get this
party started!

SO YOU WANT TO THROW A PARTY?

There are umpteen reasons to throw a party: birthdays, weddings, baby showers, bridal showers, bar mitzvahs, bat mitzvahs, new jobs, leaving jobs, family get-togethers, holidays, new homes, relocating—or just because you enjoy good friends, great food, and entertaining.

No matter what your reason, making the event a fully themed affair or adding little touches here and there transforms the normal "chips, dips, coats here, bathroom there, have a drink, thanks for coming" party into something much more entertaining. We want to show you how to do it all for less time and less money. Whether you're throwing an over-the-top extravaganza or just a simple chili night, the basics of hosting a good party remain the same. This chapter gives a brief overview of all the things you'll need to consider when developing a party. We discuss brainstorming for ideas and bringing a theme to life in every detail of the party. Most importantly, though, we provide the guidelines for developing a budget. This book is not called *Do It for Less!* for nothing. We want to share our secrets for shaving costs and working efficiently on large parties, and give you the tools, recipes, and confidence you need for success with your own events.

hosting advice

The first thing you need to do is relax. Sadly, the very idea of hosting a party causes some people to panic. How often have you heard a host remark, "I'm so nervous—guest X is such a good cook" or "I hope everyone likes the way the house looks"? Enough misplaced worries! You are inviting people into *your* home to eat *your* food, drink *your* wine, and have a pleasant evening. Even a world-renowned chef would be happy to be invited to a party where he or she doesn't have to cook or plan anything. Being invited to a party is a treat, a night away from the stove, something to look forward to and enjoy. So, relax—your guests will be happy to be there. And remember—*you*, not *they*, will be your harshest critic.

MAKING LISTS AND LOTS OF 'EM!

Lists are indispensable for a smoothly flowing party. Everyone forgets things; have a place to jot down those last-minute ideas or errands. There is something very satisfying about crossing off items as you complete them. Here are the "do it for less" must-have lists for a great party:

- **Guest List.** Use this as a guide when sending invitations and thank-you cards, planning a menu, and making seating arrangements.

- **Grocery List.** See page 64 for tips on writing a fail-safe grocery list.

- **Beverage and Bar List.** See page 87 for estimating beverage needs.

- **Food To-Do List.** This should include all make-ahead preparation plus all those last-minute details that can sometimes get overlooked, like bringing the butter to room temperature so that it is spreadable.

- **Party To-Do List.** This should be in a convenient place where you can quickly add anything that comes to mind, from making sure you buy extra trash-can liners to hosing down the driveway.

- **Emergency Numbers List.** This should include numbers for the police and fire departments, the nearest hospital, a reliable taxi service, and 24-hour plumbers and electricians.

MORE BANG FOR YOUR BUCK

Having a budget and sticking to it will prevent you from having to refinance your home just to throw a party. We are all guilty of getting too excited or anxious about entertaining, which ultimately leads to overspending. What starts out as an intimate, simple dinner party for eight friends can grow and grow—and so can the expenses. Before you know it, you have a different bottle of wine for each course, you're up until 2 a.m. the night before making party favors, and a man in a white tuxedo is at the front door wanting to know where he can set up the baby grand. When the party is finally over, you realize it would have been cheaper to take everyone out to a nice restaurant.

so how do you create a budget?

The first step is to decide how much you can afford and how much you want to spend. Write this amount at the top of a sheet of paper. Aim to stay within this limit without going over. As you read through the book and develop your own party plan, keep all these budgetary components in mind.

You can tailor any extravagant idea to fit even a modest budget with a bit of creativity and ingenuity.

What should be included in your budget? It depends on the type of party you are giving, but it can include some or all of the following:

- Invitations, including postage.

- Location rental fee.

- Food.

- Beverages, including alcohol and bar.

- Caterer.

- Specialty cakes.

- Rentals, including such things as tents, tables, chairs, linens, flatware, plates, and glasses.

- Disposable goods, including such things as plastic glasses, plates, and napkins.

- Decorations and party favors.

List the ones that apply to you on the same sheet of paper as your budget amount. Do some price-checking and come up with a projected cost for each item. When in doubt, overestimate the cost. Total the amounts, and then add an extra 10 percent for any extras that you may have forgotten. What do you do if your budget is $500 and the final total is $655? Well, you could cut down the number of guests (do your in-laws really have to come?), or you could trim costs elsewhere.

Use our sample budget worksheet on the right as a guideline for outlining your party expenses. See page 54 for more help with menu budgeting, and add items that are specific to your type of party as needed.

budget worksheet

Item	Cost per Item	Quantity	Total Cost
Invitations			
Postage			
Appetizers			
Soup/salad			
Entrée			
Side #1			
Side #2			
Dessert			
Soda/juice/water			
Wine			
Beer			
Coffee/tea			
Ice			
Tabletops			
Tablecloths			
Napkins			
Plates			
Glasses			
Cups/saucers			
Flatware			
Serving pieces			
Ice buckets			
Flowers			
Centerpieces			
Balloons			
Furniture			
Tableware			
Location			
Music/band/DJ			
Games/prizes			
Party favors			
Valet			
Tips			
Miscellaneous			
Tax			
		Final Cost	

DEVELOPING A PARTY PLAN

be inspired

Inspiration is everywhere. If, in your mind's eye, a clambake can only be held on a veranda in Cape Cod with guests dressed in white and navy linen, think again. Find a way to make extravagant ideas fit into both your budget and your lifestyle. Magazines like *Bon Appétit, Country Living, Martha Stewart Living, InStyle, O, Real Simple,* and *Vanity Fair* often have seasonal articles loaded with new twists on casual and elegant social affairs alike. Use them to spark your imagination and spur fresh ideas for a one-of-a-kind party.

Also, take a walk through your local party store. Many an idea has come to mind just from wandering along the aisles. For example, some oversized playing cards can lead to a game night party with Twister tablecloths, place cards spelled out in Scrabble letters, and giant dice used as centerpieces.

Maybe the inspiration is right under your nose. If you collect something, you could base the party around your collection. Here are some "show off your collection" party ideas:

- **Cookie jars.** Have a "hand in the cookie jar" dessert party and fill each jar with a different cookie, candy, brownie, or cupcake. Fill one with oversized lollipops or flowers for a centerpiece.

- **Elvis and friends.** If you're an obsessed fan, embrace your inner movie star and throw a party in honor of your favorite celebrity. You can dress the part and serve all their favorite foods. For an Elvis party, for instance, you could order his trademark sunglasses to use as both place card holders and party favors. Serve peanut butter and banana finger sandwiches, miniature Hawaiian hamburgers, cherry soda, and more twists on his old favorites. Use your velvet Elvis as a tablecloth or a backdrop to the buffet. Play Elvis hits from start to finish, and rent a karaoke machine to keep the party rolling late into the night.

- **Photographs, postcards, and greetings cards.** For a wedding anniversary, birthday, or high school reunion, display your collection of photographs on a table and protect them with a sheet of glass or clear Plexiglass. The same idea would also work for a "foods from around the world" party, where you could display a collection of postcards, postage stamps, or menus you have acquired.

- **Pitchers, teapots, tureens, and trophies.** A simple but effective way to utilize these collections is to lay down a table runner and position the items on top. Fill one with flowers, one with breadsticks, one with cookies, and one with folded napkins.

- **Seashells.** Beach lovers take note: You can put all those shells you've collected every summer to good use. Decorate the table in a sandy-white sheer, and top with starfish and mother-of-pearl shells. Arrange a variety of cream-white pillar candles in glass bowls and pour in white sand to stabilize the pillars. Use a raw silk runner for a splash of ocean blue throughout your otherwise all-white theme.

If you do not have a collection of anything, use a single item to set a theme. Take daisies: You can cut an invitation in the shape of a daisy from yellow card stock, or write the invitation on a postcard and glue it to a packet of daisy seeds. Use bunches of daisies in vases to adorn the table, or cut the stems off several bundles and tuck the flower heads around your serving trays in bunches. Rest the place cards against bud vases with a single daisy, which then becomes the party favor. Serve daisy-shaped cookies for dessert. Without too much thought, you have created a theme for a children's party or a bridal shower. This can work with any flower.

Still need inspiration? Choose from some of these themes: Asian, Tuscan, Moroccan, black and white (or other monochromatic look), beach or luau, indoor/outdoor picnic, western barbecue, costume, high tea, decade (1950s, for example), cooking, masked ball, tailgate, sushi and sake, movie and TV-inspired (*Star Wars, Rocky Horror Picture Show, I Love Lucy*), Mardi Gras, poolside, retro, pasta, disco, safari/jungle, south of the border, toga, hillbilly, gothic, Greek, girls' night out, karaoke, pajama, wine and cheese, all chocolate, all dessert, or fondue.

Invitations

Guests love to get invitations in the mail, and sending eye-catching invitations will get everyone excited about your upcoming party. Set the tone for the party with the first impression: a creative, thoughtful, *inviting* invitation.

If you and your guests have access to the Internet, an easy way to invite people is to use an online service and send virtual invitations. Of course, not everyone is computer savvy, in which case mailed invitations are a better bet. You can buy invitations or make them yourself. See page 228 in our Resource Guide for more on all types of invitations.

Handwritten invitations are the definitive personal touch. They will save you printing costs, but not necessarily time. Making your own invitations can set a distinctive stage for your party. Unique designs and clever wording create an invitation that guests will keep as a treasured memento long after the party is over.

You can purchase plain note cards and envelopes at an office supply or paper store and decorate them according to the theme of your party. Coordinate the look of your invitations with menu cards, napkin rings, or party favors by using extra fabric you have on hand. If you have the time to hand-deliver your invitations, you do not have to make them fit into envelopes. For a graduation party, for example, you could buy gold-bordered certificate paper from an office supply store and print your invitations to look like diplomas. Roll them up and secure with a fancy ribbon, and hand-deliver or mail in a tube.

party favors

- **Mulling spices.** Cut a 10 by 5-inch rectangle of cotton cheesecloth and fold it in half to create a 5-inch square. Place a small bay leaf, a stick of cinnamon broken into small pieces, four whole cloves, three whole allspice, a strip of dried lemon peel, and two strips of dried orange peel in the center of the cheesecloth. Gather the corners together and tie with cotton twine. This is a great party favor for the holidays. Include a hand-made tag with the person's name and directions for using the spices.

- **Organza gift bags.** These inexpensive and beautiful sheer fabric bags can be found at craft and gift stores. Fill them with candy, sugared almonds, bath salts, or potpourri.

- **Travel kits.** For a bridal shower, fill inexpensive plastic make-up bags from your local drug store with travel-size essentials like nail polish remover, lip gloss, Q-tips, and hand lotion.

- **Mini picture frames.** If you have a Polaroid camera, take a photo of each guest as he or she arrives at your party. Before the night is over, slip each photo into a small, inexpensive frame and place in a gift bag for each guest to take home.

- **Frisbees.** For a picnic or barbecue, give each of your guests a Frisbee. They are cheap and fun for all ages, and Fido likes them too.

- **Candles.** For an anniversary or special dinner, give your guests a small votive candle wrapped in a piece of tulle. Secure with a piece of ribbon for an inexpensive, yet elegant favor.

- **Fun-in-the-sun gifts.** If you are having a beach party or luau, send your guests home with a fun-in-the-sun gift. Roll a travel-size tube of sunscreen, protective lip balm, and a small bottle of water in a small towel.

- **Garden-to-go.** Make your centerpieces into party favors. If you have eight guests at one table, have eight small terracotta flowerpots with a flower or herb planted in each. Tie a gingham ribbon around each pot. Arrange the pots in a circle in the center of the table, with the one in the center on a small platform so it sits higher than the others. Or, fill 4-inch terracotta pots with packets of seeds, paperwhite or hyacinth bulbs, and a small container of plant food. If you have the time, buy a large bag of potting soil and fill resealable plastic storage bags to put in the pot with the bulbs. You can even write guests' names on the pots and use them as place cards. After the party, hand out one pot to each guest. The blooms will be a reminder of the party.

- **Child's play.** For children, forgo the candy and instead fill a small plastic bucket with things they can play with—stickers, crayons, yo-yos, small coloring books, play jewelry, or modeling clay.

- **Bird's-eye view.** When partying among close friends or at a birthday, give each guest her own disposable camera and prepay for the film to be developed. Wrap it with a small photo album, and at the next party, invite everyone to bring back her album to share.

- **Simply chic.** Place a gardenia at each place setting with a corsage pin. The flowers will scent the room and make for delicate corsages and boutonnieres for your guests.

- **Edible name cards.** Write each guest's name on a big sugar cookie with cake decorating gel. Prop the cookie next to the guest's water glass for a delicious seating guide. Write each guest's name on a small strip of paper and slip the end of the paper in a chocolate-covered fortune cookie. Handmade truffles make for a special gift, dessert, or party favor as well. When making the truffles, slightly flatten the bottom and make a slit in the top to use as a place card holder. For more information on truffles, see page 137.

flowers

Floral arrangements can be costly, especially for a wedding or large event. Consider ordering just one or two arrangements from a florist for the most prominent places and making the centerpiece arrangements for the tables yourself. They can be made the day before it stored in a cool place overnight. Here are some "do it for less" tips for successful flower arranging:

- **Homegrown.** Do you have flowers in your garden you can use? If not flowers, do you have a bush or tree with great leaves that can be used for filler? Check out the local farmers' market just before closing time for great deals on flowers.

- **Pruning and preserving.** Remove any foliage that will be under the water line and cut the stems on an angle. Use warm water and add fresh-cut flower food, available from your florist, to prolong the life of the arrangement.

- **Stay put.** When trying to arrange and secure branches, grasses, and bamboo stalks, mold a square of chicken wire across the top of the vase to hold the stems in place.

- **Short and sweet.** It is much easier to make short arrangements than to make tall ones. An easy arranging trick is to hold the flowers tightly together in a small bouquet, then cut all the stems so they are an even length and arrange in the vase. If you're unsure about what flowers will work, take the vase along to a florist and ask for advice.

- **In season.** Cut flowers such as sunflowers or lilies always say "summer." Arrange them in small galvanized vases or buckets for a rustic display. For an alternative, use an empty and cleaned coffee can with the label removed. Tie with a bow of raffia or paint the cans in bright primary colors to complement the flowers. This will also work with empty jam or mason jars.

- **Color safe.** If you are overwhelmed by the sheer choice and variety of flowers, try sticking to one type and color. An all-white arrangement will work with almost any décor.

- **A plant in every pot.** Potted flowering plants also work well for tabletop décor. Hyacinth, azaleas, and chrysanthemums make some popular choices. No need to re-pot them; just place the plant in an inexpensive terracotta pot that is slightly larger than the plastic pot in which it was purchased. Plant the arrangements after the party or give them away as favors.

- **Tweaking.** Turn back the petals of tulips or roses to give the flowers a more open, airy look.

- **Vases and containers.** Use clear vases or containers that have narrow necks and wide bases. This way you only need a minimum number of stems to fill them. Fill a glass vase with cherries, pebbles, or thick slices of lemons and limes to help keep the flowers in place and add another dimension to the floral arrangement.

entertainment

There is nothing like having a live band at your party. There is nothing like having a *bad* live band at your party. You can select a band from word-of-mouth referrals or from a booking agent found in your local yellow pages. Try and see the band play live if you can. You will be able to judge whether their music will be compatible with your guests and how well the band members interact with the audience. If that is not possible, then ask for a demo tape and client referrals. Any professional band should have a demo tape, photo, and press kit available. For most live bands, the more musicians and the longer they play, the greater the cost. Suddenly that one-man band sounds very tempting! Be aware, too, that bands bill weekends and holidays at higher rates than normal.

Musicians typically break up the evening into sets with a short intermission in between. If you want continuous music, you must inform the musicians beforehand. There may be an extra charge if you want the band to play continuously, so you may prefer playing recorded music during the breaks to save some money.

You should decide exactly how long you want the band to play. If you expect the musicians to play beyond the agreed time, they should be paid overtime, usually in half-hour increments.

The band will need time to set up the equipment and possibly run a sound check before the guests arrive. If you are renting a location, make arrangements for them to get into the venue early. It is customary to feed and tip the band, but it is totally up to you. If you are not providing them with dinner, you should let them know ahead of time.

One of the most popular choices for entertainment is a DJ. With a good DJ you can avoid out-of-tune, would-be lounge singers. Instead, you can expect a fairly compact equipment set-up with a selection of music you want to hear. As with a band, word-of-mouth referrals or the yellow pages are easy ways to find a good DJ. Another excellent resource is the American Disc Jockey Association, a non-profit organization that will help you find an approved DJ in your area. (See page 229 for more information.) All the DJs in the association are fully insured, have experience, carry back-up equipment in case of technical difficulties, and are very versatile and punctual.

Some DJs just play music with a little chitchat in between, while others can emcee and provide full entertainment with games, light shows, and props to accompany different songs. You should dictate beforehand the level of interaction that you want between DJ and guests. Also suggest a play list, giving guidelines as to what you want and do not want to hear. Usually you will be able to select the CDs from their inventory list. If it is a formal affair, then ask him or her to be dressed appropriately. As with a band, you will need to allow time for set-up and breakdown.

The cheapest and simplest form of entertainment is playing a few CDs on your own audio system to create ambiance at your party. Try to be diplomatic and reserved in your choices, and select music to match the mood. For a sit-down dinner party, soft classical or jazz sets a nice tone, as guests will not have to compete with the lyrics of a song when trying to hold a conversation. To find the perfect music for your theme, visit any number of music download websites. You can burn your own party mix from their vast music libraries that include everything from Celtic bagpipes to authentic Hawaiian. (See the Resource Guide on page 229 for specific sites.)

valet parking

First impressions are lasting impressions. At larger events, the guests' first encounter is usually with the valet parking attendant, so it is important to make this first moment as pleasant as possible to help set the tone of the party. If you are going to need valet parking service for your event, then opt for a professional valet company. This is one of the few exceptions where things are best left up to the professionals. Resist the temptation to have a friend or a neighbor park the guests' cars, regardless of your friend's perfect driving record.

The number one question to ask any valet service is, "Are you and all of your drivers fully insured, licensed, and bonded?" Ask to see proof or a copy of the insurance policy. Do the employees receive any formal training, and are all driving records checked as part of the hiring procedure?

Select a company that has been in business for at least three years, and ask for references from previous clients. Make follow-up calls to check out the references. Ask the previous clients if the valets were courteous, appropriately dressed, and prompt with car returns. Inquire if any vehicles sustained damage.

Insist on meeting with a representative from the company at the party site. This will help to verify parking lots, possible location problems, and the need for any additional equipment, such as traffic cones, signs, and guide ropes.

Discuss the duration of the event and the approximate finish time, and give an accurate headcount of expected guests. You don't want to end up short-handed, but you certainly don't want to pay for extra drivers either. Many companies "stagger" their employees, which means as the evening slows down, the valet parking crew will thin out. Make sure that if you say the party is going to end between midnight and 12:30 a.m. that it does. If it unexpectedly goes until 2 a.m., you may have only a skeleton crew of valets trying to retrieve all of the cars at once.

It is becoming more and more popular for the host to have the valet service leave a party favor or gift such as a Sunday newspaper and fresh croissants in each guest's car. If you plan to do this as a party favor, discuss it with the valet company before the party. Most companies will be happy to oblige, while others may charge a fee. It is appropriate to feed the valet attendants a meal and offer them a non-alcoholic drink during the 5 to 6 hours that they will be working.

party locations

HOSTING AT HOME

Ah, the perfect vision of entertaining . . . your house is spotless, the wine is chilling, the weather is warm—but not too hot. The aroma of baked Brie wafts through the air, and, yes, at exactly 7:31 p.m., ding-dong, the doorbell rings and the first guests arrive at what is to be the event of the year.

Now the not-so perfect vision . . . at 8:30 a.m. the following morning, you are on your hands and knees trying to get that red wine stain out of your new Berber carpet. When you walk into your bathroom, you are greeted by an emergency-on-call, $100-an-hour plumber's crack as he lovingly snakes your toilet that, unfortunately, could not handle the attention of 100 guests. You could do with a drink, but then you remember someone took the last bottles of wine as a parting gift.

Okay, maybe it's not that bad, but there are certain hazards to having a party at home. A few easy precautions can save a lot of stress and money:

- **Breakables.** If your guests are likely to spring to their feet at the opening bars of the "Macarena" and you anticipate lots of dancing, remove all breakables and delicate items before the guests arrive. Common items that may be damaged include table lamps, picture frames, candle holders, glass and porcelain anything, and, of course, potted plants, whose soil will be strewn everywhere by the party's end.

- **Privacy.** If you have a special attachment to a certain piece of furniture or carpet and you think that throwing a tarp over it may offend your guests, either move it to another room or close the door and hang a polite sign that says "private area."

- **Clogged pipes.** Have your toilet snaked before the party, especially if you expect a lot of guests. Better to spend $40 now than to risk having to spend hundreds of dollars to call an emergency plumber during the party.

- **Toiletries.** Stock the bathroom with plenty of paper napkins, tissues, and toilet paper. Provide a trash can, and check on it every hour to make sure it doesn't get too full. Using a pump dispenser for soap will keep the sink area cleaner than using bar soap. A scented votive candle burning in the bathroom makes for a nice touch as long as it is checked often. It is, however, dangerous to leave an unattended candle burning anywhere.

- **Neighbors.** As a courtesy to your neighbors, alert them to your upcoming party. Invite them to stop by if it's appropriate. They are less likely to be annoyed by your guests' parked cars, loud music, or any other inconveniences if they're part of the fun.

- **Garbage.** Make sure your trash cans and recycling containers will be as empty as possible before the big day. Set up a recycling system at the party with each trash can labeled "glass and cans" or "paper only." Not only will this help to alleviate a mountain of trash, but you will also be helping the environment. If you run out of space for trash cans, double-bagged, heavy-duty trash liners are a great alternative that should last until trash day. Put a few extra trash bags in the bottom of a trash can before lining it. This way you can replace the bag quickly and have it back in working order immediately. Do not let trash cans become too full. They look unsightly, and trash bags can burst when you change them.

BACKYARD PARTIES

One alternative to having hordes of people stampede through your house is to hold the party in your backyard. This works well if **a)** the weather is warm enough, **b)** your backyard is large enough, and **c)** you have a backyard. Your guests will still have to use the house bathroom, but you'll have much less indoor traffic.

Outdoor dining is generally casual, so don't worry if your yard looks nothing like a botanical garden. If you can't get your garden landscaped or spend a lot on décor for your backyard party, here are a couple of ideas to enhance the mood:

- **Plant rentals.** Find out if your local party rental company or nursery rents out trees. Huge ficus trees are not necessary; large shrubs or 3 to 4-foot trees will do. Use them to create areas, make dividers, and hide unsightly spots. Strategically placed, shrubs and trees can create the illusion of a lushly landscaped yard.

- **Ferns.** Boston ferns are also great fillers. Inexpensive and very showy, they can be hung or placed on walls and tables for a green accent.

- **Blooms.** Flowers really add a summery feel, but there's no need to spend a fortune. If you are lucky enough to have flowers in your garden, cut small bunches or individual stems and place them in several small bud vases. Group the vases together or place them in a row along the middle of the table. If you don't own bud vases, you can use shot glasses. Just don't use heavily scented flowers that will overwhelm the flavors of your food.

- **Furniture rentals.** If you do not own enough tables and chairs, they can be rented for a minimal fee. Most rental companies waive the minimum order fee if you pick up and return the rentals yourself.

- **Picnic.** No tables or chairs? Throw blankets or tablecloths straight on the grass and scatter with pillows for a picnic feel.

- **Classic cloths.** Plastic red-and-white-checked tablecloths give a classic outdoor look and are available in most grocery stores. Some even come with elastic edges to form-fit the table. If not, be sure to tape or staple them to the underside of the tables if it's a little breezy, or use tablecloth weights.

Having your party at night will hide a multitude of backyard sins. A bare wall twinkling with the Christmas lights from your attic will be instantly transformed from "whatever" to "wow." Place a small card table in front of the lit wall, drape with a tablecloth, place a tub full of ice on top, and use the table for an illuminated, self-serve drink station. Twinkle lights also work well in trees, along the lawn to make a path to the eating area, or taped to the underside of a market umbrella. Plastic-hose twinkle lights are ideal for placing on the ground.

No twinkle lights? The next best things are votive candles used with glass holders so the wind won't blow out the flame. You can purchase votives and holders in bulk at restaurant supply, craft, and club stores. If you are using votives, invest in a long-stemmed lighter or long fireplace matches to make lighting easier. Remember: it takes a long time to light a hundred votive candles, so start lighting before the guests arrive.

If you feel that this is all too overwhelming and the party you've planned isn't going to work in your studio apartment or your miniscule balcony, then maybe you should consider moving the party to another location.

tablecloth weights

These handy items for outdoor parties are often overlooked. By keeping tablecloths from blowing up onto food, weights keep tablecloths looking neat. You can quickly and easily make weights for your next party with wooden clothespins, which can be purchased at craft supply stores, where you can also find supplies to decorate the clothespins. For example, you can use small, painted wooden ladybugs, cacti, stars, and Christmas trees to hot-glue onto the clothespins. You can paint the clothespins any color you like to complement your décor. For a fancier party, for instance, we painted our clothespins black and hot-glued plastic gems and small satin bows onto them. For a barbecue, we left the clothespins in their natural state, glued on a small button in the shape of a chicken, and tied a bow around them with twine. For a garden party, we cut flowers out of felt. For a holiday party, we filled a hollow, plastic ornament with sparkly gold ribbon and tied the ornament to the clothespin with more festive ribbon. You can fill plastic ornaments with shells, sand, marbles, coins, or candy. And don't be afraid to let your kids get in on the decorating activities.

LOCATION, LOCATION, LOCATION!

The number-one rule for parties in another location is to visit the site before the party. And by "before" we do not mean the day before. You will want time to assess any problems that may arise, such as parking, access for guests and staff, workspace for kitchen or catering staff, sufficient amenities, and any necessary permits that may be required. Consider these alternatives for party locations:

free locations

- **Friend's home**. Maybe you have a close friend or relative who has a fabulous home or yard and would be only too happy to let you throw your party on her property. As an incentive, offer to pay for a maid service to come to the house the day after for a professional clean-up. Consider the deal closed when you hear the words, "I insist; consider it my gift." You should repay this kind gesture with a thank-you gift of flowers, your best homemade jam, a gift certificate to a favorite store, or a day of massage and pampering at a spa.

- **Local park**. Another popular freebie is a local park. Usually in a convenient location, parks have all the basic necessities: picnic tables and benches, bathrooms, plenty of space, trash cans, and lots of trees for shade. Some even have barbecue grills, so all you need to bring is the charcoal.

  If your local park is a popular place for a party, consider sending out a scout a few hours before to stake out a plot. Outline your designated area with balloons and brightly colored bunting. Please be considerate of other park users. Don't cordon off the whole park, and leave the "keep out" signs at home.

- **Beach**. The beach has always been a favorite and, most importantly, free party location. Plenty of shade is a must. If your budget doesn't stretch to include a canopy, ask each guest to bring a beach umbrella. The different colors and sizes will make your party look very festive. You can incorporate swimming, boogie boarding, Frisbee throwing, kite flying, sand-castle building, and even limbo dancing into the party, if you wish. Stock up on plenty of sunscreen, water, and towels for your guests, and urge them to apply sunscreen regularly, especially after swimming. Check with your local fire department for rules and regulations, as some states prohibit alcohol, barbecues, bonfires, and fireworks on their beaches. Also, check with the lifeguard station for surf conditions and high tide times.

- **Rooftop.** If you live in a city and crave the great outdoors, consider throwing a rooftop party. Some apartment buildings have rooftop garden areas designated specifically for residents' use. Of course, consideration for neighbors and permission from the resident committee, landlord, or owner is a must.

- **Block party.** The classic block party takes advantage of a great free location. As well as inspiring a sense of community in the neighborhood, it keeps the festivities close to home, simplifying the logistics of setting up and taking down. You usually need permission and a permit from your local permits and regulations department.

rental locations

When renting a location, always insist upon a rental agreement. It should cover fees, deposit, hours of rental—including set-up and clean-up time for caterers and bartenders—and insurance coverage. If one of your guests accidentally breaks a piece of art in the gallery you have rented, who is responsible for the breakage? Are your guests covered for any injury that may occur on the property? All these details should be outlined in the rental agreement. Any additional insurance should be negotiated and included in the rental fee. And remember, renting a location out of season can be much less expensive.

- **On the water.** If you live near water, you can rent a boat—not an ocean liner and not an inflatable dinghy, but a riverboat, small or large yacht, pontoon, barge, ferry, or something big enough to accommodate your guests comfortably. Some of these boats may or may not be seaworthy, but you will be surprised by how many dry-docked vessels are for rent at reasonable prices. Check with the dock masters at local marinas for information. If you feel adventurous, rent a self-drive boat and turn the party into a river cruise. Not everyone has sturdy sea legs, so check with guests before planning a party on the water and setting sail. You may want to buy motion sickness tablets or patches and pass them out to your guests on a silver tray.

- **Place of worship.** Depending on the type of event you're throwing, the local church hall may be appropriate for your party, especially if you are a member of the congregation. Most religious institutions welcome the extra income or donation, especially if the hall is empty on the day you plan to hold your party. Many church halls have tables, chairs, and sometimes kitchen and parking facilities. Even though your party will not be in the sanctuary itself, approach the religious administrator only if the event you plan to hold is suitable and respectful of church-owned property. Ladies' high-tea or a child's birthday party, yes, bachelor party or rave, no.

- **Art gallery.** If you plan to hold a cocktail party or corporate event, contact art galleries in your area. Many gallery owners are very open to holding events, as it brings in potential customers. At most galleries, seating is at a minimum, so this location works well for meet-and-greet parties where guests will be standing only for an hour or so.

- **Coffee house.** A fun place to hold an intimate party can be your local coffee house. If you have an independently owned coffee bar in your area, ask if you could rent it on a slow mid-week evening or after hours. Throw a coffee and dessert party with everything provided in-house. Hire their expert cappuccino maker for the night, and either pass out the desserts or set up a simple buffet.

- **Botanical gardens.** Botanical gardens make a great location for off-season parties. Even during the fall or winter months when many plants and flowers are out of bloom, you'll still find lots of color and textures. Some gardens have special event areas with waterfalls, lanais, or gazebos. Also, check for after-hours deals during the spring and summer.

- **Country club or hotel.** If you have a bigger budget, you might consider a country club or hotel. They have excellent grounds and facilities for weddings and larger events. They will usually provide everything from parking and professional event planners to party favors, all for a fee. Be aware that most of these locations insist that you use their catering facilities and staff as part of the deal. Country clubs and hotels charge high prices for a full-service affair, but, with everything covered and included in one price, you are paying for the convenience.

restaurant parties

For a successful company party, restaurants always make a good choice. It could be the one you frequent for lunch, a favorite choice of the birthday person in your office, or a well-reviewed restaurant you have been eager to try.
These "do it for less" tips will get you started:

- **Negotiate.** Work out a deal with the special events or catering manager. A 15 percent service charge may be applied to your total bill. You may think this is a little high, but this may be cheaper than renting equipment and having it delivered.

- **Careful menu selection.** Plan a menu that is cost effective for the restaurant. If necessary, speak with the chef to find out about upcoming seasonal specials.

- **Shave costs.** If the menu has eaten up most of your budget, propose bringing your own wine and bottled water. There might be a small corkage fee for the waiter to open and serve your wine. Check around for price breaks if buying wine by the case. Save money by bringing your own centerpieces, party favors, and after-dinner chocolates.

- **Valet.** For a special touch, arrange pre-paid valet parking for guests if your budget allows.

- **Pre-arranged seating.** Designate seating by having place cards that take the guesswork out of who sits where.

- **Capture the moment.** A picture says a thousand words, so invest in a few disposable cameras. Have them on every table, and designate a camera wrangler to collect them at the end of the party. Display the photographs in a collage at the office until next year's company party.

ways to party

TO BUFFET OR NOT TO BUFFET?

If space is an issue, you may want to consider buffet-style service. A buffet can be set up in one room with the tables and chairs set up in a different room. Ideally, the buffet should be as close to the kitchen as possible to make replenishing the food easier. Try not to set up close to any area that you anticipate will be busy (next to the bar or near frequently used doors) to avoid congestion. Never block exterior doors or a potential fire exit. If space permits, allow the buffet to be free-standing and away from a wall to allow access from both sides and to create a smooth flow of guest traffic. If need be, remove any unnecessary furniture and breakables. A single 6 to 8-foot buffet should be large enough to accommodate up to fifty guests. If you feel at home in the kitchen, but feel at a complete loss when it comes to arranging a buffet, don't despair. Your buffet can look as good as your food by following only a few simple guidelines.

choosing tablecloths

Make sure the tablecloth is the correct size—not only for the top surface, but also for the drop if you need it to drape all the way to the floor. Don't lessen the ambience of an elegant evening with unsightly metal table legs peeking out from under a too-short tablecloth. Once the tablecloth is in place, box it for a tailored look. (See page 53 for more information on tablecloth sizes and boxing instructions.)

reaching new heights

For a dramatic look, create height on the buffet by elevating the food. Place a riser or pedestal on the tablecloth, and then cover it with another piece of cloth or fabric. The riser should be something sturdy like bricks, small crates, empty boxes, upturned baking pans, chafing dish inserts, telephone books, or even stacks of paper plates. Decorative risers need not be covered. Glass bricks,

available from building supply stores, create both height and ambiance when illuminated from behind with votive candles. You can make your own risers by covering or painting empty coffee cans. For very inexpensive risers, use upturned terracotta flowerpots.

For safety's sake, elevate cool or room-temperature food only and resist the temptation to build too high.

the focal point

A classic buffet may have a centerpiece of flowers or an ice sculpture. This works if you have plenty of space on your table. If buffet space is tight, consider using several smaller flower arrangements and stagger them at different heights using risers. Or have the florist make a garland-style arrangement and snake it through the buffet. Flowers can also be placed behind the buffet, on stands, or even suspended, if space permits. Use lemon greens, Hawaiian leis, clumps of grapes, small apples and pears, twinkle lights, chile peppers strung on twine—anything that fits the theme of your event.

For a thrifty alternative to flowers, use baskets of beautifully arranged bread, fruit, or vegetables. Save the produce to use the next day.

Fill a clear glass bowl with water and float three gardenias for a simple centerpiece. Gardenias will stand out best against a dark-colored or black tablecloth.

Pillar candles or candelabras set at different levels will add a sense of drama to your table. Group different types of candlesticks: short with tall, crystal with brass, silver with ceramic. Use similarly colored candles to tie them together. Allow enough space for the guests to serve themselves safely. Check local fire codes and use fire-retardant cloths when using candles. Invest in a small fire extinguisher and keep it under the table in case of emergencies.

If your buffet looks bare, fill in any spaces with something that can be scattered such as rose petals, loose flowers, candy, crackers, bunches of fresh herbs, or dried whole chile peppers. Or use an item that ties in with your theme such as chocolate coins for a pirate party, shells for a luau, or fortune cookies for an Asian buffet. But don't junk it up—simple is usually better.

A great way to enhance the mood of the party is to place a portable tape or CD player under the buffet. Most record stores carry special effects and ambiance tapes and CDs (see the Resource Guide on page 229). Play sounds of the ocean for a luau, a babbling brook or water for an Asian theme, scary sounds for a Halloween party, or any soft music that works with the theme.

flaunting the food

Try using plates and bowls that complement the color of the food. White will work with almost anything, so invest in a few basic platters, cake stands, plates, and bowls. You'll find that these basic pieces become mainstays in your repertoire.

Display a beautiful, multi-colored salad in a large glass or plastic salad bowl. Marble, used in counter tops and available at hardware and tile stores, can be used for a number of great food presentations. Look for damaged or broken pieces and ask the store to break them into different sizes for you. Because the surface of marble stays reasonably cool, it is perfect for a cheese and fruit display. Use longer pieces, supported by risers, to create a series of dramatic-looking shelves for the food.

Beveled mirrors or mirror tiles can also be used for cheese. Place mirrors under bowls of food to give a suggestion of depth to the buffet.

Baskets are a must for any party thrower. They are inexpensive, come in all different shapes, and are available everywhere. They can be easily recycled by spray painting or wrapping the handles with fabric, silk ivy, and flowers. Line your basket with a linen napkin or aromatic herbs before adding food. If you are building crudités, you can line the basket with non-toxic leaves. Try lemon leaves, ornamental purple or green kale, bok choy, banana leaves, curly green lettuce, or Savoy cabbage.

If hot food is being served on a buffet, you will almost certainly need a chafing dish (see page 100). To avoid the usual industrial look of multiple chafing dishes, use different shapes or mix copper with silver and place dishes at different angles. Make your own rustic-looking chafing dish by stacking red bricks to form a base and place a cast-iron griddle or skillet on top. For the heat source, use a canned or gel fuel like Sterno, or votive candles set on a terracotta plant saucer and placed underneath. Another alternative to a chafing dish is a crock-pot or slow cooker. Set on low, it can be used to keep stews, soups, chowders, chili, or even beans warm. If the design of your crock-pot doesn't match your party décor, wrap it in a small tea towel, napkin, or piece of fabric.

go with the flow

For the buffet to flow smoothly, food placement is important. See our buffet flow diagrams below and right.

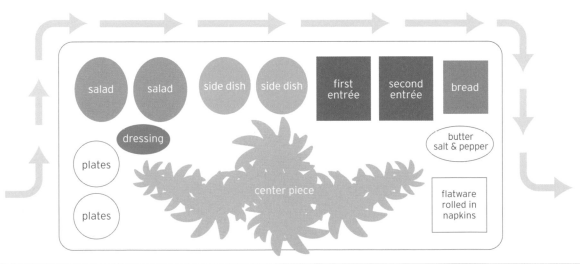

salad · salad · side dish · side dish · first entrée · second entrée · bread

dressing

plates

plates

center piece

butter salt & pepper

flatware rolled in napkins

maintaining your buffet

Provide your guests with the correct serving utensils. Tongs are the most guest-friendly utensils for a buffet. They can be used for everything from salad and rolls to chicken breasts and pastries.

Select utensils that are the correct size for the serving dish. Too short can be very messy; too long is unwieldy. Provide a spoon rest or small saucer for the utensils that may drip and ruin the tablecloth. A 3-inch-wide offset spatula is a must for easy maneuvering of lasagna. Score the surface of the lasagna into portion sizes to act as a guide.

The food should be in manageable-size pieces that will fit the plates and make it from the buffet to the table. For example, if you are using large chicken breasts, consider slicing them first before adding to the chafing dish. Cut whole corn in half and trim broccoli into florets before serving. Avoid round foods such as peas that may roll off the plate. If soup is on the menu, use deep bowls or mugs and provide a ladle that gives the correct portion.

Check on the buffet occasionally to monitor the food. Are you going to run out of Boeuf Bourguignon? If you are expecting a rush of guests, keep an extra pan or two of the hot beef in a cooler under the buffet. Because coolers are insulated, they will keep hot food hot for limited periods of time. Having the hot food this close will ensure a quick change-out when one pan becomes low. Put the pan of food into the cooler just before serving. This method of storing food should only be a 15 to 20-minute temporary measure when you expect a quick turnaround. If you do run out of something, simply remove the plate or tray. Fill the space with an extra breadbasket or another bowl of salad.

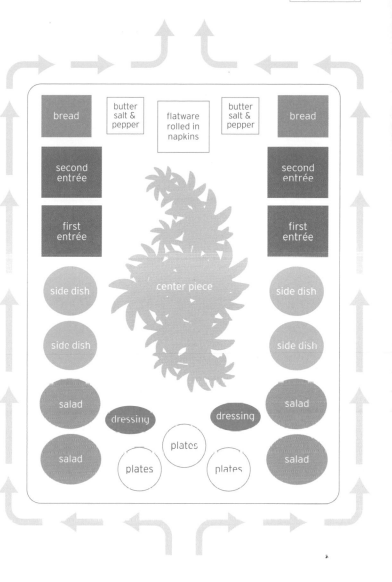

 Place the most expensive food (or the food that you have least of) at the end of the buffet line. This way your guests will have filled their plates and will have limited space left for the more expensive item.

building a crudités display

Crudités is the French word for mixed salad. It is commonly used to describe a tray of carrots, celery, and other vegetables. If you are short of time, buy a prepared crudités tray from your grocery store, and make it look homemade by arranging the vegetables in a tureen or large shallow bowl with the dip served in a small bowl or cup placed in the center. Alternate colors so you don't have broccoli next to celery. Instead, have red bell pepper strips or carrots between the broccoli and celery. Stand vegetables upright instead of laying them flat. Add tiny yellow tomatoes or snow peas to your display—whatever is in season and available. Blanch broccoli and asparagus for half a minute in boiling water; they will turn a lovely, bright green.

the ease of cheese

Caterers frequently depend on cheese trays to supplement more time-consuming dishes. Cheese and crackers work as well for an early brunch as they do for an after-play reception. Group several cheeses together, mixing colors, shapes, and textures. Choose at least one semi-hard cheese, one blue cheese (such as Gorgonzola, Roquefort, or Stilton), and one soft cheese. (See the Cheese Glossary on page 82 to help you navigate the wide variety of cheeses available and choose appropriate fruit and wine pairings.)

Cheese displays can be built on any clean surface. Use clean pieces of marble, wood cutting boards, or large tiles. (Chill the marble to keep the cheese cool.) You can line the board with clean leaves from lemon trees or rose bushes, or buy leaf-shaped cheese paper from a cookware store. Make sure that any fresh leaves you use come from non-toxic, pesticide-free plants. Serve the cheese and crackers with bunches of different-colored grapes, slices of firm pears and apples (spritzed with lemon juice to prevent browning), dried fruit such as figs, apricots, and dates, and whole nuts like almonds and walnuts. Allow six to ten crackers per person, depending on the length of the party and the extent of the menu. If your cheese display surface is large enough, arrange the fruit and crackers around the cheese. If you don't have enough space on the cheese board, then put the fruit and crackers in separate bowls, or scatter the crackers directly onto the tablecloth itself.

making an ice bowl

For a stunning and easy dessert presentation, make a bowl of fresh flowers or fruit suspended in ice. Ice bowls make particularly attractive and practical serving dishes for ice creams and sorbets. You will need flowers, leaves, a lemon, a half-gallon of distilled water, and two bowls. One bowl should be small enough to fit inside the other bowl, with about an inch of space all around. Use glass bowls if you have them, as it will be easier to see the arrangement as you work.

To make the ice bowl, place a $\frac{1}{2}$-inch slice of lemon on the bottom of the larger bowl and set the smaller bowl inside. Wedge the flowers and leaves in the space between the two bowls, turning the petals so that they press against the outside bowl. Fill the space between the bowls with distilled water, which freezes clearer than regular tap water, and place in the freezer. Place a dinner plate on top to weigh down the smaller bowl. Flowers will float to the top if not wedged in, so be sure to check the bowl after 40 minutes and push any slipped flowers down with a wooden skewer or add more flowers before the water freezes completely. Let it sit in the freezer until completely frozen, at least four hours or up to a week.

To unmold, fill the sink with very warm water. Lower the bowl into water so that the entire outside (but none of the inside) of the larger bowl is immersed. Hold the bowl in the hot water for 20 seconds. Remove from the water and push the ice until it slides out of the bowl. If it doesn't slide out, return to the water for 10 seconds longer, and then try again. When the outside bowl is removed, fill the inside bowl with hot water and let it sit for 20 seconds. Pour the water out and slide the inner bowl out. If the inner bowl sticks, refill with hot water and try again.

To even out the rim of the ice bowl, run hot water over a large knife for 10 seconds. Rub the flat of the knife over the uneven rim of the ice bowl. Repeat until any large lumps are smoothed out. Place the ice bowl in the freezer until ready to serve.

For a dramatic ice cream presentation—and to save time when serving—scoop the ice cream up to a day in advance, and place in a single layer on a baking sheet. Store in the freezer and cover with plastic wrap once the scoops have set. Just before serving, place the scoops into the ice bowl, and put the ice bowl in a large shallow bowl or on a tray with sides to catch any melted water. Expect the ice bowl to last from 45 minutes to 2 hours, depending upon the room temperature.

practically homemade specialty cakes

If you want a three or four-tiered wedding cake with basket-weave decorations and intricate details, then be prepared to pay hundreds of dollars. But you don't have to spend a lot of money on a special-occasion cake. Call your local supermarket bakery and ask if they make wedding cakes. You will be surprised by how reasonable their prices can be compared to a high-end bakery. If you like the price of grocery store wedding cakes but want something more personal, buy a plain white cake with a simple border. Add fresh roses or rose petals in colors that match the theme of the wedding for a simple, but very elegant look. Try adding French ribbon, dragées (edible gold or silver balls), and strings of faux pearls or fresh, non-toxic flowers.

To make a white lily cake, purchase a single-layer, half sheet cake from a supermarket and cut it in half. Spread raspberry jam or white frosting on the top of one half, and then place the other layer on top. Cover the whole surface with frosting, and then gently press shredded coconut into the frosting. Garnish it with three lilies to create an elegant and easy cake.

For a professional look, try covering unfrosted cake layers with fondant, a white, pliable frosting that is used to give special occasion cakes that smooth, flawless look. It can be colored with food coloring or flavored using extracts. You can find it at cake decorating, craft, and party stores.

To make a "do it for less" baby shower cake, you will need a whole, unfrosted two-layer sheet cake from the grocery store. Cut it into two squares, one slightly bigger than the other (freeze any trimmings and use them later for a trifle or fondue). Paint the top and sides of each cake with warm jam that has been strained to remove any seeds. This helps the fondant to stick. Wearing disposable plastic gloves, you can color the fondant by kneading in food coloring, a few drops at a time, until the right color is achieved. Roll out the fondant on a work surface dusted with powdered sugar until it is $\frac{1}{8}$-inch thick. Then, carefully lift the fondant in one piece on top of the cake. Smooth down the sides and trim the edges. Repeat with the second cake, using a different color fondant. Roll out the trimmings and cut into polka dots, crescent moons, or other shapes using small cookie cutters. Glue the shapes in place with a little melted chocolate or jam. Place one cake on top of the other.

You can use the same technique for a "do it for less" wedding cake: Buy one 12-inch round, unfrosted, double layer cake; one 8-inch round, unfrosted, double-layer cake; and one 4-inch round, unfrosted, double-layer cake. You will also need cardboard cake rounds to match each cake size. Most bakeries will gladly sell you unfrosted cakes and the matching cardboard cake rounds. Cover each cake with white fondant as described for the baby shower cake, and place on cake rounds. Use a dab of melted chocolate or jam on the cake round to glue the cake in place. Roll any unused fondant into a long, thin coil and place around the base of each cake for a finished look. Place four skewers in the center of the 12-inch and 8-inch cakes for supports (you will need to trim the skewers). Decorate with silver dragées, edible fresh flowers, or petals. Assemble the cake at the venue to avoid the headache of trying to transport it.

white lily cake

COCKTAIL PARTY

No room for a buffet? Have a cocktail party instead. Cocktail parties are very space-efficient, and all you need to serve are hors d'oeuvres and drinks. The hors d'oeuvres can either be passed on trays or placed in different stationary locations.

By using a few stand-up cocktail tables, you'll give your guests some places to congregate, while giving yourself more surface space for serving hors d'oeuvres. Party rental companies often offer these at a low rate. Cover with a small tablecloth or place mat and use for your placed hors d'oeuvres, an ice-filled tub of drinks, or a tray of pre-poured wine glasses.

Provide your guests with small, sturdy plastic or paper plates and plenty of cocktail napkins. Have several trash cans on hand.

Avoid food that is awkward or too big to eat. Finger food should be small enough to be eaten within one or two bites. People will be balancing a drink in one hand and possibly a plate in the other, so select food that isn't going to roll off the plate. Whenever possible, serve food that can be eaten easily without a plate like cubes of cheese and meat on toothpicks or skewers.

If you have the time, make a centerpiece to use with a shrimp cocktail. Line a large ring mold with plastic wrap. Place lemon rounds neatly around the bottom of the mold. Add chopped ice, additional lemon slices, and distilled water; freeze overnight. To unmold, dip the ring mold in warm water and turn out the ice ring. Remove the plastic wrap. Place the ice ring on a serving platter or tray with a lip to catch any melting water. Pour the cocktail sauce into a clear bowl in the middle of the mold, and arrange the shrimp around the ring.

 Buy a few wooden tray tables for serving your cocktails. They cost less than $10 in home furnishing and hardware stores

in-a-flash hors d'oeuvres

These "do it for less time" hors d'oeuvres can be made in five minutes or less.

- **Artichoke dip.** Chop a jar of drained artichoke hearts and mix with Boursin cheese. Microwave on high for a hot and tasty dip.

- **Bruschetta.** Rub French baguette slices with store-bought roasted garlic cloves. Top with a tomato slice and a fresh basil leaf. Look for jars of pre-roasted garlic in the produce section of grocery stores.

- **Caprese salad skewers.** Place a 1-inch piece of fresh mozzarella, a fresh basil leaf, and a small cherry tomato on a toothpick or small skewer.

- **Caviar and toast points.**

- **Cheese ravioli.** Skewer cooked cheese raviolis or tortellini and serve with a dipping sauce made from a jar of drained and puréed roasted red bell peppers.

- **Cheese, fruit, and crackers.** See page 36 and 85.

- **Chips and salsa.** Take store-bought salsa and add chopped fresh cilantro for a "just made" taste.

- **Cream cheese dip.** Top an 8-ounce block of cream cheese with your favorite chutney and microwave until melted. Stir and serve with crackers or apple slices.

- **Edamame.** Sprinkle pre-cooked edamame (soy beans in shells) with sea salt. Serve warm or cold.

- **Endive.** Fill Belgian endive leaves with purchased tapenade (olive spread) or flavored cream cheese.

- **Fresh mozzarella dip.** Pour your favorite marinara sauce in a serving bowl. Top with a $1/2$-inch-thick slice of fresh mozzarella and microwave until the cheese is almost melted. Scoop with slices of crusty French baguettes.

- **Fruit with blue cheese.** Buy crumbled blue cheese and add a little mayonnaise. Spread on fruit slices or serve as a dip.

- **Ham and Swiss pinwheels.** Spread slices of ham with a thin layer of cream cheese and top with a layer of thinly sliced Swiss cheese. Roll up jellyroll fashion. Chill, and then cut into $1/2$-inch pieces.

- **Hummus with pita bread triangles.**

- **Olive bar.** Dress up plain olives by tossing with a mixture of lemon or orange zest, dried thyme, salt, and pepper.

- **Prosciutto and melon cubes.** Wrap 1-inch cubes of cantaloupe with prosciutto or thinly sliced ham and secure with a toothpick.

hummus

salmon pinwheels

- **Salmon dip.** Combine finely chopped smoked salmon with cream cheese, pipe onto cucumber rounds, and garnish with a sprig of fresh dill. For an even faster recipe, buy salmon-flavored cream cheese from the deli section of your grocery store.

- **Salmon pinwheels.** Spread whipped cream cheese over thinly sliced smoked salmon. Roll up jellyroll-style, wrap in plastic wrap, and chill to firm slightly. Slice into $\frac{1}{2}$-inch-thick pieces and skewer with slices of cucumber, if desired, on individual serving picks.

- **Sausage skewers.** Slice pre-cooked chicken sausage and place on skewers. Microwave for one minute, or until warm, and dip in Dijon or honey mustard.

- **Shrimp cocktail.** Thaw pre-cooked shrimp, toss in a little freshly squeezed lemon juice, and serve with cocktail sauce. Make a quick cocktail sauce by mixing ketchup with lemon juice and prepared horseradish. Serve on a lemon ice ring. (See page 39 for instructions.)

- **Tapenade.** Spread store-bought tapenade (olive spread) on Melba toast or crackers.

- **Tiropitakia.** Cut thawed phyllo dough into 2-inch squares. Place a teaspoon of feta cheese, oregano, and thyme mixture in the center. Squeeze corners of dough together to form a purse. Mist with vegetable or olive oil cooking spray and bake at 375 degrees until golden.

- **Tortellini skewers.** Buy tortellini salad from the deli section of your grocery store and thread onto skewers. Dip into store-bought pesto, balsamic vinaigrette, or your favorite dressing.

- **Vegetable crudités and dip.** See page 36 to learn how to transform a store-bought crudités platter for your party.

12 classic cocktails (All recipes make one serving)

black russian

1½ ounces vodka

¾ ounce coffee liqueur

Pour the vodka into a tumbler filled with ice. Add the coffee liqueur and stir.

bloody mary

1½ ounces vodka

2½ ounces tomato juice

Dash of Worcestershire sauce

Dash of Tabasco sauce

Dash of salt and pepper

Celery stick for garnish

Pour the vodka into a highball with ice. Pour the tomato juice on top. Add the Worcestershire sauce, Tabasco sauce, salt, and pepper. Garnish with a celery stick.

cosmopolitan

½ ounce Cointreau

½ ounce triple sec

1 ounce vodka

½ ounce freshly squeezed lime juice

½ ounce cranberry juice

Lime wedge for garnish

Fill a mixing glass halfway with ice. Pour in all the ingredients, shake vigorously, and strain into a chilled martini glass. Garnish with a lime wedge.

daiquiri

1½ ounces light rum

½ ounce freshly squeezed lime juice

1 teaspoon powdered sugar

Shake all the ingredients together with ice and strain into a cocktail glass.

long island iced tea

½ ounce vodka

½ ounce light rum

½ ounce gin

½ ounce tequila

½ ounce triple sec

½ cup cola

Put all the ingredients in a highball. Stir well, and add ice.

manhattan

2 ounces whiskey or bourbon

1 tablespoon sweet or dry vermouth

Dash of angostura bitters

Maraschino cherry for garnish

Pour the whiskey, vermouth, and angostura bitters into a tumbler and stir. Garnish with a cherry.

margarita

1 ounce tequila

1 ounce Cointreau

1 ounce freshly squeezed lime juice

Shake all the ingredients together with ice and strain into a salt-rimmed margarita glass or tumbler. Serve with or without ice.

martini

2 ounces gin

Dash extra dry vermouth

Cocktail onion, green olive, or
  lemon peel for garnish

*Shake or stir the gin and
vermouth with ice and strain
into a martini glass. Garnish
with a cocktail onion, olive, or
piece of lemon peel.*

old fashioned

1 maraschino cherry,
  stem removed

1 orange slice

1 teaspoon powdered sugar

1 tablespoon club soda

1½ ounces whiskey

2 dashes angostura bitters

*Place the cherry, orange slice,
sugar, and club soda in a tumbler
and mash the fruit with a spoon to
extract the juice and dissolve the
sugar. Fill the glass with ice, add
the whiskey and bitters, and stir
until ice cold.*

singapore sling

1½ ounces gin

½ ounce Bénédictine

½ ounce grenadine or
  pomegranate juice

Squirt of freshly squeezed
  lemon juice

Club soda as needed

½ ounce cherry brandy

1 maraschino cherry for garnish

*Pour the gin, Bénédictine,
grenadine, and lemon juice into a
highball with ice, and stir well. Fill
almost to the top with club soda,
and pour the cherry brandy on
top. Garnish with a cherry.*

tequila sunrise

½ ounce grenadine or
  pomegranate juice

1½ ounces tequila

Orange juice as needed

Orange slice for garnish

*Pour the grenadine into a highball,
and then fill with ice cubes.
Gently pour in the tequila, and
then gently pour in the orange
juice until the glass is filled. The
color should turn from bright red
to deep orange to light orange.
Garnish with a slice of orange.*

vodka martini

2 ounces vodka

Dash of extra dry vermouth

Green olive or lemon peel
  for garnish

*Shake or stir the vodka and
vermouth together with the
ice, and strain into a martini glass.
Garnish with an olive
or lemon peel.*

SIT-DOWN SERVICE

For a truly special, all-out event, nothing seems quite as elegant as sit-down service. But plated service does require a lot of planning. Besides preparing the food, you will also have to set the table. This includes placing linens, name cards, flatware, glasses, and china, as well as folding the napkins, arranging the seating, and placing the centerpieces.

On the positive side, pre-plating food not only gives you the artistic freedom to create stunning presentations but also gives you control over food portion sizes. This can be essential when serving an expensive entrée. Sit-down dinners also allow you to set the pace of the party. If the guests are chatting too much and you fear they may be staying for breakfast, serve that pre-plated dessert and coffee as quickly as possible.

If you are the chef for the night, be prepared to spend time in the kitchen, but keep in mind that time in the kitchen is time away from your guests. The idea is to enjoy yourself and be a guest at your own party. With careful planning, you can design a make-ahead menu that takes a minimum of effort on party day. For example, place trays of cold or room-temperature hors d'oeuvres throughout the entertaining area. Then start the meal with a salad that can be plated before guests arrive. Dress the salad just before serving. Choose a stew-style main course such as coq au vin that can be held in a warm oven. Accompany it with potatoes au gratin, which can also be made ahead and kept warm in the oven. Brown the top under the broiler just before serving. For dessert, bring a pre-sliced cake to the table. If you do feel overwhelmed, consider hiring a waiter to help out if your budget allows. Better to hire a server than appear overworked at your own party. (See page 108 for hiring tips.)

everything in its place

The tradition of lavish ten-course banquets has sadly faded away over time. As our food has simplified, so has the flatware. Gone is the arsenal of flatware such as celery forks, knife rests, and finger bowls. But the same rules still apply: Start from the outside, using the first knife and fork for the salad, and work your way inward. The knife and fork closest to the dinner plate is for the main course. When setting the table for your party, refer to the diagrams on the next page for the correct placement of flatware and glasses. If possible, set the table and decorate the day before the party to save time and energy.

formal dinner setting

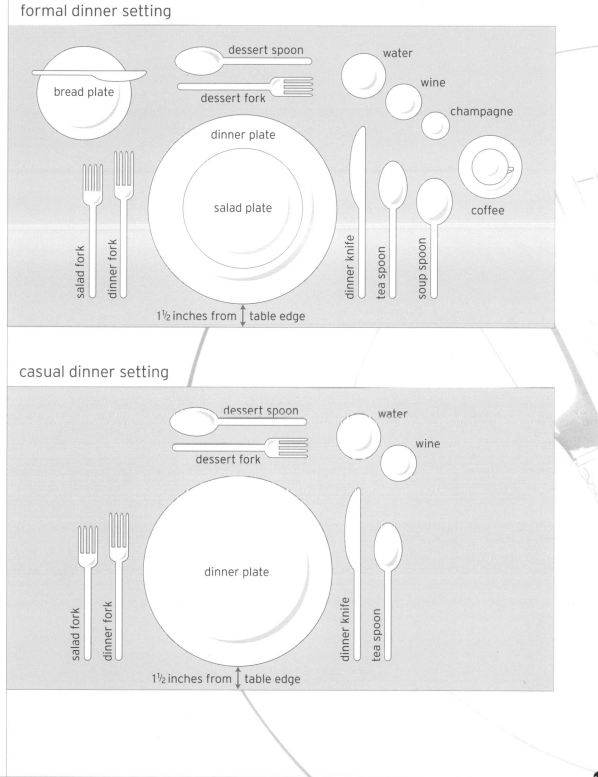

bread plate

dessert spoon

dessert fork

water

wine

champagne

dinner plate

salad plate

coffee

salad fork

dinner fork

dinner knife

tea spoon

soup spoon

1½ inches from table edge

casual dinner setting

dessert spoon

dessert fork

water

wine

dinner plate

salad fork

dinner fork

dinner knife

tea spoon

1½ inches from table edge

napkin folds

Folding napkins into decorative shapes will add a special touch to any party without adding cost. Buy cheap cloth napkins and fold them a week before your party (Search online at Ebay for great deals or borrow from friends and family). No need to have dozens of napkins in the same color or pattern; mix and match for an eclectic look. Use pastels and floral patterns for spring parties, anniversaries, and Mother's Day; use bright colors and patterns for summer parties, luaus, and fiestas; mix red, green, and gold for holiday parties. For formal parties, mix solid black and white napkins or add one color to the black and white that complements your décor.

the bishop hat	fan in goblet	the clown hat	the rosebud	the candlestick	the pyramid

FAMILY STYLE

Family-style service is the usual choice for holiday dinners and potlucks, but remember that this casual style of passing dishes around the table may not be compatible with formal or business-related gatherings. If dishes or plates are hot, supply an oven pad or cloth napkin to make passing food easier. Take time before the guests arrive to find appropriate serving utensils for all the dishes. (A pair of tongs is an invaluable tool.) Trying to maneuver a huge plate of mashed potatoes can be awkward, so divide food into smaller, more manageable serving bowls or plates if need be.

easy menus in minutes

For an informal party, use an old standby with a few personal twists. Pizzas can be modified to suit just about anyone. Order a variety of toppings or just buy basic cheese or tomato and add your own toppings. Reheat to create your own customized pizzas and serve a selection of premium and microbrewery beers to complement your designer pizzas.

You can buy pizza dough fresh or frozen. Make mini pizzas using the bread-type packaged crusts, or use pita bread to make a lovely, thin-crust pizza. Pizzas are a great way to use leftovers. Simply chop meat and veggies, scatter over the dough, and sprinkle with cheese—an easy and colorful main dish. Not all pizzas need a tomato sauce; many are better with flavorful alternatives that can be purchased at your market. Instead of tomato sauce, try black or green olive tapenade, sun-dried tomato pesto or basil pesto, Alfredo sauce, or chutney. Here are some tried-and-true pizza ideas for your next casual party:

- **Grilled pizza.** Pesto, grated mozzarella cheese, leftover grilled vegetables (really, anything works: eggplant, zucchini, tomatoes, corn cut off the cob, onions, and mushrooms).

- **California barbecue pizza.** A great way to use leftover or rotisserie chicken. Purchase barbecue sauce, shredded or diced cooked chicken, thinly-sliced red onion, and chopped cilantro, and dribble a little extra sauce on top.

- **Fresh tomato pizza.** Thin slices of ripe tomatoes, fresh basil leaves, and slices of a good-quality, soft mozzarella.

- **White pizza.** Alfredo sauce, crumbled goat cheese, grated mozzarella, grated fontina cheese, and a little Parmesan.

- **Seafood pizza.** Pesto, chopped leftover fish like salmon or shrimp tossed with a little olive oil and chopped garlic, and mozzarella cheese.

build your own tart bar
Buy small, pre-baked tart shells or individual shortcakes from a bakery or restaurant supply store. Place on a tray with a selection of fresh berries, nutella, whipped cream, and chopped nuts. Let guests build their own tarts.

- **Pine nut pizza.** Green olive tapenade or store-bought pesto, pine nuts, crumbled feta cheese, and green onions.

- **Easy vegetarian pizza.** Add goat cheese and grilled veggies from the deli section of your grocery store to a basic cheese and tomato pizza to create a hearty vegetarian pizza.

PLANNING A POTLUCK

Nothing beats an old-fashioned potluck dinner. Having a potluck simplifies the party preparation. Hosts have fewer responsibilities and more time to enjoy the festivities. Potlucks create a communal experience for the guests because everyone has a small part in making the party a success. Make sure each guest brings something that will highlight his or her culinary talents, but that also goes with the menu you have decided upon. A potluck menu should flow just like any other menu. Decide what type of dishes you want ahead of time, and let people know at least a week in advance what you would like them to bring. It is always a good idea to make the main entrée yourself to ensure that there will be enough servings for everyone.

Ask your guests to let you know if they decide to make any changes to their contribution. You will need to have plenty of time to make up unexpected holes in your menu. If only you had known ahead of time that your sister-in-law had decided not to bring the buns and condiments for your barbecue, choosing instead to get creative with a Jell-O salad, you could have asked someone else to bring those items or could have gotten them yourself.

Some potlucks are very catch-as-catch-can affairs, but people rarely seem to mind. With these flexible dinners, anyone can bring anything. But if your menu is more specific, you will want to give your guests guidelines for the dishes they bring. Doing so allows you to organize the necessary refrigeration and cooking space and to find the appropriate serving dishes and utensils. For example, if your menu theme is Mexican fiesta, you should write out a desired menu just like you would if you were making it all yourself. Take, for instance, this menu:

Guacamole, Salsa, and Tortilla chips

Caesar Salad with Chile-Spiced Croutons

Pork Enchiladas

Chicken Taquitos

Chile-and-Cheese Tamales

Caramel Flan

Now, that might be what you want, but unless you are specific with your guests, what you'll get is:

No guacamole, six bags of chips
Potato Salad
Tamale Pie
Tamale Pie
Tamale Pie
Tamale Pie
Brownies and a stale, store-bought cake

You can see the problem. If the menu concerns you, be specific. It might not matter if the enchiladas are chicken or beef instead of pork. But it certainly does matter if four people bring the same thing. By providing guidelines, you'll make it easier on your guests and on yourself.

If you have invited guests who don't enjoy cooking and only go into the kitchen to make microwave popcorn, then ask them to bring wine, bottled water, beer, soda, ice, a bouquet of flowers, pretty paper napkins, dessert plates and plastic forks, a store or restaurant-bought dessert, or something else that is easily purchased. They also could bring an extra coffee maker and some freshly ground coffee and cream. Be specific if you ask a guest to bring wine. Suggest red or white, a Merlot or Chardonnay, or something that complements the menu.

MIX 'N' MATCH

Remember that this is your party. You can serve *whatever* you want, *however* you want. In the end, you may find the most practical and successful idea involves mixing all of the above serving styles. Choose the combination that best meets your time and budget restrictions. You could start by passing the hors d'oeuvres on trays or placing them on a buffet. Seat your guests for a sit-down, pre-plated dinner, and then have a dessert buffet and coffee service in another room or in the garden. This will give you time to greet your guests when they arrive and mingle with them during dessert. Whatever you choose, enjoy yourself. The more fun you have, the more fun your guests will have.

got enough room?

SEATING GUIDES

Once you have decided on a location—whether it be your home or elsewhere—careful placement of the food, bar, and seating will ensure a free-flowing event with no overcrowding. The size of the venue will also dictate the number of guests to invite and the most suitable and practical style of food service: buffet, cocktail, or sit-down.

Let's say you want to invite twenty-five people over for a sit-down dinner party in your home. You know you will have to rent tables, but how many should you rent? And will you have enough space in your dining room for them? First make a rough floor plan of the room, including length and width measurements. Use the seating chart on the next page as a guide to plan how many guests can fit around certain sizes and shapes of tables.

If you choose six 36-inch round tables that can seat five people each, draw six circles on your floor plan to represent the tables. Add about 2 to 3 feet to the diameter of each table to represent space taken up by chairs. Keep 2 to 4 feet between chair backs, and try to allow easy access to the kitchen and restroom areas. Try different configurations until the tables fit with the necessary amount of space between each one.

What can you do if, no matter how hard you try, you just can't fit all the tables in unless you take out a load-bearing wall? Try using a smaller table so that you can make use of more floor space. Instead of round tables, you could use two 96 by 30-inch buffet tables that can seat up to fourteen guests each, placed end to end to form one long banquet-style table. Alternatively, you could place three 60 by 30-inch tables in a "U" shape in one half of the room. This will leave room for dancing or a dessert and coffee buffet. If you decide to rent tables and chairs, many rental companies will draw a free computer layout for you.

seating diagrams and guides

round tables		
diameter	guests	maximum
24 inches	2	2
30 inches	2	4
36 inches	4	5
48 inches	6	8
54 inches	7	9
60 inches	8	10
72 inches	10	12

square, rectangular, or oblong tables		
length and width	guests	maximum
36 x 36 inches	4	4
48 x 48 inches	6	8
60 x 60 inches	8	10
60 x 30 inches	6	8
72 x 30 inches	6	8
96 x 30 inches	8	10

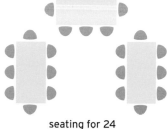

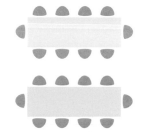

seating for 30
(each 36-inch table seats 5 guests)

seating for 24
(8 guests per 60 x 30-inch table)

seating for 20
(10 guests per 96 x 30-inch table)

PARTY RENTALS

You may find that you simply don't own enough tables and chairs for your guests. Although she didn't complain, Grandma may not have enjoyed sitting on an upturned milk crate at last year's Thanksgiving feast. Maybe you had better look into renting extra seating this year.

For a sit-down dinner with rented tables, chairs, linens, china, flatware, and glasses, expect to pay at least $15 and up per person for rentals, depending on what part of the country you live in and how luxurious your choices are.

Not sure where to start? Look in the yellow pages under "party rentals." Call a nearby company first because the closer they are, the less expensive the delivery charge. Explain the basics of your party to the representative, who will ask you a host of questions so he can give you a quote. A trained representative should be able to determine if you need anything other than the obvious, such as tenting or a dance floor. If your party does require a tent, then the rental representative should inspect the party site to accurately measure the area and ascertain the need for any fire department permits. Always check that the company has liability insurance.

Ask them to mail, fax, or e-mail the quote to you. Look it over and see if there are any places to save some money: Plain white chairs are less expensive than the gold ones they suggested. Do you really need five patio heaters? You can provide your own large trash bags much cheaper than the rental company will.

Once you have the quote trimmed down to a manageable price that includes all the services you need, call other companies and get a second or even third quote. This will give you some bargaining leverage when you point out that Company A has a cheaper delivery charge than Company B. Most companies will be only too happy to match or beat a rival company's quote in order to earn your business.

Some larger rental companies have a minimum order policy, but some will waive this if you offer to pick up and return the rentals yourself. This works okay for smaller items like linens, plates, and flatware, but it can be a problem if you are trying to haul tables and chairs without a 40-foot truck.

renting smart

- **Hidden fees.** What is the cost of pick-up and delivery, and does that fee include setup, too? Make sure all this is clear before you sign the rental agreement.

- **Hours of operation.** Not all companies work on Sundays. If your party is on a Saturday night, be prepared to have the rentals delivered on Friday afternoon and then possibly not picked up until Monday morning.

- **Contact information.** Make sure you always have the name and phone number of a contact person or representative on hand, plus pager and cell phone numbers for after-hours emergencies.

- **Company policies.** Find out the company's payment, reservation, and cancellation policies. If you cancel less than 24 hours before the event, expect to lose most or all of your deposit. Look into the insurance coverage provided by your contract. If necessary, get additional insurance.

DRESSING THE TABLES

It's a good idea to invest in a couple of neutral, machine-washable tablecloths that can be used at more than one party. A standard black tablecloth can be used for evening and formal events or as a base on which to add more tablecloths.

Overlay different colors and textures of cloth on top of a basic tablecloth. Look in the bargain bins at fabric stores for remnants that can be used to add layers. Another great alternative to buying tablecloths is to use bed sheets in different patterns and colors. Plain white sheets can be decorated with stencils and fabric paint if you have the time.

You may want to use something other than a standard tablecloth to complement the theme of the party, such as burlap for a rustic feel, an oversized Italian flag for our Authentic Toscana party, Hawaiian shirts for a luau, or a Mexican serape for a "south of the border" look.

what size tablecloth do I need for my table?

First, you will need to measure your tabletop. Measure the length and width for rectangular and oval tables; the diameter for round tables; and one side for square tables. If you will be using the leaves on your table, remember to include their lengths in with your measurements. For the overhang or drop, add an extra 20 inches to the length and to the width for oval, rectangular, and square tables. For round tables, add 20 inches to the diameter. This will give you the minimum of a 10-inch drop for the tablecloth. For a longer drop of about 14 inches, add 28 inches instead of 20 inches to your measurements. For a fold-up table, be sure to use a floor-length tablecloth to hide the legs. The chart below allows for a minimum of a 12-inch drop; use it as a starting point for finding the perfect tablecloth for your party.

tablecloth sizing

⭕ round tables

diameter of table	guests	tablecloth size
36 to 48 inches	4	60 inches
46 to 58 inches	6	70 inches
64 to 76 inches	8 to 10	90 inches

▭ rectangular tables

length and width of table	guests	tablecloth size
36 x 78 inches to 48 x 90 inches	6 to 10	60 x 102 inches
36 x 96 inches to 48 x 108 inches	8 to 12	60 x 120 inches

◻ square tables

dimensions of table	guests	tablecloth size
28 x 28 inches to 40 x 40 inches	4	60 x 60 inches

⬭ oval tables

length and width	guests	tablecloth size
28 x 46 inches to 40 x 58 inches	4 to 6	52 x 70 inches
36 x 58 inches to 48 x 70 inches	6 to 8	60 x 84 inches
36 x 78 inches to 48 x 90 inches	8 to 10	60 x 102 inches
36 x 96 inches to 48 x 108 inches	12 to 14	60 x 120 inches

tablecloth boxing

For a tailored finish to your tablecloth, box the corners.

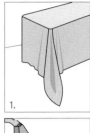
1.

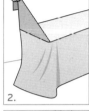
2.

3.

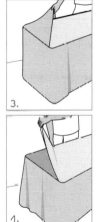
4.

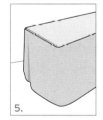
5.

what's cooking?

The date is set, the invitations have been mailed, and your remodeled bathroom is ready for its close-up. Now, what are you going to serve for dinner? In Chapter 3, we discussed what kind of service—buffet, cocktail, or sit-down—would be most suitable for your party. Armed with that information, you can now build a fantastic menu. If you consider yourself a gourmet chef, then you can build the whole menu around your famous cassoulet recipe. But not everyone is kitchen-savvy. If you're more comfortable making reservations than dinner, planning a menu and preparing food for a party can be quite daunting. With a few guidelines and thoughtful food selections, you can easily put together delicious and memorable menus that will wow your guests.

MENU BUDGETING

A major factor in menu planning is budget. You may not be aware of how much this is all going to cost, so make the extra trip to the grocery store to check prices so that there will be no expensive surprises the day before the party. Depending on the type of party, you may or may not have separate budgets for food and drink. Alcohol is probably going to be the high-ticket item of the party. (See the Beverage Consumption Guides starting on page 87.)

If you have never bought alcohol for a large party, take a trip to the liquor section of your grocery or club store. Ask the manager about discounts for buying wine by the case. Remember to take a note pad and write down the prices of all the alcohol you will be serving. And don't forget disposable glasses, napkins, ice, lemons, limes, and olives.

With the bar expense figured, you can now calculate your food cost. Do you know how much that leg of lamb is going to cost? Unlike clothing, groceries cannot be returned in most circumstances, not even for store credit, so careful shopping is a must.

One of the best "do it for less" tips we can give you is to shop with seasonality in mind. For example, do not promise raspberries for a New Year's party unless you have your own hothouse in the backyard. If you don't know what fruit and vegetables are in season, ask the produce manager of your local grocery store or take a look at our seasonality guide below. If you buy produce in season, it will taste better, be cheaper, and be more readily available. If you decide you have to have peaches in the middle of winter, you are going to pay extra for shipping them from wherever they are grown—and they won't taste as good because they had to be picked while unripe to survive their journey.

seasonal produce guide

spring	summer	fall	winter
vegetables	**vegetables**	**vegetables**	**vegetables**
asparagus	basil	broccoli	avocados
avocados	beans	brussels sprouts	broccoli
basil	beets	cabbage	brussels sprouts
beans	chile peppers	cauliflower	cabbage
beets	corn	celery root	cauliflower
broccoli	cucumbers	chile peppers	celery root
cabbage	summer squash	cucumbers	chicory
chile peppers	sweet peppers	fennel	fennel
cucumbers	tomatoes	greens	greens
head lettuces	**fruit**	leaf lettuces	mushrooms
peas	apricots	mushrooms	spinach
radishes	berries	spinach	sweet potatoes
shallots	cherries	sweet peppers	**fruit**
spinach	dates	sweet potatoes	grapefruit
sweet peppers	figs	winter squash	oranges
turnips	grapes	**fruit**	pears
fruit	mangoes	apples	tangerines
berries	melons	cranberries	
mangoes	peaches	dates	
oranges	plums	grapes	
papayas	watermelon	nuts	
		oranges	
		pears	
		persimmons	

a word about catering

Many caterers are also event planners, which means they supply more than just the food. They usually buy their supplies wholesale and have industry contacts, which can result in some great deals. They may be able to offer you a package that includes food, alcohol, rented items, wait staff, flowers—the whole shebang. Ask the caterer for a breakdown of each item; then, if you feel you can supply the flowers cheaper, do so.

Ask for a contract, and make sure you understand it. There may be a per-slice cake-cutting fee and overtime for wait staff if they stay beyond a prearranged time. Some caterers specify that a guest count can go up but not down. This means that if you told the caterer that one hundred guests are coming but only seventy-five show up, then you are still going to be charged for the full hundred. If, on the other hand, you tell the caterer that you are expecting another ten guests the day before the party, you will be charged for these extra guests. These fees are usually not applied until your final invoice.

Many caterers will provide a drop-off food service. All the food arrives fully or partially cooked with reheating instructions.

 As an alternative to a full-service catered event, buy an entrée and several side dishes, and make your own salad and dessert.

Know that leaner cuts of meat are usually more expensive than the fattier cuts, as are trimmed and pre-portioned steaks. It is typically cheaper to buy a whole beef tenderloin from a club store and trim and cut it into steaks yourself than it is to buy prepared filet mignon. But you have to decide whether the extra cost is worth the convenience and time you save by buying prepared foods.

Less popular meats, such as lamb and veal, are usually more expensive than chicken or beef. Chicken can be substituted for veal in many recipes. Seafood as a whole can be pricey, so careful selection is essential. (See page 94 for tips on selecting seafood.)

If a recipe calls for cooked shrimp, look in the freezer case for deveined and pre-cooked shrimp. You'll find prepared shrimp very cost-effective in the time saved in shelling, deveining, and cooking. These only need to be thawed according to package instructions and refreshed with a squeeze of fresh lemon juice to be recipe-ready.

ESTIMATING FOOD QUANTITIES

The length of your party plays a big part in determining food quantities. For a reception lasting an hour and a half, followed by a dinner, you should calculate seven pieces of canapés and hors d'oeuvres for each guest.

If a reception is earlier in the day (right after office hours), people tend to be hungrier, so plan for ten to twelve pieces of canapés and hors d'oeuvres per guest. Receptions are expected to last until the usual time for dinner, say 6:30 to 7:00 p.m.

When your reception starts at about 6:00 p.m. and is not followed by dinner, much more food is needed. Estimate twelve to fourteen canapés and hors d'oeuvres per guest, and choose recipes that seem more filling and substantial on an empty stomach—warm turkey and pesto panini, for instance, instead of carrot sticks with curry dressing.

When service is butler-style—that is, plated and served by wait staff—you have much more control over the flow of food. When the budget is tight, butler-style service can actually end up being cheaper because you can control portions and timing. In contrast, buffets can be picked clean in a very short time and, when not replenished, quickly reveal that there was not enough food.

Accurately estimating quantities can be difficult. You could either run out of food too early or have food left over. It helps if you monitor the food intake of your guests. For your peace of mind, have some extra food in reserve for unexpected demand. How much food people will eat on any given occasion is, for the novice entertainer, difficult to estimate, but it helps to take the following issues into consideration:

- **Age of guests.** Older people tend to eat less than younger people, and certainly less than hungry teenagers.

- **Type of food.** Light foods go more quickly than rich foods.

- **Time of day.** Guests tend to eat more at an after-work party than at an after-dinner open house. Not everyone has the time or the disposition to eat a European three-hour, five-course meal. On the other hand, salsa and chips are not going to satisfy a hungry dinner crowd. As a rule, people tend to eat lighter, smaller portioned meals at lunchtime than at dinnertime. Try to schedule the meal so that the main course will be served at a reasonable time. We have all been to parties where the cheese and crackers are devoured in the first thirty minutes. Hunger can turn a crowd of happy party revelers into a disorderly mob. You have been warned.

PLANNING YOUR MENUS

Food magazines often have recipes in a menu format. This can be great inspiration when creating your own menus. If you don't like the whole menu, then just pick the items that appeal to you and make your own substitutions.

For an easy "do it for less" alternative, follow the "buy something, make something" route. If your green bean recipe is legendary, then serve it as a side dish next to a store-bought, pre-cooked rotisserie chicken and roasted potatoes from the deli. Who's going to know? Who's going to tell? Remember, when asked for a recipe for something you haven't cooked yourself, the answer should always be, "It's my Aunt Fanny's secret family recipe that I promised never to reveal to another living soul." Even the most prolific professional caterers do not make everything from scratch—it's just not cost or time-effective.

Do you really need six courses? Simplifying the menu should save you some money. Look at the menu ingredients: Can you make a substitution for an expensive piece of meat or fish? Can the veal in the scaloppine be replaced with a chicken breast? Sure it can. Try serving a one-course meal such as a hearty stew or clam chowder. Served with a crusty bread you have just warmed in the oven, this menu is sure to please everyone during chilly months. Go the potluck route and ask your guests to bring a dessert or side dish. Or, change the style of the party. Instead of an evening event, make it a breakfast, brunch, or afternoon event, where most people will expect less fancy fare. Or, have a dessert and coffee party as a "do it for less" alternative. Start mid-evening, say 8:30 p.m., after your guests have already eaten dinner.

uncharted territory

While it's ambitious to want to try a new recipe, keep in mind your cooking abilities, the amount of time you have to prepare the food, and the quality of the recipe itself. The recipes in *Do It For Less! Parties* evolved from years of catering, and we tested each recipe twice while compiling the book. But not all recipes out there receive the same level of attention, so you should always try to do a trial run of any recipes you'll be serving to guests. You'll work out all the kinks and reduce the potential for "operator error" well before party time.

the balancing act

Once you have decided on your menu, write it down. How does it sound? Do the courses flow naturally? Does reading the menu make you hungry? It should! (See page 60 for menu samples.) Menus should be an interesting balance of temperature, appearance, and texture. This takes practice, but here are a few tips to help you on your way:

- **Temperature.** Everything doesn't have to be served hot. Many flavors, in fact, are overwhelmed by high heat and blossom only when served at room temperature. Likewise, a cool salad or sauce can offer a much-needed relief from a spicy dish.

- **Flavorful.** Flavors should complement each other and flow from appetizer to entrée to dessert. If your first course is Caesar salad and the dessert is tiramisu, save the green tea-smoked red snapper with fried rice for another day. Instead, follow the salad with lasagna. Establishing a theme really helps with menu planning.

- **Color-coordinated.** Think of how the finished plates will look. Is all the food one color? If so, what can you add to make the plate more colorful? That plate of steak with potatoes au gratin and sautéed mushrooms is going to look rather bland with all that brown on brown. Serve the steak on a raft of beautiful blanched asparagus and garnish the top with a small dice of roasted red bell peppers. Now your meal has color as well as flavor.

- **Vary the textures.** Many hosts forget to consider the various textures of the foods they're serving. As with flavor and appearance, try not to repeat foods with similar textures throughout your menu. If you are serving a creamy sauce with your entrée, don't serve a thick, creamy soup to start. A clear soup or a salad would be a better choice.

- **Don't be repetitive.** Avoid repeating a single food item, food color, flavor, or cooking procedure (e.g., fried everything) throughout the whole menu. For example:

> Warm Herbed Goat Cheese Salad
>
> Gorgonzola Stuffed Chicken Breast with Seasonal Vegetables
>
> Potatoes au Gratin
>
> Individual Caramel Cheesecakes
>
> Assorted Breads and Parmesan Grissini

As you can see, this menu is a little heavy on the cheese and, for most of us, would taste too rich. Now, there is nothing wrong with having a party planned around cheese. It sounds delicious and many restaurants do just that with several small courses, but be aware that less is often more when it comes to food, especially with strong and spicy flavors. When serving fatty foods, serve something tart or acidic as an accompaniment. This will help cut through the richness. Mint sauce with lamb and orange sauce with duck are classic examples.

selling the sizzle

Including a well-written menu with your invitation can "close the sale" and entice people to want come to your party. Make sure that it sounds appealing, appetizing, and interesting. We call this "selling the sizzle."

Instead of,

Chicken with Sauce and Vegetables

Impress your guests with,

Sautéed Breast of Free-Range Chicken
with a Lemon-Tarragon Beurre Blanc
and a Selection of Farm-Fresh Seasonal Vegetables

The following are examples of delicious, easy-to-make, "do it for less" crowd-pleaser menus included in the book that can be adapted for any party. Use the whole menu or interchange with your own favorite recipes to make your party a hit.

Authentic Toscana (p. 114)

Classic Caesar Salad

Chilled Penne Pasta with Pesto
 and Pine Nuts

Italian Meatball Lasagna

Sweet Potato Gnocchi
 with Sage Butter Sauce

Assorted Grissini

Tiramisu

Chocolate-Almond Biscotti

Coffee Service

Starry Night (p. 126)

Creamy Herb Mushrooms

Baby Spinach, Walnut, and Orange
 Salad with Raspberry Vinaigrette

Brie-Stuffed Chicken Breast with
 Herbed Breadcrumbs

Rosemary-Roasted Red Bliss Potatoes

Baked Asparagus in Garlic Butter

Baskets of Assorted Artisan Breads

Poached Bosc Pears in Cabernet
 Sauce with Vanilla Bean Ice Cream

Chocolate-Orange Truffles

Asian Inspiration (p. 138)

Egg Rolls with Sweet and Sour Sauce

Beef Saté Skewers with Spicy
 Peanut Dipping Sauce

Stir-Fried Ginger-Pineapple Chicken

Jasmine Rice with Scallions

Garlic Snow Peas and Almonds

Mango or Coconut Sorbet

Chocolate-Dipped Fortune Cookies

Arabian Nights (p. 148)

Tabbouleh Salad

Moroccan Lamb Tagine
 with Honey and Lemon

Mint Yogurt Sauce

Curried Rice

Marrakech Chicken

Toasted Almond and Feta Zucchini

Pita Bread

Chocolate Baklava

Iced Mint Tea

Down-Home Barbecue (p. 160)

Roasted Potato Salad with
 Dijon Mustard and Chives

Kentucky Sweet-Talkin'
 Barbecued Chicken

Five-Alarm Chili

Coleslaw with a Kick

Buckaroo Beans

Fresh Corn on the Cob
 with Sage Butter

Double-Fudge Brownies with
 Creamy Fudge Frosting

Ice-Cold Lemonade

Garden Elegance (p. 174)

Baby Greens with Champagne
 Vinaigrette

Pecan-Crusted Halibut Fillet
 with Dijon Cream Sauce

Lemon Rice Pilaf

Garden-Fresh Green Beans

Strawberries and Chantilly Cream

Mini Chocolate-Almond Tartlets

Peach Bellinis

Bountiful Harvest (p. 186)

Butternut Squash Soup

Oven-Roasted Turkey with Herb Gravy
 and Cornbread Dressing

Creamy Mashed Potatoes

Candied Yams

Lemon Broccoli

Fresh Cranberry Relish

Pecan Pie with Spiced Whipped Cream

Spring on the Terrace (p. 204)

Walnut, Spinach, and Asparagus
 Strudel

Sesame Honey-Baked Chicken Wings

Muffuletta Sandwiches

Lemon-Caper Potato Salad

Marinated Cherry Tomato Salad

Apple-Pecan Coffee Cake with
 Apple Cider Glaze

Fresh Seasonal Fruit Salad

Sangria

On the Beach Luau (p. 216)

Coconut Shrimp

Honey-Barbecued Pork Ribs

Island-Style Chicken with Mango Salsa

Hawaiian Baked Beans

Pineapple and Golden Raisin
 Rice Salad

Macadamia and White Chocolate
 Chunk Cookies

Passion Fruit Iced Tea

By mixing and matching the recipes in this book and by adding other simple ingredients, you can create a variety of other wonderful "do it for less" menus. See our ideas below for a starting point.

Hors d'Oeuvres and Cocktails

Creamy Herb Mushrooms (p. 130)

Beef Saté Skewers with Spicy Peanut Dipping Sauce (p. 142)

Coconut Shrimp (p. 220)

Walnut, Spinach, and Asparagus Strudel (p. 208)

Vegetable Crudités with Blue Cheese Dipping Sauce (p. 36)

Cheese Board with Crackers and Assorted Breads (p. 36 and 82)

Cocktails (p. 42)

Wedding Rehearsal Dinner

Baby Greens with Champagne Vinaigrette (p. 178)

Brie-Stuffed Chicken Breast with Herbed Breadcrumbs (p. 132)

Creamy Mashed Potatoes (p. 198)

Garden-Fresh Green Beans (p. 182)

Tiramisu (p. 123)

Coffee Service (p. 125)

Serious Chocoholics' Party

Mini Chocolate-Almond Tartlets (p. 184)

Double-Fudge Brownies with Creamy Fudge Frosting (p. 172)

Chocolate-Orange Truffles (p. 137)

Chocolate Baklava (p. 158)

Vanilla Bean Ice Cream with Fudge Sauce

Chocolate-Dipped Fortune Cookies (p. 147)

Seaside Picnic

Marinated Cherry Tomato Salad (p. 212)

Garlic Snow Peas and Almonds (p. 146)

Honey-Barbecued Pork Ribs (p. 225)

French Baguettes and Sweet Butter

Strawberries and Chantilly Cream (p. 183)

Iced Mint Tea (p. 159)

Afternoon Tea Time

Cucumber and Watercress Finger Sandwiches

Smoked Salmon and Cream Cheese on Pumpernickel Bread

Skewered Chicken Tenders with Marrakech Sauce (p. 156)

Mini Chocolate-Almond Tartlets (p. 184)

Apple-Pecan Coffee Cake with Apple Cider Glaze (p. 213)

Darjeeling and Earl Grey Teas

Lemon wedges, sugar cubes, and cream

Party on the Patio

Baby Spinach, Walnut, and Orange Salad (p. 131)

Island-Style Chicken with Mango Salsa (p. 222)

Lemon Broccoli (p. 199)

Jasmine Rice with Scallions (p. 145)

Chocolate Baklava (p. 158)

Sangria (p. 215)

Coffee and Dessert Party

Macadamia and White Chocolate Chunk Cookies (p. 227)

Tiramisu (p. 123)

Apple-Pecan Coffee Cake with Apple Cider Glaze (p. 213)

Strawberries and Chantilly Cream (p. 183)

Pecan Pie and Spiced Whipped Cream (p. 202)

Chocolate-Almond Biscotti (p. 124)

Coffee Service (p. 125)

Tailgate/Super Bowl Party

Pizza (p. 47)

Sesame Honey-Baked Chicken Wings (p. 209)

Five-Alarm Chili (p. 168)

Chips and Dips

Double-Fudge Brownies with Creamy Fudge Frosting (p. 172)

Hearty Lunch

Classic Ceasar Salad (p. 118)

Fresh Corn on the Cob with Sage Butter (p. 171)

Muffuletta Sandwiches (p. 210)

Apple-Pecan Coffee Cake with Apple Cider Glaze (p. 213)

Peach Bellinis (p. 159)

Christmas Eve Dinner

Butternut Squash Soup (p. 194)

Filet Mignon with Cabernet Sauce

Rosemary-Roasted Red Bliss Potatoes (p. 134)

Baked Asparagus in Garlic Butter (p. 135)

Chocolate-Orange Truffles (p. 137)

"I don't eat anything with the letter 'e' in it"

It's considerate to inquire in advance about any special dietary needs of your guests. Some may be lactose-intolerant or allergic to foods like shellfish or peanuts. Others follow vegetarian, vegan, kosher, low-fat, or low-carb diets. Every caterer's kitchen staff has heard the words, "Do you have anything other than chicken? There's a vegetarian at table four." Of course, it helps to know this in advance and not as you are about to serve dinner to fifty guests. Just do the best you can to accommodate all your guests. Here are a few lighter alternatives that you can incorporate into the suggested menus.

appetizers

- **Artichoke dip.** Purée artichoke hearts with garlic and low-fat sour cream. Pour into an oven-proof crock, sprinkle with Parmesan cheese, and bake until browned and bubbly. For another level of flavor, stir in thawed and drained frozen spinach before baking.

- **Crudités with hummus.** High in fiber, full of flavor, and an interesting change from the usual ranch dressing.

- **Chicken saté with curried yogurt dipping sauce.** Thaw frozen chicken tenders and skewer on wooden or metal skewers. Grill until cooked through. Combine low-fat plain yogurt with a good-quality curry powder, and serve with the chicken for a quick, flavorful, and nearly fat-free starter.

salads

- **Create-your-own green salad.** Add your favorite brightly-colored fresh produce to mixed greens, baby spinach leaves, or crisp curly lettuce and serve with a few specialty low-fat or low-calorie salad dressings, like raspberry, lemon poppyseed, or mandarin orange vinaigrettes.

- **Fresh seasonal fruit salad.** Look for fruits on special sales and use them to bulk up the salad. Great fruit for bulk are melons, bananas, apples, and grapes. Apples and bananas will discolor after they're cut, so toss them in a little lemon juice ahead of time or cut them at the last minute. Add little accents of color and flavor with chopped kiwi fruit or mango. Try to include unusual fruits, such as pineapple or papaya. Allow about 6 to 8 ounces of whole, unprepared fruit per person. For a taste of pure summer, wash a selection of raspberries, blackberries, blueberries, and strawberries. Hull and slice the strawberries, and toss with the other berries. Dress them up by drizzling with orange liqueur or brandy an hour before serving. Allow half a pint of berries per person. For an exceptional presentation, hollow out a watermelon, honeydew melon, cantaloupe,

flavored syrup

While it will add some calories, an infused syrup will also add flavor to your fruit salad. Combine equal parts of sugar and water in a saucepan. Bring to a boil for 2 minutes. Add flavorings like zest from lemons, limes, or oranges; whole scraped vanilla beans; fresh mint; or cinnamon sticks. Allow the syrup to cool to room temperature, and then strain and toss with the fruit.

grapefruit, or coconut to create a hand-made serving dish. Cut wedges into the rim for a decorative look, and fill with the fruit salad.

- **Greek-style pasta salad.** Layer pasta, feta cheese, chopped cucumbers, raisins, walnuts, and cherry tomatoes on a bed of fresh spinach. Drizzle with oil and vinegar.

entrées and sides

- **Faux fried chicken with coleslaw.** Coat the chicken with herbed breadcrumbs, mist with olive oil, and bake until golden brown and cooked through for a healthful "fried" chicken. Serve with coleslaw made with low-fat mayonnaise.

- **Flank steak with asparagus.** Marinate flank steak, one of the leanest cuts of beef, in light soy sauce, orange juice, and ginger for 1 to 2 hours. Remove from the marinade, pat dry, and broil or grill until medium-rare. Let the meat rest for 10 minutes, and then cut against the grain into thin slices. Served with steamed or grilled asparagus.

- **Grilled vegetables.** First, make sure your grill is clean. (If you don't own a grill, you can use a grill pan over high heat, or place vegetables on an oiled baking sheet and set under the broiler.) Rub a paper towel dabbed in oil on the grill grate to keep the vegetables from sticking. Try zucchini, carrots, eggplant, summer squash, portobello mushrooms, yellow onions, asparagus, bell peppers, fennel, and endive. Cut vegetables like zucchini, carrots, eggplant, and squash into thick strips lengthwise. Cut bell peppers and onions into 1-inch rings; cut tomatoes in half. Trim the woody stems off asparagus and the roots off green onions. Grill mushrooms, pearl onions, and grape tomatoes whole. Brush the vegetables with olive oil and season liberally with sea salt and freshly ground black pepper, or drizzle ribbons of grilled zucchini or summer squash with pesto. Grill over medium-high heat until crisp-tender, turning once. Grill portobellos bottom-side down. After flipping, fill with goat cheese and top with chives. If you have a mixed crowd of vegetarians and meat-eaters, add some steaks or chicken breasts to the grill after cooking the vegetables.

- **Roasted chicken three ways.** Transform store-bought rotisserie chicken into quick chicken fajitas, chicken salad, and chicken curry.

- **Salmon in parchment.** Place a salmon steak or fillet on a piece of parchment paper. Top with lemon and fresh dill. Pull the sides of the parchment together and fold down, creating a seal that is as air-tight as possible. Bake in a 350-degree oven for 20 minutes, or until the desired degree of doneness. Serve the puffed paper packets to guests and let them unwrap them at the table.

- **Thai stir-fry.** Sauté pre-cut chicken with some curry powder in a tablespoon of olive oil until the chicken is cooked through. Remove the chicken and sauté some pre-cut vegetables with some more of the curry powder until crisp-tender, adding another tablespoon of oil if needed. Return the chicken to the pan and pour in a little chicken broth or water to make a sauce. Sprinkle with julienned basil or mint and chopped peanuts.

- **Turkey scaloppine with tomato and arugula salad.** Dip turkey cutlets in egg whites and dust with bagel crumbs. Sauté in a nonstick skillet with a tablespoon of olive oil until golden brown and cooked through. Spritz with lemon juice and top with arugula and tomatoes.

desserts

- **Fruit in phyllo.** Fill phyllo cups with a variety of low-fat fillings like fruit, sorbet, meringue, or fruit yogurt.

- **Peach cups.** Fill fresh peach halves with low-fat yogurt and fresh berries.

- **Summertime trifle.** Make colorful parfaits by layering low-fat pound cake with low-fat yogurt, fresh fruit, and reduced-fat whipped topping.

ORGANIZING YOUR GROCERY LIST

successful shopping

Always take a calculator when shopping for quantity recipes to quickly and easily calculate the most appropriate package sizes for your particular needs. In the *Do It for Less! Parties* shopping lists, most items are listed in ounces so that you are not limited to size-specific packaging if shopping in bulk.

Having your menu in black and white will help you write the grocery list. To make life easier when shopping for groceries, use the following as a guideline:

Divide a sheet of paper into columns that correspond to the different areas of a grocery store, such as produce, dairy, cheese and deli, meat and seafood, pantry items and dry goods, alcohol, and miscellaneous. Start with the first item on the menu, for example:

> Baby Spinach Salad with Toasted Walnuts,
> Caramelized Pears, and Champagne Vinaigrette

List the baby spinach in the produce section, walnuts in the pantry/dry goods section, and pears in the produce section. You'll also need sugar to caramelize the pears, so add sugar to the pantry/dry goods section. You'll need champagne vinegar and extra-virgin olive oil for the dressing, so add them to the pantry/dry goods section as well. The recipe also calls for Dijon mustard, salt, and pepper. You might already have these in your pantry, but you should check to make sure you have enough. Continue in this manner through the rest of the menu. Don't forget paper goods and extra cleaning products. Add those to the miscellaneous column.

By adopting this method, you will be sure to have everything you need. Dividing the list into sections will make tackling the job with a shopping buddy much easier. We've divided our shopping lists for the menus into non-perishable items you can buy one to two weeks ahead, and then into perishable items you should buy only one to two days before the party. We then subdivided the lists into basic grocery sections to help you shop for our menus. Take a look at our format as a guide if creating your own menu. (See an example on page 116.)

CREATING VISUAL APPEAL

Making your food look as good as it tastes is not at all difficult. Here are a few simple rules:

- **Color.** Contrasts in color and texture add interest to plates. Your poached chicken breast may be delicious, but serving it with mashed potatoes and cauliflower might not do it justice. Instead, serve it with steamed spinach or green beans and roasted red potatoes. Add diced red pepper to a corn salad. Swirl cream into colorful, smooth soups or sprinkle with chives.

- **Shape.** Cut peppers into strips or triangles. Slice carrots, green onions, and asparagus on the diagonal. Thinly slice chicken breasts and fan out on the plate.

- **Texture.** Garnish cream soups with crunchy croutons. Sprinkle toasted sesame seeds or almonds over vegetables. Top meat with sautéed mushrooms or thinly sliced and fried onions.

- **Height.** Build the plate high: Place your vegetable and starch either right next to each other in the center of the plate or one on top of the other, and then place your meat on top or leaning up against the starch and vegetable. For example, if you are serving mashed potatoes, sautéed mushrooms and zucchini, and a salmon fillet, place a small mound of mashed potatoes in the center of the plate. Spoon the vegetables over the mashed potatoes. Place the salmon on top of the vegetables so that one end is at the center of the mashed potatoes and vegetables and the other end rests on the plate.

- **Plate size.** Use a correctly-sized plate. Tiny portions on huge plates are fine if you are doing an early '90s food-as-art theme dinner, but to most of us, it looks as if the host is being cheap. Likewise, too much food piled on a small plate gives the overcrowded look of a "you can only visit the buffet once" food mountain.

portion control

If you're worried about running out of food and want to inconspicuously control portion size, shrink the size of the plate.

Standard dinner plates are normally 12 inches in diameter, and bistro plates run even larger at 14 inches. In comparison, buffet plates are only 9 inches.

By maintaining the proportion of food to plate, you can put less food on the 9-inch buffet plate without it looking meager.

garnishing

Accentuating your food with an appropriate garnish will turn your plates from blah to beautiful. You don't have to spend hours carving elaborate vegetable creations to make your plates pop. Here are a few garnishing guidelines:

- **Edible.** All garnishes must be edible.

- **Simple.** Don't gild the lily. The garnish is there to enhance the food, not to compete with it.

- **Relevant.** Use a garnish that is relevant to the dish. Take an ingredient from the recipe and use that as your garnish. If your dish has chopped chives in it, then decorate the plate with two whole chives arranged in an X shape. Add color and zing to your coffee service with lemon twirls, or garnish your flounder with a wedge or slice of lemon. Using a citrus zester, make long strings of lemon zest and arrange it in a bundle on top of the fish. Or, quickly deep-fry the zest for a crunchy garnish.

- **Blooming.** To decorate your plate, you can use edible flowers such as pansies, roses, lavender, nasturtium, and chive blossoms. Buy them from the produce section of the grocery store if they are available, or, if not, use organically grown flowers. Do not use regular flowers from a florist, as they are usually sprayed with pesticides.

- **Old stand-by.** Parsley is a great garnish. It gives life to mashed potatoes, soups, stews, and any bland-looking food that needs a splash of color. Finely chop, and then dry in paper towels to stop the green color from transferring to other food. Use whole sprigs of Italian parsley on the rim of a plate for an easy garnish.

- **Curling.** For an East-meets-West flare, make a simple green onion curl. Cut the white root end off of a green onion, and trim the green leaf end to about 3 inches. Using scissors or a sharp knife, cut through each leaf lengthways, leaving about 1/2-inch joined to the whites of the onion stem. Place the green part of the onion in a bowl of iced water for 30 minutes so the leaves will curl. The longer the onion sits in the water, the tighter the curl will be. This is a great garnish for our Asian Inspiration menu on page 138.

- **"A-peeling."** Wow your guests with a simple rose flower. Take a firm tomato, and using a sharp paring knife, peel the tomato as if you were peeling an apple. Try to keep the peel as thin and long as possible. Blot the tomato peel with paper towels. Carefully roll up the peel in a coil to make a flower shape. For more elaborate garnishes, visit your favorite Asian restaurant. They frequently make intricate food carvings out of cucumbers, carrots, tomatoes, and radishes. Purchase garnishes to use for place cards, to decorate the buffet, or to adorn dinner plates.

tableware

Choose dishes and utensils that fit the mood of the party and reflect the hours you spent planning every detail of your party, from choosing the perfect tablecloths to packaging the party favors. Disposable goods are appropriate for a casual or outdoor event like a child's birthday or a neighborhood barbecue. Other than the obvious "do it for less" advantage, plastic or paper plates are easier to dispose of or recycle and are much easier to store and transport. More formal events, however, usually call for more formal china, flatware, and glassware. Plain white dishes look great with almost any theme or table setting. You can buy them in bulk from stores like Pier One and Ikea or restaurant supply warehouses. A hostess can never own too many white plates, and you'll use them for years to come. If entertaining an extremely large crowd, renting may be a better option.

If the budget simply does not allow for real china, don't despair. You'll find a wide selection of good-looking, sturdy, stylish products on the market to set the right tone for your event. You can even mix-and-match, using real flatware with a good quality disposable plate for the buffet.

measurements and seasonings

PER-PERSON SERVING QUANTITIES

meat, poultry, and seafood serving quantities

meat and poultry	quantity per person (uncooked)
Beef, lamb, or pork (boneless)	4 to 6 ounces
Steak or leg of lamb (bone-in)	6 to 8 ounces
Pork chops (bone-in)	1 large
Pork or beef ribs or shanks (bone-in)	1 pound
Beef, pork, or lamb roasts (bone-in)	8 to 11 ounces
Beef, pork, or lamb roasts (boneless)	4 to 6 ounces
Chicken thighs, legs, or wings (bone-in)	2 (3 to 4-ounce) pieces
Chicken breast (boneless and skinless)	1 (6 to 8-ounce) breast
Chicken or turkey (whole)	12 ounces to 1 pound

seafood	quantity per person (uncooked)
Crab meat, lobster meat, octopus, shrimp, scallops, squid	4 to 5 ounces
Lobster (in shell)	$1\frac{1}{2}$ to 2 pounds
Crab (in shell)	$1\frac{1}{2}$ to 2 pounds
Mussels	12 each
Oysters and clams	4 to 6 each
Whole fish (not cleaned and guts intact)	12 to 16 ounces
Whole fish (cleaned and guts removed)	8 to 12 ounces
Fish fillets and steaks	5 to 8 ounces

hors d'oeuvres and side dishes serving quantities

other foods	quantity per person (cooked or prepared)
Potatoes	3 to 4 ounces
Salad	3 to 4 ounces or 1 heaped cup
Vegetables	3 to 4 ounces
Dessert	4 ounces
Hors d'oeuvres	4 to 5 ounces
Rice	2 ounces
Pasta	3 ounces

USEFUL INGREDIENT EQUIVALENTS

ingredient equivalents

dry goods	quantity	equivalent
Chocolate chips	5 ounces	about 1 cup
Chocolate chips	1 (12-ounce) bag	about $2\frac{1}{2}$ cups
Chocolate, unsweetened	1 ounce	1 square
Cocoa powder	3 ounces	1 cup
Coconut, flaked	1 (14-ounce) bag	$5\frac{1}{3}$ cups
Flour, all-purpose	1 pound	3 cups sifted or $3\frac{1}{2}$ to 4 cups unsifted
Flour, cake	1 pound	$4\frac{1}{2}$ to 5 cups sifted or $3\frac{3}{4}$ cups unsifted
Flour, whole wheat	1 pound	$3\frac{1}{2}$ to $3\frac{3}{4}$ cups unsifted
Rolled oats	1 pound	$5\frac{1}{3}$ cups
Shortening	1 pound	2 cups
Sugar, brown	1 pound	$2\frac{1}{4}$ cups packed or $3\frac{1}{2}$ cups not packed
Sugar, granulated	1 pound	$2\frac{1}{4}$ cups
Sugar, powdered	1 pound	$4\frac{1}{2}$ cups sifted or $3\frac{3}{4}$ cups unsifted
Sugar, superfine	1 pound	2 cups

meat and poultry	quantity (uncooked)	equivalent (cooked)
Bacon	1 pound (16 to 20 slices)	3 cups cooked and crumbled
Chicken breast	1 large	2 cups cooked and diced
Chicken (bone-in)	3 to 4 pounds	4 cups cooked and shredded

ingredient equivalents (continued)

legumes, pasta, and rice	quantity (uncooked)	equivalent (cooked)
Beans, dried	1 pound (2½ cups)	6 cups
Lentils or split peas	1 pound (2¼ cups)	5 cups cooked or 6 to 7 cups puréed
Macaroni	1 pound	8 to 9 cups
Spaghetti	1 pound	7 to 8 cups
Rice, regular white long-grain	1 cup	3 cups
Rice, brown	1 cup	3 to 4 cups

herbs and vegetables	quantity (uncooked, fresh produce)	equivalent
Beets	1 pound	2 cups cooked and diced
Bell pepper	1 large	1 cup chopped
Broccoli	1 medium-size (9-ounce) bunch	3½ cups florets
Cabbage	½ small head	3 to 4 cups shredded
Carrots	6 to 8 medium-size (1 pound)	3 cups shredded
Celery	2 medium-size stalks	1 cup diced
Eggplant	1 medium-size (14 ounces)	5 cups cubed or 3½ cups diced
Green onion	1 onion	2 tablespoons sliced
Herbs, fresh	½ ounce	¼ cup loose or 2 tablespoons chopped
Lettuce	1 (6-ounce) bag pre-washed lettuce	about 3 cups
Mushrooms	½ pound	2 cups sliced
Onion	1 large (5 to 6-ounce)	1 generous cup chopped
Onions	1 pound	3 to 4 cups chopped
Potato	1 medium-size	½ cup mashed
Pumpkin	1 pound	1 generous cup cooked and mashed
Spinach	1 pound	8 cups uncooked or 1½ cups cooked
Sweet potatoes	1 pound	1½ cups cooked
Tomatoes	1 pound	1½ cups peeled, seeded, and diced
Zucchini	1 pound	3½ cups sliced or 2 cups grated

ingredient equivalents (continued)

nuts	quantity	equivalent
Almonds or peanuts (shelled)	1 pound	3 cups
Pecans or walnuts (shelled)	1 pound	3½ to 4 cups
Pecans or walnuts	1 pound in shell	1¾ to 2 cups shelled

dairy	quantity	equivalent
Butter	1 pound	2 cups
Cheese	1 pound	4½ cups grated
Cream cheese	3 ounces	6 tablespoons
Cream cheese	8 ounces	1 cup
Egg whites	8 to 10 large eggs	1 cup
Egg yolks	12 to 14 large eggs	1 cup
Heavy whipping cream	1 cup	2 cups whipped
Parmesan cheese	3 ounces	1 cup grated

fruit	quantity (fresh)	equivalent
Apple	1 medium-size (5 to 6-ounce)	1 cup diced
Apples	2 medium-size (1 pound)	1¼ cups applesauce
Bananas	3 medium-size	1 cup mashed
Berries	1 quart	3½ cups
Cherries	1 pound	2½ cups pitted
Cranberries	1 pound	3 cups sauce
Cranberries	1 (12 ounce) bag	2½ cups sauce
Lemon juice	1 medium-size lemon	2 to 4 teaspoons juice
Lemon zest	1 medium-size lemon	1 teaspoon grated rind
Lime juice	1 medium-size lime	1½ to 2 teaspoons juice
Lime zest	1 medium-size lime	¾ teaspoon grated rind
Orange juice	1 medium-size orange	4 to 5 tablespoons juice
Orange zest	1 medium-size orange	3 to 4 teaspoons grated rind

dried fruit	quantity	equivalent
Candied fruit or peel	½ pound	1½ cups
Dates (pitted)	1 pound	2⅔ cups
Dates (with pit)	1 pound	3½ cups
Raisins	1 pound	3 cups

ingredient equivalents (continued)

miscellaneous	quantity	yields
Bread	4 slices	1 cup crumbs
Coffee	1 pound beans	80 tablespoons ground
Graham crackers	14 crackers	1 cup crumbs
Popcorn	1/4 cup uncooked kernels	5 cups popped
Vanilla wafers	20 wafers	1 cup crumbs

substitutions

ingredient	quantity	substitution
Chocolate	1 oz unsweetened	3 tablespoons unsweetened cocoa plus 1 tablespoon butter
Herbs	1 tablespoon fresh	1 teaspoon dried
Garlic	1 clove fresh	1/8 teaspoon garlic powder
Mustard	1 tablespoon Dijon	1 teaspoon dry mustard

butter equivalents table

sticks	tablespoons	cups	ounces
1/2	4	1/4	2
1	8	1/2	4
1 1/2	12	3/4	6
2	16	1	8

U.S. CONVERSION TABLES

common u.s. measurement equivalents

teaspoons	tablespoons	fluid ounces	cups	pints	quarts	gallons
1 teaspoon	$1/3$ tablespoon					
$1\frac{1}{2}$ teaspoons	$1/2$ tablespoon					
2 teaspoons	$2/3$ tablespoon					
3 teaspoons	1 tablespoon	$1/2$ ounce				
	2 tablespoons	1 ounce	$1/8$ cup			
	3 tablespoons	$1\frac{1}{2}$ ounces				
	4 tablespoons	2 ounces	$1/4$ cup			
	$5\frac{1}{3}$ tablespoons		$1/3$ cup			
	6 tablespoons	3 ounces				
	8 tablespoons	4 ounces	$1/2$ cup			
	10 tablespoons	5 ounces				
	$10\frac{2}{3}$ tablespoons		$2/3$ cup			
	12 tablespoons	6 ounces	$3/4$ cup			
	16 tablespoons	8 ounces	1 cup	$1/2$ pint		
		16 ounces	2 cups	1 pint		
		32 ounces	4 cups	2 pints	1 quart	
		128 ounces	16 cups	8 pints	4 quarts	1 gallon

quick u.s. weight conversions

ounces	pounds
4 ounces	$1/4$ pound
8 ounces	$1/2$ pound
12 ounces	$3/4$ pound
16 ounces	1 pound
24 ounces	$1\frac{1}{2}$ pounds
32 ounces	2 pounds
40 ounces	$2\frac{1}{2}$ pounds
48 ounces	3 pounds
56 ounces	$3\frac{1}{2}$ pounds
64 ounces	4 pounds
72 ounces	$4\frac{1}{2}$ pounds
80 ounces	5 pounds
160 ounces	10 pounds

METRIC CONVERSION TABLES

It's fun to buy cookbooks when you're overseas, but many foreign cookbooks use the metric system of weights and measures. The following tables give you the appropriate conversion so that you can try the recipes once you get home. Work out the math before you start cooking and double-check yourself for accuracy.

dry measurements

u.s. measurements	metric
$\frac{1}{16}$ ounce	1 gram
$\frac{1}{3}$ ounce	10 grams
$\frac{1}{2}$ ounce	15 grams
1 ounce	28.35 grams (30 grams for cooking purposes)
$3\frac{1}{2}$ ounces	100 grams
4 ounces ($\frac{1}{4}$ pound)	114 grams
5 ounces	140 grams
8 ounces ($\frac{1}{2}$ pound)	227 grams
9 ounces	250 grams or $\frac{1}{4}$ kilogram
16 ounces (1 pound)	453.6 grams (450 grams for cooking purposes)
18 ounces ($1\frac{1}{8}$ pounds)	500 grams or $\frac{1}{2}$ kilogram
32 ounces (2 pounds)	900 grams
36 ounces ($2\frac{1}{4}$ pounds)	1,000 grams or 1 kilogram
3 pounds	1,350 grams or $1\frac{1}{3}$ kilograms
4 pounds	2,800 grams or $1\frac{3}{4}$ kilograms

liquid measurements

u.s. measurements	metric
1 teaspoon	5 milliliters
1 tablespoon	15 milliliters
1 fluid ounce (2 tablespoons)	30 milliliters
2 fluid ounces ($\frac{1}{4}$ cup)	60 milliliters
8 fluid ounces (1 cup)	240 milliliters
16 fluid ounces (2 cups/1 pint)	480 milliliters
32 fluid ounces (2 pints/1 quart)	950 milliliters
128 fluid ounces (4 quarts/1 gallon)	3.75 liters

SALT AND PEPPER

Herbs and spices boost the flavor of many foods, but none are so fundamental to cooking as salt and pepper. Salt heightens and brightens the natural flavors in food. We have an inherent taste for this essential nutrient. You should always check for seasonings right before serving, tasting particularly for salt. Salt comes in many forms. The most common forms include:

- **Table salt.** A finely ground salt from mined rock salt deposits. It contains chemical additives to keep it free-flowing. Iodine is usually added, causing a slightly bitter aftertaste. Used for general cooking.

- **Kosher salt.** A purified, coarse-grained salt mined from rock salt. Preferred by many cooks because it contains no additives, it has a purer salt taste and dissolves more quickly than table salt.

- **Sea salt.** Comes in coarse to fine grains. Sea salt is not mined; rather, it is made by evaporating seawater. It contains no additives and, like kosher salt, has a pure salt taste and is preferred for cooking.

- **Fleur de sel.** A coarse-grained salt from France, "fleur de sel" means "flower of salt." It comes from the skin that forms on saline pools during summer months when weather conditions are just right. The salt is said to blossom when the skin appears. It is harvested by hand and is not processed. It has a delicate flavor and an earthy aroma that work well as a finishing touch to cooked food or as a special component to uncooked dishes like salads, dips, and cold soups.

Pepper is the next most commonly used seasoning after salt. Pungent and aromatic, pepper comes in many forms. The two basic forms are:

- **Black pepper.** An unripe peppercorn that has been dried at moderate temperature. Black pepper can be used in nearly every recipe, even on fruit or in chocolate dishes.

- **White pepper.** A fully ripened pepper fruit with its outer hull removed. White pepper is most often used in sauces where black pepper would spoil the color. It is also used whenever pungency is preferred over the peppery taste and intense aroma of black pepper.

FOOD SEASONING GUIDES

Nutmeg isn't just for cookies. Have you tried it on spinach or carrots? Not only will this guide help you decide how to flavor those chicken breasts you have sitting in your fridge, but it will also inspire you to try different herbs and spices on foods you never imagined. We've given you classic food and seasoning pairings to spark your creativity. In most large grocery stores, you can find fresh herbs as easily as you can find a head of lettuce. If you wish to buy dried and ground herbs from the spice shelf instead, make sure to buy in small quantities. Bottled herbs and spices can lose their flavor and potency as quickly as six months from the day they are packaged. To bring out the flavor of dried spices or seeds, toast them in a heavy skillet over medium heat, stirring continually until fragrant and a shade darker. Watch carefully, as they can burn quickly. See the Resource Guide on page 231 for reputable purveyors of herbs and spices.

vegetable seasoning guide

food	seasoning
Beans (dried)	Bay leaf, black pepper, cumin, garlic, parsley, thyme
Beets	Basil, dill, ginger, mint, mustard, parsley
Carrots	Cinnamon, cloves, dill, mint, nutmeg, parsley, savory, tarragon, thyme
Cauliflower	Chives, curry powder, nutmeg, parsley
Corn	Basil, chives, chile powder, dill, mint, parsley
Eggplant	Basil, cilantro, cumin, garlic, parsley, thyme
Green beans	Basil, black pepper, garlic, marjoram, savory, thyme
Peas	Basil, marjoram, mint, parsley, savory, tarragon
Potatoes	Chives, dill, garlic, rosemary, parsley, thyme
Spinach	Curry, garlic, nutmeg
Summer squash	Basil, chives, garlic, marjoram, oregano, parsley, savory
Winter squash	Allspice, cinnamon, cloves, mace, nutmeg
Tomatoes	Basil, chives, garlic, marjoram, oregano, parsley, savory, tarragon, thyme

meat, fish, and poultry seasoning guide

food	seasoning
Beef	Bay leaf, black pepper, chile powder, cumin, garlic, ginger, thyme
Chicken	Basil, bay leaf, chives, cilantro, cinnamon, cloves, cumin, curry powder, garlic, ginger, marjoram, mustard, rosemary, sage, tarragon, thyme
Duck	Parsley, sage, thyme
Fish	Basil, bay leaf, chervil, chives, cilantro, cumin, curry, dill, marjoram, mint, mustard, oregano, paprika, parsley, saffron, savory, tarragon, thyme
Lamb	Cumin, curry, garlic, mint, oregano, rosemary
Pork	Allspice, bay leaf, cumin, fennel, garlic, ginger, marjoram, mustard, rosemary, sage, thyme
Turkey	Bay leaf, rosemary, sage, savory
Veal	Basil, bay leaf, lemon, parsley, savory, tarragon, thyme

meat, seafood, and cheese

MEAT, MEAT, AND MORE MEAT

Many factors affect the quality of meat: the age of the animal, its diet, its breed, how it was slaughtered, how it was stored, whether or not it has been aged, and the packing and shipping conditions. Of course, these are all out of your control. What is in your control is where you buy your meat, what cut of meat you buy, and how you prepare it. Because of high turnover, many warehouse club stores offer excellent quality, low-cost meat. When buying meat, look for external fat that is white, not yellow. Look for beef or lamb that is red to brownish-red, with marbling (thin lines and flakes of fat) throughout. Pork and veal should be fine-grained and pale pink.

Seasoning with salt and pepper is the single most important step in flavoring meats. Meats should be seasoned before cooking so that the flavors have a chance to mellow and develop while the meat is cooking. This is especially the case with salt. Pepper actually becomes less pronounced with cooking, so you may want to add a little extra pepper when cooking is completed.

Dry rubs are mixtures of spices and herbs that are rubbed into meat before cooking. Meat can be cooked immediately or refrigerated for up to a day or two. The longer a rub sits on the meat, the more the flavor of the rub will permeate the meat.

Wet marinades are used primarily for flavor, although they do have some tenderizing effects, especially on thin cuts of meat. They also work well on sirloin, chuck, top round (London broil), flank steak, and chops. The tenderizing components of any marinade are the acidic ingredients: citrus juice, wine, vinegar, or soy sauce. Do not marinate tender, thin, or small cuts of meat for too long—a few hours is plenty—or the acid can break down the meat, making it mushy. Marinades are not useful for large cuts like roasts, since marinades don't penetrate far enough into the meat.

They also don't work well for tough cuts like brisket or shank, which contain too much connective tissue. No amount of marinating will break this down.

The only way to make tough cuts of meat tender is to braise or stew them. This produces a very flavorful liquid, while enhancing the texture and taste of the meat. To braise or stew meat, you should first brown the meat in a little oil over high heat before adding any liquid. Once the meat is browned on all sides, remove it from the pan and deglaze the pan by pouring in a flavorful liquid like stock or wine and scraping up any browned bits with a wooden spoon to add flavor and depth to the braising liquid. Once the pan is deglazed, return the meat to the pan and add additional liquid. Cover and simmer over low heat for several hours, or until the meat is tender.

major cuts of meat

- **Top back.** This section contains the rib, short loin, and sirloin. Steaks and roasts are cut from this section. These tender cuts have a fine-grained texture and benefit from dry-heat cooking methods like grilling, broiling, roasting, and sautéing. Filet mignon and tenderloin are the most tender and expensive. New York strip or top loin, Porterhouse, T-bone, and rib eye steaks are just a bit less tender, but more flavorful and less expensive.

- **Shoulder and side.** This section yields the chuck (or shoulder), flank, plate, and brisket (or foreshank). These tougher cuts are best braised or stewed. They are more coarsely grained with tougher connective tissue, which dissolves with moist, low-heat cooking.

- **Leg, chuck, and flank.** The leg, or the round, along with part of the chuck and flank, are in the middle of the tough-tender scale. These slightly tougher cuts (like top round) marinate very well. Rump roasts, also in this category, are great slow-roasted with dry rubs. Bottom round and round steaks are best braised.

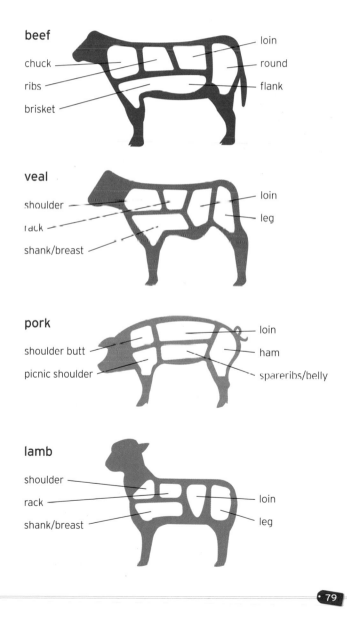

beef
- loin
- chuck
- round
- ribs
- flank
- brisket

veal
- loin
- shoulder
- leg
- rack
- shank/breast

pork
- loin
- shoulder butt
- ham
- picnic shoulder
- spareribs/belly

lamb
- shoulder
- rack
- loin
- shank/breast
- leg

COOKED MEAT TEMPERATURE GUIDE

Most new hosts and hostesses are afraid to prepare a roast beef or a leg of lamb for fear that it will under or over-cook.

Take the guesswork out of cooking meats by using the cooked-meat temperature guide below. For accuracy, use an instant-read thermometer, available at grocery and cookware stores. Please note, the following internal temperatures yield what most cooks consider to be the optimum taste and texture. However, some temperatures are lower than the 160 degrees suggested by the U.S. Food Safety and Inspection Service guidelines, at which temperature all meat bacteria are killed, though poultry must be cooked to at least 175°.

proper temperatures

chicken	temperature (°F) when done
Thigh	175° to 180°
Breast	175° to 180°

beef	temperature (°F) when done
Rare	130°
Medium-rare	140°
Medium	150°
Medium-well	165°

lamb	temperature (°F) when done
Rare	130°
Medium-rare	140°
Medium	150°
Ground lamb	165°

pork	temperature (°F) when done
All cuts	165° to 170°

veal	temperature (°F) when done
Medium	150°
Medium-well	165°

SEAFOOD SUBSTITUTIONS

Sometimes it is difficult to find the fish specified in recipes. This chart will help you make good substitutions.

delicate-textured seafood

mild-flavored	medium-flavored	strong-flavored
Cod	Black cod	Bluefish
Crabmeat	Butterfish	
Haddock	Lingcod	
Flounder	Perch (lake)	
Pollock	Whitefish	
Scallops	Whiting	
Skate		
Sole		

medium-textured seafood

mild-flavored	medium-flavored	strong-flavored
Crawfish	Mullet	Mackerel
Lobster	Perch (ocean)	Salmon (canned)
Orange roughy	Shad	Sardines (canned)
Rockfish	Smelt	Smoked fish
Sheep's head	Trout	
Shrimp	Tuna (canned)	
Tilapia		
Walleye pike		

firm-textured seafood

mild-flavored	medium-flavored	strong-flavored
Grouper	Catfish	Marlin
Halibut	Mahi mahi	Salmon
Monkfish	Octopus	Swordfish
Seabass	Pompano	Tuna
Snapper	Shark	
Squid		
Sturgeon		

brie bits

The most often asked question about Brie is, "Can I eat the rind?" The answer is "yes," but it can be easily removed with a sharp knife if you wish. Brie is at its best when served at room temperature or slightly warm.

For an easy presentation of whole Brie, remove the wrapper and label but leave the rind intact. Place the Brie back into the wooden box. With a sharp knife or cookie cutter, cut and remove a 3-inch circle from the top of the cheese. Remove the circle of rind. Place the wooden box in a preheated, 350-degree oven for 30 minutes, or until the cheese has melted. Let your guests scoop out the melted cheese using crackers or crudités.

For another easy presentation, place the whole Brie in the center of a piece of thawed frozen puff pastry. Cover the surface with pesto. Place another piece of puff pastry on top. Pinch the pieces of puff pastry together, trimming as necessary to encase the Brie. Using a sharp knife or cookie cutter, cut a 3-inch circle out of the puff pastry. Fill the hole with pine nuts. Place on an ungreased baking sheet, brush with beaten egg, and bake in a preheated, 400-degree oven for 20 to 30 minutes, or until puffed and golden. For a sweet alternative, omit the pesto and pine nuts and use apricot jam topped with fresh raspberries or dried cranberries.

CHEESE GLOSSARY

Boursin, feta, creamy, aged . . . where to begin? This cheese glossary should clear up the confusion about "Gouda" cheeses.

fresh or unripened cheeses

Fresh cheeses are uncooked, resulting in a mild and creamy texture with a slightly tart flavor.

- **Cream cheese.** A soft cow's milk cheese used throughout the kitchen in baking, dips, dressings, and confections. Popular spread on bagels and toast.

- **Feta.** A semi-soft cheese made from sheep or goat's milk. It is white and crumbly and usually packaged in brine. Use for snacks, salads, sauces, and fillings.

- **Mascarpone.** A soft cow's milk cheese with a flavor that makes it a popular addition to sweet and savory dishes.

- **Mozzarella.** A firm cheese usually made from cow's milk, but traditionally made with water buffalo's milk. Its texture works well on pizzas, salads, or sandwiches.

- **Ricotta.** A soft, fluffy cheese with small grains and a sweet flavor important to many pasta dishes and desserts.

goat's milk cheeses

With a sharp and tangy flavor, goat's milk cheeses range in texture from very soft and fresh to very hard, depending on age.

- **Chèvre.** Often refers to small, soft, creamy cheeses that come in a variety of shapes (cones, disks, pyramids, or logs). They are often coated with ash, herbs, or seasonings. They are excellent for cooking and complement a wide variety of flavors. The finest brands are Bûcheron, Chevroin (very mild), and Montrachet (tangy and soft).

soft cheeses

Soft cheeses are characterized by their thin skins and creamy centers.

- **Bel Paese.** Made from cow's milk. With its mild and creamy texture and fruity flavor, it makes an excellent snack.

- **Brie.** A rind-ripened cow's milk cheese that is rich, creamy, and oozy. Brie is the classic after-dinner cheese. It is also used in soups, sauces, and hors d'oeuvres. Brie is sold in round wooden boxes and is readily available in an 8-ounce size (sometimes called baby Brie), a 2-pound wheel, and pre-cut wedges.

- **Boursin.** A triple-cream cow's milk cheese usually flavored with peppers, herbs, or garlic. Smooth and creamy, it makes an excellent breakfast cheese or a filling for baked chicken.

- **Camembert.** A rind-ripened, creamy-smooth, cow's milk cheese It is creamy, smooth cow's milk cheese. It is similar in taste to Brie, but milder. Serve it after dinner with fruit.

semi-soft cheeses

Semi-soft cheese have a mild, buttery taste and a smooth, sliceable texture.

- **Fontina.** A cow's milk cheese. It has a dark-gold, crusty rind and a pale-gold dense interior with a nutty and rich flavor.

- **Gorgonzola.** A blue-veined cow's milk cheese with a creamy interior and bluish-green veins. It's creamier than Stilton or Roquefort, with a more pungent, spicy, earthy flavor.

- **Gouda.** A mild, buttery cheese. It's very popular for snacking and in fondues.

- **Havarti.** A cow's milk cheese, very similar to the Danish Tilsit. Pale yellow with many small, irregular holes, it has a mild flavor and creamy texture. It is often flavored with dill, caraway seeds, or pepper and is very popular for snacking and in sandwiches.

- **Pain de Pyrenees.** A pale-yellow cow's milk cheese with irregular holes and a sweet and mellow, nutty flavor.

- **Port du Salut.** A cow's milk cheese that is smooth, rich, and savory It's great for snacking or with fruit.

- **Roquefort.** A blue-veined sheep's milk cheese. Intensely pungent with a rich, salty flavor and strong aroma, it goes well before or after dinner.

- **Stilton.** Another blue-veined cow's milk cheese. It is pungent, rich, and tangy, combining the best of the cheddars and blues. It tastes best served alone with plain crackers, dried fruit, or port.

storing cheese

Most cheeses are best kept refrigerated, wrapped first in plastic wrap and then in a resealable plastic storage bag to keep odors out and moisture in. Firm and hard cheeses can be kept for several weeks. Fresh cheeses will spoil in seven to ten days because of their high-moisture content. Some cheeses that have become hard or dry may still be grated for cooking or baking. Freezing is possible but not recommended because it changes the cheese's texture, making it mealy or tough.

leftover cheese

Never throw out those leftover bits and pieces. A classic French recipe is to take bits of Brie, cheddar, mozzarella, and any other leftover cheeses and mix them together with garlic and wine. They call this *fromage fort* ("strong cheese"). To do this at home, take about a pound of assorted leftover cheese and trim off any dried-out or moldy parts. Put three or four cloves of garlic in a food processor and pulse until the garlic is chopped. Add the cheese, $1/2$ cup of dry white wine, and at least a teaspoon of ground black pepper. Process until the mixture becomes soft and creamy, about 30 seconds. Wrap tightly and refrigerate for 1 to 3 days. Spread on thick slices of bread and broil for a few minutes until brown and bubbly.

firm cheeses

Not hard or brittle as their name might imply, firm cheeses include a variety of textures such as flaky cheddars and holey Swiss.

- **Cheddar.** A cow's milk cheese with a dense, crumbly texture. The best cheddars are made from raw milk and aged for several months. Flavors range from mild to very sharp, depending upon the age. Colby and longhorn are two well-known mild, soft-textured cheddars.

- **Gruyère.** A cow's milk cheese that is moist and highly flavored with a sweet nuttiness similar to Swiss. It melts easily and is often used with meats, in sauces, or served after dinner.

- **Jarlsberg.** A Swiss-type cow's milk cheese with a mild, delicate, sweet flavor and large holes. It's popular for sandwiches, snacks, and in cooking.

- **Monterey Jack.** A cheddar-like cheese that is very mild and rich. Dry-aged Jack develops a tough, brown rind and a rich, firm, yellow interior. It tastes nutty and sharp and is dry enough for grating.

- **Provolone.** A mild, smooth cow's milk cheese. Smoked provolone is also popular, especially for snacking. Provolone works well in sandwiches and for cooking. It is often used for melting on pizza and pasta dishes.

- **Swiss or Emmentaler.** A cow's milk cheese with mellow, rich, and nutty flavors, a natural rind, and a light yellow interior full of large holes. This is the basic fondue cheese. It is also used in sandwiches and snacks, or served after dinner with fruit and nuts.

hard cheeses

Hard cheeses are carefully aged for extended periods, and their texture is the most conducive to grating.

- **Asiago.** A sharp, nutty cow's milk cheese with a cheddar-like texture. If aged, it is suitable for grating. Milder than Parmesan, it melts easily and is often used in cooking or shaved onto salads.

- **Parmigiano-Reggiano or Parmesan.** A cow's milk cheese used for grating and cooking. It is rich, spicy, and sharp and is excellent served with nuts and fruit. Its rind can be used to add flavor to rich sauces.

- **Pecorino Romano.** A sheep's milk cheese. Brittle and sharp, with a sheepy tang, it is excellent with olives, sausages, and red wine.

CHEESE PAIRINGS

Once you feel a bit more comfortable in the world of cheese, choose a wine and a few types of fruit that will embolden the flavors in the cheese. Since the matching-up can be difficult, we've put several of our top choices for cheese, wine, and fruit pairings here for you. Find your favorite wine in the list and buy the cheese and fruit to go with it, or pick a cheese that sounds yummy and follow our recommendation for the corresponding wine and fruit—whatever suits your fancy.

cheese, wine, and fruit pairings

cheese	wine	fruit
Blue cheese, Roquefort	Strong reds	Apples, grapes, pears
Brie, Camembert	Cabernet Sauvignon, Merlot, Pinot Noir, dry port	Plums, berries, apples
Colby	Port, sherry, Madeira, Burgundy	Melons, peaches, pineapple
Edam, Gouda, cheddar	Cabernet Sauvignon, Merlot, Pinot Noir, Burgundy	Apples, grapes, pears
Goat cheese, chèvre, feta	Chenin Blanc, Sancerre, Pouilly fume	Apples, pears, peaches
Gorgonzola	Sauternes, champagne	Pears
Gruyère, provolone	Chardonnay, Sauvignon Blanc, Beaujolais	Melons, peaches, pineapple
Monterey Jack	Chardonnay, cream sherry	Plums, strawberries, apples
Mozzarella	Pinot Blanc, Pinot Grigio	Melons, peaches, pineapple
Muenster	Beaujolais, Zinfandel, cream sherry	Melons, peaches, pineapple
Neufchâtel, cream cheese	Champagne	Apples, grapes, pears
Parmigiano-Reggiano	Chianti, Burgundy	Figs, grapes, apples
Stilton	Port	Pears
Swiss, Emmentaler	Riesling, Gewürztraminer	Apples, grapes, pears

cheers!

SERVING ALCOHOL

Everyone's fallen into the beverage abyss: Should you buy more red wine than white wine? How do you make a Singapore Sling? Should you use real or plastic glasses? This chapter will help you successfully plan your party's beverage needs.

First and foremost: SAFETY. Be aware of how much alcohol is being consumed and by whom. If you do not feel comfortable with this or if there are too many guests to keep track of, enlist the help of friends or a designated driver who is sober and can assess the situation. (Be sure to pay for the driver's gas.) Hiring a trained barman and/or waiters can alleviate this pressure. If you anticipate a rowdy party, you may even want to hire an off-duty police officer who does security work on the side. The officer can keep an eye on the crowd and act as a designated driver. As trained professionals, they will be able to spot any guests that have been celebrating excessively and help you deal with the situation effectively.

What and how much to buy really depends on the make-up of the guest list. For example, one would assume that the alcohol consumed by bachelor party revelers is going to be far more than the alcohol consumed at a mid-afternoon ladies' luncheon. The easiest way to find out is to ask your guests. Are they wine drinkers, beer drinkers, or teetotalers?

Alcohol is usually one of the biggest party expenses, so consider your budget. For larger groups, serving hard liquor can be less expensive than wine. A 750-ml bottle of wine will yield about five drinks, whereas a 750-ml bottle of spirits (rum, vodka, gin, etc.) will yield about sixteen cocktails.

If you anticipate all of your guests arriving at the same time or if you have a large number of guests, split the bar into two areas, or place glasses of pre-poured wine on an entry table. This way guests can help themselves and alleviate bar-traffic congestion.

choices for glassware

Budget plays an important role in choosing the glasses for a party. The tone of an elegant cocktail party can be dashed when the perfectly chilled Chardonnay is served out of Styrofoam cups. If you own enough glasses and are prepared to wash and dry them throughout the party, then go for it. If you plan to entertain frequently, you can start a collection of inexpensive glasses from home stores or discount stores. Renting all-purpose, 10-ounce glasses can be a great way to go if budget permits. If money is limited, start the event with real glasses and switch to disposable glasses for the latter part of the evening. Most rental companies request that glasses need only be rinsed and returned in the original boxes. A good quality plastic glass can be used for informal outdoor events.

iced down

How many times have you had to run out mid-party to the local liquor store for extra ice? Ice is an inexpensive part of the bar set-up, so opt for more rather than less. Estimate 1½ to 2 pounds per person. "Chilling tubs" are large, heavy-duty plastic containers that cost about $5 each from club or discount stores. Fill them with ice and a little water to chill white wine and other drinks. This takes about 30 minutes and leaves your refrigerator (and bathtub) free. It takes about 40 to 50 pounds of ice to fill one chilling tub. A great "do it for less" tip is to fill your empty washing machine with ice and chill cans in it. As the ice melts, the water drains away. Unplug the washer before the party just in case one of your tipsy guests wonders, "What would happen if I turned it on?"

BEVERAGE CONSUMPTION GUIDES

For the first hour of the party, assume 2 drinks per person. For the remainder of party, allow for 1 drink per person for each hour thereafter.

For instance, if you have 50 guests attending a 4 hour party, you should plan on serving 250 drinks:

- 50 guests x 2 drinks (per person for the first hour) = 100 servings
- 50 guests x 3 drinks (1 drink per hour for 3 hours) = 150 servings

100 servings for the first hour
+ 150 servings for the next 3 hours
250 servings total for a 4-hour party

cool ice

If your party is fairly small and you feel creative, try making ice cubes to match the drinks you are serving. Freeze orange juice in ice cube trays and add to sangria, or place pieces of fruit in the ice trays before adding water to make colorful and flavorful ice cubes for a summer fruit punch.

bar essentials

Don't forget other bar essentials like paper cocktail napkins (five per guest), lemons, limes, bottle openers for wine and beer, ice buckets, and tongs.

cocktail extras

For a cocktail party, you may want to add olives, cocktail onions, cherries, celery sticks, a blender, cocktail shaker, and salt for margaritas.

87

bottle yields

bottle size	beverage type	yield	serving size
750 milliliters	Champagne	6 servings	4 ounces
750 milliliters	Wine	5 servings	5 ounces
750 milliliters	Spirits	16 cocktails	1½ ounces
1 liter	Spirits	22 cocktails	1½ ounces
1½ liters	Spirits	33 cocktails	1½ ounces
1 liter	Mineral water	4 servings	8 ounces
2 liter	Soda	8 servings	8 ounces
12 ounces	Beer	1 serving	12 ounces

bar service

Inevitably someone will ask for a "sex on the beach" or a "monkey's uncle" cocktail. Unless you have a fully stocked bar and a whiz of a bartender, avoid this by asking your guests, "Would you like a drink?" followed by, "We have wine, beer, or soda."

partial bar (chart is based on a 3 to 3½-hour-long event)

ingredients	12 guests	25 guests	50 guests	75 guests
White wine	7 (750-ml) bottles	15 (750-ml) bottles	30 (750-ml) bottles	45 (750-ml) bottles
Red wine	4 (750-ml) bottles	8 (750-ml) bottles	16 (750-ml) bottles	24 (750-ml) bottles
Beer	18 (12-ounce) bottles	32 (12-ounce) bottles	64 (12-ounce) bottles	96 (12-ounce) bottles
Mineral water	3 (1-liter) bottles	5 (1-liter) bottles	10 (1-liter) bottles	15 (1-liter) bottles
7-Up or Sprite	1 (2-liter) bottle	3 (2-liter) bottles	6 (2-liter) bottles	9 (2-liter) bottles
Cola	2 (2-liter) bottles	4 (2-liter) bottles	8 (2-liter) bottles	12 (2-liter) bottles
Diet cola	2 (2-liter) bottles	4 (2-liter) bottles	8 (2-liter) bottles	12 (2-liter) bottles
Glasses	30 (10-ounce) glasses	75 (10-ounce) glasses	150 (10-ounce) glasses	225 (10-ounce) glasses
Ice	18 pounds	38 pounds	75 pounds	115 pounds

full bar (chart is based on a 3 to 3½-hour-long event)

ingredients	12 guests	25 guests	50 guests	75 guests
White wine	4 (750-ml) bottles	9 (750-ml) bottles	18 (750-ml) bottles	27 (750-ml) bottles
Red wine	3 (750-ml) bottles	7 (750-ml) bottles	14 (750-ml) bottles	21 (750-ml) bottles
Beer	5 (12-ounce) bottles	12 (12-ounce) bottles	24 (12-ounce) bottles	36 (12-ounce) bottles
Gin	1 (750-ml) bottle	2 (750-ml) bottles	4 (750-ml) bottles	6 (750-ml) bottles
Rum	1 (750-ml) bottle	2 (750-ml) bottles	4 (750-ml) bottles	6 (750-ml) bottles
Vodka	1 (750-ml) bottle	3 (750-ml) bottles	6 (750-ml) bottles	9 (750-ml) bottles
Scotch	1 (750-ml) bottle	1 (750-ml) bottle	2 (750-ml) bottles	3 (750-ml) bottles
Bourbon	1 (750-ml) bottle	1 (750-ml) bottle	2 (750-ml) bottles	3 (750-ml) bottles
Mineral water	4 (1-liter) bottles	6 (1-liter) bottles	12 (1-liter) bottles	18 (1-liter) bottles
7-Up or Sprite	1 (2-liter) bottle	2 (2-liter) bottles	4 (2-liter) bottles	6 (2-liter) bottles
Cola	1 (2-liter) bottle	3 (2-liter) bottles	6 (2-liter) bottles	9 (2-liter) bottles
Diet cola	1 (2-liter) bottle	3 (2-liter) bottles	6 (2-liter) bottles	9 (2-liter) bottles
Tonic	1 (2-liter) bottle	3 (2-liter) bottles	6 (2-liter) bottles	9 (2-liter) bottles
Glasses	30 (10-ounce) glasses	75 (10-ounce) glasses	150 (10-ounce) glasses	225 (10-ounce) glasses
Ice	24 pounds	50 pounds	100 pounds	150 pounds

coffee service

If you are serving coffee, stock up on half-and-half, sugar, and sugar substitutes. Consider adding flavored syrups or liqueurs to the selection such as Irish cream and Kahlúa, or chocolate mint sticks as stirrers.

The measurements below allow for one 5-ounce cup of coffee, 2 teaspoons of cream and sugar, and 1½ packets of sugar substitute per person. If you have large coffee mugs or expect your guests to drink two cups of coffee each, double the recipe. Party-size coffee pots often have measurements included on the inside.

coffee service

ingredients	12 (5-ounce) cups	25 (5-ounce) cups	50 (5-ounce) cups	75 (5-ounce) cups
Ground coffee	4 ounces (1¼ cups)	8 ounces (2½ cups)	1 pound (5 cups)	1½ pounds (7½ cups)
Bottled or filtered water	2 quarts plus 1 cup	1 gallon plus 1 pint	2 gallons plus 1 quart	3½ gallons
Half-and-half or cream	½ cup (4 ounces)	1 cup (8 ounces)	2 cups (16 ounces)	3 cups (24 ounces)
Sugar	½ cup (3½ ounces)	1 cup (7 ounces)	2 cups (14 ounces)	3 cups (21 ounces)
Sugar substitute	18 packets	36 packets	72 packets	108 packets

how much?

For water, fill the glass almost full. For wine, fill the glass one-third to one-half full. This allows guests to aerate their wine.

reds, bordeaux

water

burgundy

whites, sauvignon blanc

champagne flute

A FEW WORDS ON WINE. . .

Trying to choose a wine from the thousands of bottles on display can be overwhelming. Unless you know exactly what your guests like, ask the wine manager to recommend a good selection that fits your budget.

- **Season.** Low-alcohol wines are best in summer. Choose light, refreshing whites and rosés, or even some light reds in warm weather. Choose more robust wines in cooler weather.

- **Extending your dollar.** If serving large numbers, combine wine with chilled fruit juices. Hot punches and mulled wine make good use of inexpensive wines as well.

- **Temperature.** Champagne should be served from 45 to 50 degrees, white wine from 50 to 55 degrees, and red wine from 55 to 65 degrees. If you are chilling a fairly expensive bottle of wine or champagne in an ice bucket, slip the bottle into a clear plastic bag to protect the label.

wine glossary

- **Barbera.** Light and fruity Italian red wine.

- **Cabernet Sauvignon.** Rich and full-bodied red wine, often tasting of black currant and sometimes mint and eucalyptus. Improves with age. Best served with red meat.

- **Chardonnay.** Depending upon how it's made, this white wine is either dry and light or full-bodied and buttery. Excellent served with creamy sauces.

- **Chenin Blanc.** Can be dry to sweet. Sweet Chenin Blanc generally tastes of honey. Dry Chenin Blanc is fresh and fruity. Dry versions are excellent with shellfish.

- **Gamay.** Also know as Beaujolais. Most are light, fruity reds that are meant to be consumed while the wine is young. The taste of pears, bananas, and raspberries can often be detected in Gamays. Great for summer picnics.

- **Gewürztraminer.** Spicy, full-bodied white wine that can be dry or sweet. With its rose perfume and litchi flavor, Gewürztraminer is one of the few wines to go well with spicy foods.

- **Merlot.** Rich and smooth red wine.

- **Muscat.** Musky white wine, often very sweet. Sweet varieties make excellent dessert wines. Tastes of peaches and apricots, and sometimes pineapple. Excellent with fresh fruit.

- **Pinot Grigio.** An Italian white wine that's aromatic, light, and smooth. Excellent served with fish dishes.

- **Pinot Noir.** Light to medium-bodied red wine with a strawberry aroma and hints of red currants and cherries.

- **Riesling.** White wine that can vary from bone-dry to extremely sweet. Light in body, yet strongly flavored. The high acidity balances the richness of this wine. Wonderful paired with spicy foods.

- **Sangiovese.** Also known as Chianti, an Italian red wine.

- **Sauvignon Blanc.** Also known as Pouilly Fumé or Fumé Blanc. Very dry, fresh white wine. Tastes of green grass and gooseberries. Good with fish and with salads dressed with vinaigrettes.

- **Sémillon.** Dry to very sweet white wine. Makes some of the best sweet dessert wines. Serve with fruit.

- **Syrah.** Also known as Shiraz. Dark, full-bodied red wines that are less tannic when aged. Aromas of black currant, raspberry, cedar, black pepper, and spice.

- **Viognier.** A perfumed and full-bodied white wine.

- **Zinfandel.** Can be a light white or rosé wine, or a massive and tannic red. Always with a berry-like flavor.

hostess gifts

When a guest brings wine as a hostess gift, do you have to open it? The choice is completely yours. You can say, "Would you like me to open this now so we can both enjoy a glass?" Or, if you prefer, tell them that you're going to save it for the next special occasion, when it can be appreciated on its own. Either response is appropriate.

leftover wine

Your party's over, and the guests are leaving—and leaving behind half-empty bottles of wine. Pour those partial bottles into a saucepan and bring to a boil. Lower heat and simmer until the wine reduces by three-quarters. The alcohol will be mostly boiled out and the flavor will become very intense. Cool, pour into ice cube trays, and place in the freezer. When frozen, store in resealable plastic storage bags for future use. Reduced wine adds a lovely depth to sauces, gravies, soups, or even dessert syrups.

the logistics of
quantity cooking

The themed menus in *Do It For Less! Parties* all serve 12, 25, 50, and 75 guests and include shopping and do-ahead lists to make your preparation experience as stress-free as possible. We know all the recipes work—and work well, having tested them to rave reviews. Even when you're armed with quality recipes and menu countdowns, cooking for a crowd can be quite a daunting responsibility. It demands a different set of skills than does cooking for a family of four. So take the time to read this chapter thoroughly. Even the most experienced party-givers will find some words of wisdom here to improve their process of cooking for a crowd.

SAFETY AND SANITATION 101

Have you ever felt queasy a few hours after eating at a barbecue? The cause may not have been overeating; some unseen bacteria may have snuck into your coleslaw. Food contamination and food poisoning can be a serious problem. Follow this list of considerations to keep your food and guests safe.

personal hygiene

Without getting into gory details about the risks of contracting a nasty virus like Hepatitis A or a bacterial infection like salmonella, it is crucial to mention that meticulous personal hygiene is essential in any kitchen.

- **Clean hands.** Wash hands before, during, and after handling food, using soap, a nailbrush, and hot water. Wash hands after using the restroom, smoking, coughing, sneezing, or scratching, and don't cook with lotion on your hands.

- **Avoid jewelry.** Jewelry can get caught in appliances and end up in the soup. Use common sense and discretion when cooking while wearing any jewelry, or better still, remove your jewelry altogether.

- **Secure hair.** The rule for jewelry applies also to hair. If you don't want hair in the food, either tie your hair back or wear a hat.

- **Cover wounds.** Cover any cuts or open wounds with proper dressing. Wear disposable plastic gloves over the dressing to prevent any infection from spreading. Remember to change your gloves when switching from raw meats and unwashed produce to cooked foods.

- **Avoid eating while cooking.** If you are hungry, stop and take a break. Chewing food, gum, or toothpicks while cooking can lead to unwanted surprises in the food.

- **Tasting protocol.** Fingers are for pointing, spoons are for tasting. Use a spoon and not your finger to taste the sauce for seasoning. After tasting, wash the spoon before using again. No double-dipping. Alternatively, use plastic disposable spoons and discard after each use.

keep it clean

Keeping your work area clean will reduce the risk of contamination.

- **Disinfect surfaces.** Always wash cutting boards thoroughly with hot, soapy water when preparing different types of food. You don't want to contaminate your fruit and vegetables with chicken juices. Nor do you want your brownies to taste of garlic. Surprisingly, wooden cutting boards are safer to use than plastic for meats and poultry. Wash counters and work surfaces with hot, soapy water and an anti-bacterial cleanser or diluted bleach.

- **Clean as you go.** Get into the habit of washing pots, pans, and dishes as you go to keep things running smoothly and prevent a huge pile of dishes at the end of the day that nobody wants to clean. If you have a dishwasher, always empty it before you start cooking. Stopping to put clean dishes away while you work will only slow you down.

LOOK BEFORE YOU BUY

There are strict health and safety guidelines enforced by government agencies for anyone selling food of any kind. Always buy from a reputable grocery store or supplier.

The first step to sanitation starts in the grocery store. When buying packaged meats or other high-protein foods such as milk and deli products, cream, cheese, or tofu, check the "use by" or "best before" dates to ensure

helpful hint:
Bacteria can thrive on kitchen sponges, rags, and dishtowels, so they should be washed frequently, preferably in a bleach solution. To quickly disinfect a sponge or rag, dampen and then microwave on high for at least 1 minute.

optimum freshness. Sometimes if you look further back into the refrigerator case you will find fresher products. Beef, veal, and lamb should be red and fresh-looking. Ground beef, turkey, or chicken that has a gray tone is usually a few days old.

As tempting as it seems, avoid buying fish or shellfish from vendors parked in a truck stop or on the side of the street with a cooler and one of those "100 shrimp for $10" signs. There is a reason why that shrimp is so unbelievably cheap.

When buying whole fish, look for a fresh, mild ocean smell. The eyes should be clear and shiny, not cloudy or sunken. Look for a red or pink color around the gills and shiny, bright scales that are tight on the skin. Pass on any fish that is soft to the touch. When pressed, the flesh should be firm and elastic; it should not dent easily.

As most recipes call for fillets or steaks, and that is most likely how you will be buying your fish, you must rely on your sense of smell to judge freshness. If in doubt, don't buy it; choose frozen fish instead. It is often the freshest fish on the market because it is frequently frozen on the boat immediately after being caught.

CROSS-CONTAMINATION NATION

Once you have selected your meat, place it in the lowest rack of the shopping cart where the juices will not drip onto ready-to-eat or raw foods. Meat "sealed" in plastic packaging can still drip everywhere and may contain bacteria that, if not thoroughly cooked or washed off of fruits and vegetables, could cause a guest to become sick. This transfer of bacteria is called cross-contamination and is responsible for many outbreaks of food poisoning. Be aware of cross-contamination when preparing food. If you use a cutting board to prepare raw chicken, do not use the same board for cutting lettuce unless it has been thoroughly washed with hot, soapy water. A safer and more hygienic solution is to have cutting boards designated for specific duties, e.g., one for raw meats, one for cooked meats, and one for fruits and vegetables. Look for plastic cutting boards in a variety of colors, and allot one color for each duty. If you have only one cutting board, choose wood. Another alternative is to use disposable cutting boards available in grocery stores.

FOOD STORAGE AND HANDLING

There are two reasons to store food properly: sanitation and expense. Holding foods at the proper temperatures in the proper containers will keep them from dehydration and spoilage. Spoiled food is money wasted; you want your food to last as long as possible in its ideal condition.

Proper refrigeration at all times preserves freshness and keeps bacteria at bay. Perishables must be kept at 40 degrees or less and frozen food at 32 degrees or less. Bacteria thrives between 40 degrees and 140 degrees. We call this the "danger zone." Foods should not be kept in this range for more than 4 hours. Keep this in mind when serving a buffet, storing leftovers, and grocery shopping.

Temperatures vary widely for properly cooked, safe-to-eat chicken, pork, and beef. See the guides on page 80 for proper cooking temperatures. For packaged goods, read the label. Many product labels display the correct cooking temperatures on them.

ideal temperatures

location	temperature (°F)
Freezer	0°
Refrigerator	8° to 40°
Cool room temperature	65°
Warm room temperature	70° to 75°
Lukewarm or tepid liquid	95°
Warm liquid	105° to 115°
Hot liquid	120°
Boiling water	212°
Rising bread	80°
Low/slow oven	180° to 225°
Warm oven	300° to 325°
Moderate oven	350° to 375°
Hot oven	400° to 450°
Very hot oven	475° to 500°

Leftover food should be cooled, placed in airtight containers, and refrigerated as soon as possible. Eat refrigerated leftovers within three days. Be sure to reheat them to a temperature of 170 degrees to destroy any bacteria.

Plan your grocery-shopping trip so that perishables are unrefrigerated for the shortest time possible. You may want to consider having a cooler packed with ice or reusable cooling packs in your car if you have delicate items such as seafood that need to be refrigerated. A cooler will also come in handy if you are shopping in the middle of summer or the ride home is a long one. Once home, store all food in proper, well-sealed storage containers. Below are guidelines for you to follow when storing food:

 Buy coolers at the end of summer when they go on sale.

- **Breads.** Bread dries out faster in the refrigerator than at room temperature, but is less likely to get moldy. Store in paper or plastic. Alternatively, wrap tightly in plastic wrap, cover with aluminum foil, and freeze.

- **Canned goods.** Opened cans of food may be safely stored if covered tightly with plastic wrap. The exceptions are acidic fruits and vegetables like tomatoes, pineapple, and sauerkraut. These need to be stored in glass or plastic containers.

- **Chocolate.** Wrap tightly in parchment paper, and then in foil. Store in a cool place, but not in the refrigerator; 60 degrees is ideal. Chocolate chips are low in cocoa solids, so they are less sensitive to temperature. Store chocolate chips in an airtight container at room temperature.

- **Cooked food.** Refrigerate cooked food immediately. Pour warm foods into pans so that the food is no more than 2 inches deep. Stir large pans occasionally while they cool to hasten the cooling process. Set a hot pan in an ice bath to cool the food faster and safer. Contrary to popular opinion, letting the pan cool at room temperature merely allows it to spend longer in the bacteria-breeding range of 40 to 140 degrees.

- **Dairy.** Milk should be stored below 40 degrees to prevent bacterial growth. Moving a gallon container of milk in and out of the refrigerator many times will shorten its life and increase the chance of bacterial growth. Don't pour milk that has been left out back into the container, as it can contaminate the whole container. Hard cheese can be stored at room temperature if room temperature is below 80 degrees. Wrap cheese in plastic to prevent mold. Eggs will usually keep for a few weeks if refrigerated. Store eggs on the interior refrigerator shelves and not in the door. The constant opening and closing can make the door the warmest part of the refrigerator. Butter picks up flavors from other foods, so always store it in a container or wrap it well.

- **Dry goods.** The ideal storage temperature for dry goods is 50 degrees.

- **Fruits and vegetables.** Rinse in cold water and pat dry. Remove any dead leaves. Use a salad spinner to dry greens as much as possible, Store the cleaned greens in a resealable plastic storage bag, and layer with paper towels. Most fruits keep well if refrigerated. To store soft berries, put them in one layer onto a cookie sheet lined with paper towels. Throw away any moldy ones. Cover lightly with additional paper towels, then refrigerate. Thick-skinned fruits can be kept at room temperature. All fruits should be checked daily. Remove and use over-ripe or bruised fruit right away. Do not refrigerate tomatoes. Potatoes and onions are best stored in a dark place at room temperature. Do not store potatoes and onions together; doing so makes each spoil faster. Potatoes that are refrigerated need a week or more at room temperature to restore their normal starch-sugar balance. Fresh mushrooms should be stored in a paper bag in the bottom of the refrigerator.

- **Herbs.** Stand fresh herbs upright in small glasses or plastic cups with an inch of water in the bottom, and then place a plastic bag loosely over the herbs. Alternatively, rinse fresh herbs and pat dry, then wrap in damp paper towels and put in resealable plastic storage bags. Dried herbs should be kept in as dark a place as possible and discarded after six months.

- **Meats, poultry, and fish.** Store meat, poultry, and fish in containers with sides to prevent dripping. Always store raw protein in the lowest section of the refrigerator, away from cooked food to prevent contamination from stray drips. Use disposable aluminum trays and pans to store wrapped meats. Store fish, liver, and ground meats loosely wrapped in the coldest part of the refrigerator, and do not store for more than one day. Remove the giblets and rinse fresh chicken before storing. Rewrap chicken well and use within two days.

- **Spices.** Buy spices in small amounts and store in cool, dark places. Bright lights and warm temperatures will shorten an already short shelf life. Most spices need to be replaced every six months.

freezing food

Remove excess air from freezer bags to prevent freezer burn. Different foods benefit from different freezing methods. Follow these guidelines below for best results:

- **Berries.** You can freeze cranberries in their original packaging. For blackberries, blueberries, cherries, raspberries, and hulled strawberries, wash, dry, and then spread in a single layer on a baking sheet and freeze. When frozen, pour into resealable plastic storage bags.

- **Cakes.** Freeze frosted cakes uncovered until frozen solid before wrapping well to preserve the frosting.

- **Meat.** Separate pieces of meat with waxed paper before freezing to prevent them from sticking together.

thawing food

- **Use the refrigerator.** For safety, thaw frozen foods in the refrigerator. Avoid the temptation to thaw food on the kitchen counter at room temperature or to run hot water over the food. This method gives bacteria an invitation to the party.

- **Alternate thawing methods.** You can also run cold water over food that is tightly wrapped in plastic or use the microwave defrost setting. These methods of thawing must be followed with immediate cooking.

kitchen scissors

Well-made, sturdy kitchen scissors have 10,000 uses and should be kept in tip-top condition. To quickly sharpen kitchen scissors, cut through sheets of aluminum foil or fine sandpaper several times.

CHOOSING GOOD EQUIPMENT

A few thoughtful investments in quality equipment will make your life easier and your "do it for less" endeavors more successful. Choose the most useful, basic pieces of equipment to splurge on: a great knife, a stockpot, and a sauté pan. These tools will repay your investment many times over. You'll find the efficiency they bring to your preparation indispensable, and, with proper care, they can last you a lifetime.

Employ the help of a salesperson to demonstrate the products if you feel overwhelmed by the vast assortment of choices. Take advantage of sales and special offers, and don't be afraid to return a satisfaction-guaranteed product to the store or manufacturer if it doesn't meet with your approval.

knives

A good 8 to 10-inch chef's knife is your most important piece of equipment. High-carbon stainless steel is expensive, but it is the best choice for cutting most types of foods. Look for a blade that is riveted through the handle. Hold knives to check for balance, and buy one that feels good in your hand. Make sure the blade is wide and heavy for crushing garlic or cutting through chicken bones. Avoid any knives that claim to never need sharpening.

For your own safety, keep your knives sharp. Dull knives slip and cause accidents; they mutilate food instead of neatly slicing, and they add expensive minutes (and frustration) to preparation time. Once you've had the great pleasure of prepping with a totally sharp blade, you'll become intolerant of a dull one.

To keep your knife in top condition, always wash it by hand and completely avoid using the dishwasher. Straighten the blade with a steel before each use. As you slice and dice, the knife's metal tends to get tiny nicks and bends. By using a steel, you realign all the metal, which results in a sharper knife. To truly sharpen a knife, though, you need to grind the blade with a sharpener or a stone. Sharpening on a stone takes some practice, so if you're short on time (or talent), we recommend you take your knives to a professional. Some meat departments and butchers offer free sharpening for knives, but you can also go to a knife store, hunting shop, or even a taxidermist. Get frequently used knives sharpened every month or two, or every six months at the least.

pots and pans

When shopping for pots and pans, look for heavy-bottomed, high-quality pieces. Measure skillets or baking pans across the top, not the bottom. Check for oven-safe handles for stove-to-oven cooking. Avoid buying all-inclusive sets, as different brands have different strengths. Instead, focus on accumulating a collection of the best versions of each type of pan. *Cook's Illustrated* and www.epicurious.com both review cookware on a regular basis. They can offer you a starting point for pricing and dependability. The following materials form the foundation of good equipment. Look for them as you shop.

- **Stainless steel.** Not only is stainless steel a basic kitchen workhorse, but it also looks great. Look for 18/10 stainless steel with a copper core in the base to conduct heat evenly. Stainless steel skillets should always be preheated before using. To keep foods from sticking, add the butter or oil to the hot pan, and then add the food. As the food cooks, it will begin to release from the pan, leaving those delicious browned bits known as fond. A good-sized stockpot makes cooking for twelve to twenty-five guests a one-pot dinner. Find a pasta insert for your stockpot to simplify blanching a lot of vegetables or cooking pasta in batches. A heavy-gauge bottom will keep food from burning.

- **Nonstick.** Everyone should have a good nonstick sauté pan for cooking crèpes, eggs, pancakes, and delicate seafood. Unlike stainless steel, nonstick skillets should not be preheated empty. Place butter or oil in the pan, and then turn up the heat. Buy a range of sizes, starting with a 2-quart pan. Store a paper towel on top of the nonstick surface to protect it from getting scratched. Good-quality, nonstick bakeware is indispensable in muffin tins and Bundt pans.

- **Cast iron.** As far as cast iron is concerned, the heavier the better. Buy pots with two handles so you will be able to lift them when they are filled. Before using, brush the pot very liberally with vegetable oil and place over a low heat for about an hour. Cool, then wipe with a paper towel. Cast iron becomes more stick-resistant with regular use. Always wipe the pan with a little oil before storing to prevent rust.

- **Copper.** Expensive but superb for conducting heat, copper pots and pans should be lined with stainless steel for best durability.

- **Glass.** You'll find buying a selection of heatproof glass baking dishes and casseroles to be one of your least expensive purchases, but one of the most practical additions to your kitchen. You can bake, microwave, serve, refrigerate, freeze, and reheat food all in the same piece. A 13 by 9 by 2-inch pan is a good, all-purpose size.

- **18 by 12-inch stainless steel baking pans.** Often called half-sheet pans, these can be found in restaurant supply and cookware stores for about $10. Use them for baking cookies, roasting poultry, or freezing berries in a single layer. They will fit in most household-size ovens.

other essentials

- **Citrus reamer.** Available in wood, glass, or metal, these neat and inexpensive devices will ensure that you get every drop of juice from lemons, limes, oranges, and grapefruits.

- **Cooling racks.** Skip the small racks and stock up on several large, commercial-quality, oven-safe versions. Look for metal ones with small

chafing dishes

If you entertain a lot, you may want to invest in a chafing dish, which is a frame that holds a pan of water heated with a canned or gel fuel, like Sterno. The resulting steam heats a pan of food placed directly above the water. You have probably seen chafing dishes keeping food warm on buffet lines. They can be found on Ebay and in club, discount, and restaurant supply stores. A basic stainless-steel model will cost about $45 to $50. They are also available in much pricier silver and copper. Flame-resistant covers for chafing dishes are available from companies listed in the Resource Guide on page 230. Chafing dishes should only be used to keep food warm, as they do not reach a high enough temperature to cook food thoroughly.

square holes. Besides cooling baked goods, the racks can be used for roasting meats and poultry—just set the racks above a tray to catch the tasty drippings. Meats roasted this way develop a crispy crust on all sides.

- **Kitchen scale.** For accurate, consistent recipes, a good-quality scale is a must. We prefer a scale with a digital display for an accurate read. Look for a scale that can measure weight up to at least 5 pounds.

- **Stainless steel bowls.** Very durable and inexpensive, these bowls work for everything from whipping cream to tossing salad. Buy various sizes for different uses.

- **Thermometers.** We find that an oven thermometer, a meat thermometer, and a small candy thermometer are indispensable. Digital instant-read thermometers will help you be most accurate in your cooking. All ovens are not created equal, as an oven thermometer quickly illustrates. An oven that is a few degrees too hot can mean the difference between juicy, succulent turkey breast and turkey jerky; an oven that is too cool can skew cooking times and result in under-cooked meats and poultry. Buy an oven thermometer that hangs from the oven racks to optimize oven space. A meat thermometer will save you the hassle of cutting through pieces of meat to guess at how much longer they need to be cooked, and using recommended meat cooking temperatures will help you protect the health of your guests. (See page 80 for proper cooking temperatures.) Candy thermometers can be used when frothing milk for espresso, making candy to use as holiday gifts, and testing the temperature of oil for frying.

- **Utensils.** Our most valuable players are wooden spoons, in several sizes, and a pair of tongs that feels comfortable in your hand. Get a set of glass or clear measuring cups made for liquid ingredients and a set of nesting metal or plastic cups that can be leveled off with a knife for dry ingredients.

where to purchase equipment (See page 230 for specific resources.)

- Antique malls
- Auctions and estate sales
- Department stores (look for promotional sales and discounts)
- Discount stores
- Garage sales
- Online auction sales (www.Ebay.com)
- Online cooking stores (www.cooking.com or www.chefs.com)
- Party supply stores
- Restaurant supply stores
- Swap meets (great for copper cookware)
- Storage companies (selling unclaimed items)

cleaning your equipment

- **Aluminum.** For aluminum pots or pans that are discolored, fill with water and add a cut onion, the juice of a lemon, or the peel of an apple. Bring to a boil, remove from heat, and let sit for a few minutes. Rinse well.

- **Burned pots and pans.** Fill with water and dishwashing machine detergent and let set for a few hours. Bring to a boil, and scrape up any burned bits with a wooden spoon.

- **Cast iron.** After cleaning and drying well, rub a little oil into the inside of cast-iron pots and pans to keep them seasoned. If the cast iron is rusty, rub with a solution of 2 teaspoons lemon juice or vinegar mixed with 1 cup water, or a mixture of salt and oil. The outside can be cleaned with a commercial oven cleaner.

- **Coffee grinder or spice grinder.** Grind white rice or white bread to absorb odors and clean the blades of the machine. Throw out the ground rice or bread, and then wipe the interior clean with a dry cloth.

- **Coffeemakers.** Pour vinegar through the coffeemaker as if you are making coffee, then rinse twice with clean water.

- **Copper.** Rub copper with the cut side of half a lemon dipped in salt to remove tarnish. Alternatively, dissolve 3 tablespoons of salt in 1 cup of any variety of vinegar, pour into a spray bottle, and spray onto the tarnished copper. Let sit a few minutes before rubbing clean.

- **Graters, garlic presses, strainers, citrus zesters, and pastry tips.** Keep an old toothbrush handy to clean the small holes in your equipment.

- **Stainless steel.** Stainless steel can pit if soaked. Dry stainless steel well after washing. To shine, rub with flour.

- **Silver.** If silver flatware has come in contact with salt, egg yolks, broccoli, or fish, it will tarnish. Rinse and dry as soon as possible after using. To clean silver, put strips of aluminum foil in a large bowl. Place silver on top of aluminum. Cover with boiling water, and then add ¼ cup baking soda. Let soak for 10 minutes. Rinse well before drying.

removing stubborn wax

Tabletops. Set a hairdryer on its lowest setting. Blow hot air directly toward the wax spill for a few seconds, then scrape off with a credit card.

Fabrics. Peel off as much of the wax by hand as you can. Stretch the fabric over a sieve or colander and secure it with clothespins or a rubber band, with the wax-stained side down. Pour a kettle-full of boiling water over the wax, and then scrape the fabric with a credit card.

Candle holders and menorahs. To prevent candle stubs from sticking, spray holders with vegetable cooking spray before inserting tapers and wipe off excess.

Glass votive holders. If you have old wax build-up in your votive holders, place them in warm water in a saucepan and bring to a gentle boil. The wax will come off easily. Alternatively, freeze the votive holders overnight, turn upside down, and tap on the bottom until the wax pops out.

COOKING FOR A CROWD

how many *gallons* of soup?

Cooking for a crowd can be overwhelming if you are used to cooking for only a handful of people. The main obstacles for "do it for less" party givers include refrigeration, cooking space, and manpower. As the average household doesn't have a walk-in refrigerator and an arsenal of stoves, how can you throw the wedding that you promised for your niece? It would be nice to rent a restaurant kitchen for a day or so, but most liability insurance contracts prevent the restaurant from allowing anyone other than trained employees into the work area. Some larger places of worship in your community may have kitchen facilities available for rent. If so, do all the main cooking there, taking advantage of any available refrigeration, and save the simple tasks for home.

If you are going to use a non-commercial kitchen, here are some ways to fully utilize what you have to work with:

- **Menu planning.** Plan your menu carefully. Choose dishes that do not require refrigeration or that you can keep frozen until you are ready to put it in the oven.

- **Prep ahead.** Do as much cooking and preparation ahead of time as possible.

- **Freeze ahead.** Freeze as much of the prepared food as you can.

- **Clear space.** Clear as much refrigeration space as possible. If you live in a small apartment and have apartment-sized appliances, rent a refrigerator from a party rental supply company and put it on your porch or balcony.

- **Test sizes.** Make sure the storage containers you are using will fit in the refrigerator, or keep your party food in resealable plastic storage bags in the refrigerator. These use much less space than plates, bowls, or other containers.

- **Adjust refrigerator.** Set the temperature control to a cooler setting to compensate for the additional food if necessary.

- **Ask for help.** Ask family, friends, or neighbors if they have a spare refrigerator or freezer in their garage that you can use if you are still short on space.

- **Alternate cooling options.** Fill a plastic or galvanized tub with ice for your beverages so they don't take up valuable refrigerator space. If you don't have a plastic tub, use your washing machine or bathtub. Make sure it's sparkling clean, and line your tub with plastic if you have any worries. Keep extra ice in a small cooler for guests.

- **Refrigerate protein.** Keep all protein refrigerated at all times.

- **Storing produce.** Store produce in a cooler lined with ice or ice packs. Find a place to store unrefrigerated produce and dry goods as well.

- **Measure ahead.** If you plan to use roasting or baking pans, check the dimensions of the oven and the refrigerator to make sure they fit.

- **Adjust cooking times.** The more you fill the oven, the longer the food will take to cook, so allow for extra cooking time if necessary.

- **Proper temperature.** Use meat thermometers whenever possible for accurate doneness.

- **Creating baking space.** Invest in an extra cooking rack for your oven to create more space.

- **Know your limits.** If you need help, enlist friends, family, or neighbors. Check the yellow pages for cooking schools in your area. Many culinary students will welcome the experience. Post a notice for a chef's assistant on the school's bulletin board for help a few weeks before the event.

mise-en-what?

Before starting any recipe, read it thoroughly to fully understand each procedure. Next, prepare your "mise en place." This French term translates into having everything in place and ready to go, from ingredients and equipment to a preheated oven. Professional kitchens use this procedure to ensure a smooth operation. Keep the recipe close at hand and refer to it often. Set out standard plastic or metal measuring cups for measuring dry ingredients, and glass or Pyrex measuring cups for fluid ingredients.

the importance of uniform slicing and dicing

The knife cuts shown on the right give the professional standard for sizing. It is good to know the difference between "small dice" or "julienne." Not only does the finished dish look better if your cuts are uniform, it will also turn out better. Any recipe you make will have been written with these sizes in mind, and uniform shapes also allow for even cooking.

standard knife cuts

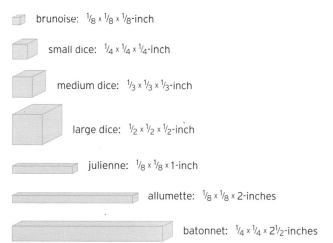

brunoise: $1/8 \times 1/8 \times 1/8$-inch

small dice: $1/4 \times 1/4 \times 1/4$-inch

medium dice: $1/3 \times 1/3 \times 1/3$-inch

large dice: $1/2 \times 1/2 \times 1/2$-inch

julienne: $1/8 \times 1/8 \times 1$-inch

allumette: $1/8 \times 1/8 \times 2$-inches

batonnet: $1/4 \times 1/4 \times 2 1/2$-inches

FIRST AID FOR FOOD

We all want our food to be perfect but sometimes, through stress, or just plain bad luck, disaster strikes. If you are on the verge of a culinary catastrophe, don't wait another second to administer our first aid for food.

- **Burned food.** Burned food doesn't necessarily mean disaster. Rice and slow-simmering stews can burn on the bottom if the flame is too high or the pot you are using has a very thin bottom. If you smell burning, remove the pot from the heat. Carefully ladle or pour the food into a fresh saucepan, taking care not to disturb or scrape the burned part from the bottom. Adding a little sugar to the recipe may remove any lingering burned flavor. However, if you burn onions or garlic, throw them away and start again. There's no rescuing the bitter taste of burned onions or garlic.

- **Crystallized honey.** If your honey has seen better days and now looks like a solid amber mass, place the jar in a bowl of hot water for several minutes or in the microwave for 30-second intervals. Stir until smooth.

- **Lumpy gravy.** "Why did my gravy turn lumpy?" Here is the rule to follow: Whenever you add the thickening agent (usually an equally weighted amount of flour and fat) to the liquid or pan drippings, make sure they are at the same temperature. Make a roux (a paste used to thicken gravy and sauces) by combining equal amounts flour and butter or pan drippings in a skillet over medium heat. Stir frequently until the roux turns pale brown. Whisk the hot liquid into the hot roux (or vice versa).

  You can also make the roux ahead of time and refrigerate. In that case, whisk the cold roux into cold stock or other pan liquids. Heat on medium-high, whisking constantly, and bring to a simmer. Let cook several minutes until the gravy thickens to the desired consistency and the raw-flour taste cooks out.

  So what can be done to lumpy gravy? The easiest and quickest solution is to pour it into a blender and blend until smooth. Return it to the saucepan and cook until the raw-flour taste cooks out.

- **Over-baked cake.** Don't throw out that over-baked cake. Cut it into cubes and use it in place of bread in any bread pudding recipe. Or, poke holes in the cake with a skewer and cover with a simple syrup. To make a simple syrup, boil 1 cup of sugar with 2 cups of water. Cook for 2 minutes without stirring, and then cool to room temperature. Make holes in the cake with a skewer, cover with the syrup, and let the cake absorb the liquid for a few hours. You can create flavored syrup by using orange or pineapple juice in place of the water. Or, make an infused syrup by adding citrus peel, spices, or vanilla beans to the water before it boils. If you want to use extracts or alcohol such as rum or brandy, wait until the mixture has cooled before adding them. Serve the syrup-soaked cake with fresh cream or scoops of ice cream.

- **Over-beaten egg whites.** If you have beaten your egg whites too long and they have become too hard to fold, add an extra egg white or a teaspoon of sugar and beat again until just smooth.

- **Over-cooked vegetables.** Drain over-cooked vegetables and place in a food processor or blender. Add a little butter, salt, and pepper, and process until smooth. You now have a purée of fresh carrots or a purée of fresh cauliflower. You can even add stock, cream, or a mixture and turn them into soup. If all else fails, remember that plain puréed vegetables make nutritious baby food.

- **Over-salted food.** A soup redolent of the salty ocean air is a good thing. A soup that tastes like ocean water is not. Everyone has different taste buds, so as a rule, it is better to under-season than over-season. Salt and pepper can be added at the table, but they cannot be removed. If you have been a little too generous on the salt, add an acid to counteract it. Try vinegar or a citrus juice. You can also cut up a raw potato, add it to the dish, and simmer for 20 minutes. The potato will absorb some of the salt. Be sure to remove the potato pieces before serving.

- **Overly spicy food.** Tame that "ring of fire" chili by mixing in sour cream or plain yogurt. Serve with bread or potatoes to help absorb the fiery taste.

- **Seized chocolate.** Keep water away from chocolate when melting it. Even the smallest drop will make the chocolate harden, or seize. Add about 1 teaspoon of solid vegetable shortening to each ounce of seized chocolate, and stir until smooth.

- **Stale dinner rolls.** Dinner rolls can go stale very quickly if placed on the table too early. To revive them, mist lightly with water and wrap in aluminum foil. Place in a 250-degree oven for 10 to 15 minutes. This light steaming should bring them back to life.

- **Uneven baking.** If your cake turns out lopsided, then your oven may not be heating evenly. To save the cake, spray the underside of a nonstick baking sheet with vegetable cooking spray and place on top of the cake as it is cooling. The weight of the pan should even out any kinks. The next time you bake, be sure to rotate the cake halfway through the cooking time.

SERVING IN QUANTITY

If you look behind the scenes at a large catering event during service time, you'll see a carefully orchestrated dance as coordinated and precise as a military operation. You may not be throwing a party for several hundred, but you can apply the same serving techniques that professional caterers use for your extravaganza.

How can you plate the food, serve all your guests simultaneously, and still keep the soup hot? For plated service, you need to have a designated plating area. An extra table set up close to the dining area is perfect. If the kitchen is the only option, clear all counter-tops first, and then place a cutting board on a cool stovetop for additional space. You can also use the top of a washer and dryer if they aren't in a damp basement. If the food can be easily transported, consider using a garage or patio if weather and cleanliness permit. Cover the table with a towel or tablecloth to prevent the plates from slipping.

The food will stay hot longer if the plates are warm. Stack and warm them in a low oven (150 to 200 degrees), and do not be tempted to speed up the process by kicking up the heat. Hot plates not only burn fingers and take a long time to become cool enough to be handled, but they may also crack if too hot. If you are having a smaller gathering, run the plates through the quick cycle of your dishwasher and remove while still warm. Cool dessert and salad plates in the refrigerator or in a cooler.

Salads can be tossed just before plating or plated and pre-set on the dining table. The easiest way to serve a mixed green salad is to wear disposable plastic gloves and place a handful of leaves within the inner rim of each plate. Clean any stray splatters of dressing from the rim before serving. If you are tight on space, consider plating half the salads just before serving, then plate the rest as the first half are being served.

If you are plating for more than ten guests, an extra pair of hands will help. Draw a plate presentation on a chart like the one at the right for the servers to follow, or make an actual sample plate of food before the serving begins. If you are suddenly called away to deal with a crisis, then whoever is left in charge of serving has a presentation plate they can copy. The most efficient system of plating is to have a team working in sequence. Each team member is responsible for one food item. With all the warm plates laid out, one team member starts by portioning out the food that will stay hot the longest—mashed potatoes, for example—and serving them on every plate. Then a second follows with the green beans. A third adds the chicken breast, and a fourth follows with the sauce. If there are only two in a team, one person serves the mashed potatoes and the second person serves the green beans. While the green beans are being served, number one follows with the chicken breasts and number two finishes with the sauce. With this style of plating, the food can be served to the guests quickly and in a steady stream. Food can be unpredictable, so be prepared for some

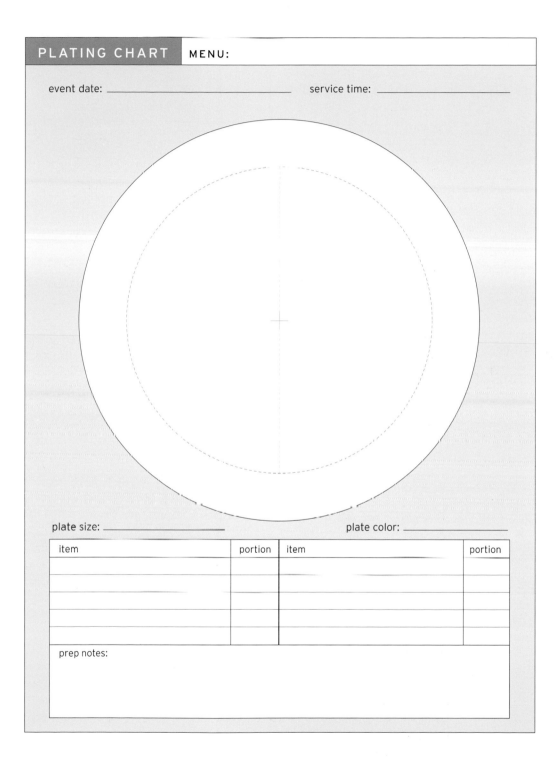

PLATING CHART MENU:

event date: _____ service time: _____

plate size: _____ plate color: _____

item	portion	item	portion

prep notes:

inconsistencies with the plate presentation. Don't concern yourself if the swirl of sour cream in one soup bowl isn't as perfect as the swirl in another bowl. The more you fuss with the food, the colder it gets.

If serving ice cream or sorbet, remove it from the freezer at least a half hour before serving. The larger the container, the longer it will take to soften. Have more than one ice cream scoop sitting in hot water, and alternate them to make scooping easier. If you have plenty of freezer space, pre-scoop the ice cream up to a day in advance and place on cookie sheets. Store covered in the freezer.

wait staff and kitchen help

If you spend most of your parties either slaving away in the kitchen or making drinks to serve your guests, then you might want to consider hiring a waiter or chef for the evening. An extra pair of hands can make all the difference at even the smallest gathering.

A staffing agency should be able to provide both waiters and chefs. Look under Bartending Services or Party Staffing in the yellow pages, or contact cooking schools or colleges with hospitality programs. Students may be able to apply the time worked to their externships. Some restaurant waiters and chefs may be available for private parties as well. And don't forget to enlist the help of teenagers, family, friends, and volunteers. If your family and friends are helping, remember that they are not there to be your servants—you get what you pay for.

The main difference between hiring from an agency and hiring on your own is that the agency will provide all the necessary insurance and legal documentation. If you hire someone privately, you may be responsible if that person becomes injured while in your employ. Check with your local employment office for legal requirements.

The following is a guideline as to how many servers to hire:

- **Butler-style reception:** one server for 20 to 25 guests

- **Buffet, assisted:** one server for 40 guests

- **Buffet, self-service:** one server for 60 guests

- **Sit-down dinner, formal:** one server for 10 guests

- **Sit-down dinner, informal:** one server for 20 to 25 guests

- **Open bar:** one bartender and one wine server for 50 to 60 guests

If you feel uncomfortable about letting a stranger into your home, arrange a short meeting with him before the day of the party. Is his appearance suitable? How many events has he worked? Does he have references? Discuss the structure of the party, go over the food, and describe the ingredients briefly: "The guests will arrive at 7:00 p.m.; we will have cocktails for an hour and then move into the dining room. The first course will be at 8:15, followed by the main course at 8:30. We'll then have a coffee and dessert buffet in the living room."

Arrange an area for the wait staff or kitchen help to change their clothes and park their cars. Be specific with your instructions for dress code, appearance, and conduct.

A waiter will alleviate some of the pressure, especially if you are one of those entertaining whirlwinds that does absolutely everything for the party except harvesting the grapes to make the wine. Use a waiter during that all-important half-hour to one hour before the party. This should be time for you to get your party clothes on and have a moment to relax before the curtain goes up. Give the waiter a to-do list of last-minute jobs while you get ready. The list could include heating up appetizers, lighting candles, filling up the ice bucket, or opening the red wine.

An experienced chef or kitchen helper can be a great investment to any dinner party. You can make as much food as you want before the event then let the chef cook the last-minute items, leaving you more time to enjoy your company. Or, arrange for the chef to come earlier in the day or even the day before to help you prepare the food. If you and only you can make your famous beef en croûte, then have him peel the potatoes, clean the vegetables, wash the salad, make the dressing, or clean up behind you.

57 morsels
of kitchen wisdom

We've gleaned the best-of-the-best tips and hints for you from our years of cooking and catering, and we hope the sum of our experiences makes your foray into the world of big parties all the more successful. Thank cooks everywhere—from grandmas to chefs de cuisine—for these ingenious solutions to everyday culinary problems. Good luck in the kitchen!

1. Blah berries. To bring out the flavor of mediocre berries, place washed berries in a bowl and sprinkle with 1 to 2 tablespoons of sugar for every pint. (Hull and slice strawberries first.) Let the berries sit at room temperature for a minimum of 15 minutes, and up to an hour. The sugar draws moisture from the berries, creating a natural syrup.

2. Freezing extra vegetables. Bring a large pot of water to a boil. Add the vegetables and boil for 30 to 45 seconds. Strain the blanched vegetables and immediately shock in ice water to stop the cooking and preserve their color. Drain and pat dry. Place in a single layer on a baking sheet and freeze. Once frozen, store in resealable plastic storage bags.

3. Bread crumbs forever. Slice fresh or day-old bread or tear into chunks and let sit out overnight. Place in a food processor fitted with a metal blade or a blender with salt, pepper, and dried herbs, if desired, and process until the desired texture is reached. Spread the crumbs out on a baking sheet. Bake in a 300-degree oven for 10 to 15 minutes to toast. Let cool completely before storing in an airtight container. The breadcrumbs will keep for up to four days at room temperature, one month in the refrigerator, or six months in the freezer.

4. Browning equals flavor! Moisture causes meat to steam instead of sear, so be sure to blot meat with paper towels before browning for a crispy brown exterior. Brown in small batches to avoid crowding, as this will lower the heat of the pan. Use a large, heavy pan for best results.

5. Deglazing. With deglazing, use a liquid like water, stock, or wine to dislodge and dissolve the fond—browned bits of sautéed food that have become stuck to the bottom of the pan, usually from searing meat. To make a simple pan sauce (also called a reduction) after sautéing a piece of meat, remove the cooked meat from the pan and turn the heat to high. Pour in a cup of stock or wine, and scrape the bottom of the pan with a wooden spoon. Allow the liquid to reduce slightly and intensify in flavor. Remove from the heat, season with salt and pepper, and stir in a pat of cold butter for a velvety finish. Pour over the cooked meat and serve immediately.

6. Got buttermilk? If you need buttermilk but don't have enough time to run to the store, you can make it yourself. Add a tablespoon of cider vinegar, distilled white vinegar, or lemon juice to each cup of milk needed. (Any fat content will work.) Let stand at room temperature for 10 minutes. When the milk curdles, it is ready to use.

7. Fresh outta crème fraîche? Combine 1 cup whipping cream with 2 tablespoons of buttermilk. Let stand at room temperature for 8 to 24 hours, or until thick. The taste should have a slight twang.

8. Reviving ailing vegetables. Carrots, celery, or green onions that seem a bit limp can be revived by a submerging in an ice-water bath for 30 minutes. Pat dry and store in the refrigerator.

9. Adding crunch. Most casseroles have a creamy, soft texture that benefit from a crunchy topping. Sprinkle a mixture of buttered breadcrumbs and Parmesan cheese over the top for the last 5 minutes of baking, or until the crumbs turn golden brown.

10. Creamy white. Add a few drops of lemon juice or milk to the cooking water to help cauliflower, artichoke hearts, and potatoes retain their creamy-white color.

11. Dehydrated onion soup or ranch dressing mix. A package of either mix makes a tasty, easy seasoning for soups, stews, hamburgers, or meatloaf.

12. Egg whites. To increase the volume in beaten egg whites, use room-temperature eggs.

13. Nuts to you. The natural oil in nuts makes them spoil or go rancid quickly. Store them in resealable plastic storage bags in the freezer until ready to use.

14. Mo' better gravy. Baste your beef roasts with beef stock and poultry with chicken stock. When it's time to make the gravy, there will be plenty of richly flavored drippings to mix with the roux.

15. Whipped cream. Put the bowl and beaters in the freezer before whipping cream. Heavy whipping cream doubles, and often triples, in volume when whipped correctly.

16. Quick ripening. Place pears, avocados, or peaches in a brown paper bag, fold to close, and let stand in a warm (but not hot) place until ripe.

17. Heavenly corn. To remove kernels from the cob without having them fly all over the kitchen, place the ear in the funnel of an angel food cake pan, and push the cob down. The kernels will fall in the pan.

18. No wash, no waste. When beating egg whites and egg yolks separately, always beat the egg whites first. You can use the same bowl and beaters for the yolks without washing them first.

19. No-slide cutting boards. Place a damp towel under a cutting board to keep it from sliding.

20. Messy measuring. Before measuring molasses, honey, or syrup, spray the measuring utensil with vegetable cooking spray for easy clean-up.

21. Extra flavor. For a richer flavor, cook noodles, rice, or grains in vegetable, chicken, or beef stock.

22. Crispy, please. For extra-crispy fried potatoes, soak the slices in cold water in the refrigerator overnight. Pat dry before frying.

23. Perfect pancakes. Use a clean turkey baster to make pancakes. Squeeze the batter onto the griddle for perfectly shaped pancakes every time.

24. Stop the cracks. To prevent shells from cracking when boiling eggs, add a pinch of salt to the water before cooking. For easy peeling, crack the eggshells and run under cold water.

25. It's not easy being green. To avoid an unappetizing green rim around your yolk, prepare your hard-boiled eggs as follows: Start with room-temperature eggs and place in a pot or saucepan. Cover them with cold water, an inch above the tops. Bring the water to a boil, then immediately turn off the heat and cover. After 15 minutes, remove the eggs from the pans and run under cold water to stop the cooking and prevent discoloration.

26. Hard brown sugar. To keep brown sugar soft, store with a slice of fresh apple.

27. Bakery finish. For a glossy finish to pastry crusts and baked goods, brush with beaten egg whites before baking.

28. More juice. To get more juice out of any citrus fruit, microwave it for a few seconds until barely warm. Roll the fruit under your palm on the counter before squeezing. Use a citrus reamer to get the most juice possible.

29. Zesty toppings. A citrus zester is a very useful kitchen tool. Use lemon, lime or orange zest to garnish salads with a flash of color, add zip to cookies, or sprinkle on roasted chicken for a burst of citrus flavor.

30. Five great things to do with a carton of eggnog.

1. Use it as a batter for making French toast.

2. Serve it warm with brandy when it's cold outside.

3. Pour it over warm, cooked oatmeal on Christmas morning.

4. Use it as a sauce, slightly warmed, over your best holiday cobbler.

5. Serve it icy cold over fresh fruit or berries.

31. Three easy champagne cocktails.

1. Slice strawberries and soak in brandy. Place in the bottom of champagne glasses and cover with bubbly.

2. Add a tablespoon of chilled Limoncello for a lemony splash.

3. Add a tablespoon of pomegranate juice in each flute with a twist of lime peel.

32. Delicate foods. For slicing goat cheese, angel food cake, or any delicate food, slice with unflavored dental floss or fishing wire stretched tight.

33. Separating eggs. For best results in separating eggs, use cold eggs.

34. Resting roasts. Always let cooked roasts stand at room temperature about 15 minutes before carving. This allows the juices to settle and the meat to firm up for easier slicing.

35. Mashed potatoes. Always mash potatoes while they're hot—cold potatoes can turn out gummy.

36. Eggs fromage. For decadent scrambled eggs, cut a 3-ounce bar of plain or chive cream cheese into cubes. Melt in a buttered pan before scrambling eggs. (This quantity of cheese works with six to eight eggs.)

37. Christmas goodies. Bake your Christmas goodies in November, and then wrap well and freeze until the holidays.

38. Dusting cake pans. When a cake mix calls for flouring the pan, use a bit of the dry mix instead to eliminate any white residue on the outside of the cake.

39. No budget for bottled water? Freshen up plain tap water by slicing English cucumbers and/or lemons and floating them in a pitcher of chilled water.

40. Fish stinks. Rub your hands and your cutting board with the cut half of a lemon after working with raw fish.

41. Easy hors d'oeuvres cleanup. Generously slice the ends off of a lemon or lime, and then slice the fruit in half. Use the thick rounds as pin cushions on serving trays for guests to put their used toothpicks.

42. Beautiful breadbaskets. Line breadbaskets with blooming rosemary for color and aroma.

43. Not enough candlesticks for the holidays? For an innovative candlestick holder, buy a small bushel of large red apples. Core the apples, trim the bottoms so the apples sit flat, and insert the tapers of your choice. For safety, make sure that the candles aren't too top-heavy.

44. Mobile kitchen. When you host your next bridal shower, string everyday kitchen tools from wire hangers to make a mobile and hang above the buffet as a special party favor for the bride.

44. More room for your party food. Add extra shelves to your refrigerator by placing baking sheets on top of food containers.

45. Refrigerator and freezer space. To maximize storage space in your refrigerator or freezer, store all party food in heavy-duty resealable freezer bags. Be sure to double-bag soups. Squeeze out any air, press flat, label with a permanent marker, and stack in your refrigerator or freezer.

46. Wafting scents. Dab your fingertip with vanilla extract or essential oils of lemon or orange. Pat the extract on several light bulbs before turning them on. When the lights warm up, you will have sweet smells for an hour.

47. Water protection. To protect your table from water, cut a layer of thick sheet plastic from the hardware store and lay it on the table under the tablecloth.

48. Delicate buffet surface. Protect the top of the buffet table by placing an old blanket under the tablecloth.

49. Cleaning service. Give yourself a much-needed break: arrange for a cleaning service to come for both the day before and the day after the party. It'll be worth every penny.

50. Party gloves. Use disposable plastic gloves when slicing fresh chiles, cooking seafood, or tossing salad.

51. Smelly garbage can. Put a sheet of fabric softener in the bottom of the trash can to keep odors at bay.

52. Choosing hues. Pick up free paint color chips from your local hardware store and keep them handy for matching invitations, linens, and flowers.

53. Misplaced lids. Do your pots need lids? A 12-inch pizza pan will work as a cover on almost any pot.

54. Messy kitchen or floral-arranging jobs. Put an open newspaper over the counter while arranging flowers or under the cutting board while prepping food. When it's time to clean up, roll up the newspaper and throw it away.

55. Cleaner dishes. Before you wash china and glasses, run an empty dishwasher with 2 cups of white wine vinegar in place of soap to clean the interior and lessen any hard water deposits on dishes and glasses.

56. Disposal sparkle. To freshen up your sink and sharpen the blades of your garbage disposal, grind a quartered lemon and 6 ice cubes in the disposal.

57. Easy party clean-up. Set up a scullery area for your guests to leave dirty dishes.

Classic Caesar Salad

Chilled Penne Pasta
with Pesto and Pine Nuts

Italian Meatball Lasagna

Sweet Potato Gnocchi
with Sage Butter Sauce

Assorted Grissini

Tiramisu

Chocolate Almond Biscotti

Coffee Service

authentic toscana

An ideal buffet menu for an office luncheon, a late afternoon or early evening dinner, or a casual Sunday family get-together.

authentic toscana menu:

classic caesar salad
chilled penne pasta with pesto and pine nuts
italian meatball lasagna
sweet potato gnocchi with sage butter sauce
assorted grissini*
tiramisu
chocolate-almond biscotti
coffee service

* Allow 1 to 2 grissini (Italian for "breadsticks") per person.

decorating ideas:

party colors. Sun-baked orange, rich purple, moss green, earthy brown, and a splash of merlot.

invitations. Color-copy a rustic wine label onto linen paper, or print an antique map of Italy in sepia tones.

table linens. Use real linen fabrics in whites, creams, and the rich earth tones listed above.

decorations. Group assorted boules of breads along the center of the table or place in breadbaskets lined with fresh rosemary. Use blooming or dried lavender arranged in jugs of rustic pottery. Place bunches of wildflowers in empty metal tins for olive oil or clear milk bottles tied with a grosgrain ribbon. Arrange Italian wine bottles with beautiful labels next to bunches of black and red grapes, whole salami, and wedges of Parmesan that can all be eaten during or after the party. Set a minimalist tone with four small bowls of Italian olives garnished with fresh lemon curls set on a brown linen runner. Set groups of

richly-colored pillar candles evenly spaced along the length of the table, or assemble a collection of long, cream-colored tapers in pewter or wooden bases as a centerpiece. Tie napkins with a ribbon and tuck a sprig of rosemary, thyme, oregano, or lavender into the napkin.

place cards and favors. Cut a slit in the base of a wine cork and insert a simple name card to designate your guests' seats. Place small bunches of grapes in front of each place setting and nestle a name card between the grapes, or use miniature potted rosemary plants as name card holders. Find a classic recipe for pizza dough, print it on nice linen paper, and tie it around a small bunch of flowers or herbs to give to your guests as favors. Give each guest a small bag of homemade biscotti to take with them.

entertainment. Play light Italian opera, the soundtrack from *The Godfather* or *Moonstruck*, or popular Italian artists.

menu countdown

1 week before:
• Shop for non-perishables.
• Buy beverages.

3 days before:
• Make space in refrigerator and freezer.

2 days before:
• Shop for perishables.
• Prepare gnocchi dough and refrigerate.
• Prepare biscotti and store in airtight container.

1 day before:
• Set up tables and décor.
• Prepare Caesar salad dressing.
• Prepare chilled penne pasta.
• Clean and dry lettuce for salad.
• Prepare sauce for gnocchi.
• Prepare and cook lasagna.
• Prepare tiramisu and chill.

morning of the party:
• Buy ice.
• Set up coffee service.

1 to 2 hours ahead:
• Reheat lasagna.

just before serving:
• Cook gnocchi and reheat sauce.
• Toss salad.
• Brew coffee.

authentic toscana shopping list: **1 to 2 weeks before**

ingredients	**12** people	**25** people	**50** people	**75** people
alcohol				
Cabernet Sauvignon	1 (750-ml) bottle	1 (750-ml) bottle	2 (750-ml) bottles	3 (750-ml) bottles
Coffee liqueur	1½ ounces	3 ounces	6 ounces	9 ounces
pantry items & dry goods				
All-purpose flour	9 ounces	18 ounces	36 ounces	54 ounces
Anchovy fillets (optional)	3	6	12	18
Baking powder	2 teaspoons	1 tablespoon plus 1 teaspoon	2 tablespoons plus 2 teaspoons	¼ cup
Cake flour	10 ounces	20 ounces	40 ounces	60 ounces
Canned sweet potatoes	6 pounds	12 pounds	24 pounds	36 pounds
Chicken stock	4 ounces	8 ounces	16 ounces	24 ounces
Dark chocolate bar	4½ ounces	9 ounces	18 ounces	27 ounces
Dijon mustard	¼ ounce	½ ounce	1 ounce	1½ ounces
Extra-virgin olive oil	14 ounces	30 ounces	60 ounces	90 ounces
Granulated sugar	1½ pounds	2½ pounds	4½ pounds	6½ pounds
Marinara sauce	36 ounces	72 ounces	144 ounces	216 ounces
No-boil lasagna noodles	¾ pound	1½ pounds	3 pounds	4½ pounds
Penne pasta	1½ pounds	3 pounds	6 pounds	9 pounds
Pine nuts	2 ounces	4 ounces	8 ounces	12 ounces
Semisweet chocolate chips	2½ ounces	5 ounces	10 ounces	15 ounces
Slivered almonds	3 ounces	5 ounces	10 ounces	15 ounces
Unsweetened cocoa powder	2¼ ounces	4½ ounces	9 ounces	13½ ounces
Vegetable cooking spray	1 can	1 can	1 can	1 can
Walnuts	2 ounces	3 ounces	6 ounces	8 ounces
Worcestershire sauce	¼ ounce	½ ounce	1 ounce	1 ounce
dried herbs, spices, & extracts				
Almond extract	¼ ounce	¼ ounce	½ ounce	1 ounce
Black peppercorns	as needed	as needed	as needed	as needed
Ground cinnamon	¼ ounce	¼ ounce	¼ ounce	¼ ounce
Ground nutmeg	¼ ounce	¼ ounce	¼ ounce	¼ ounce
Salt	as needed	as needed	as needed	as needed
Vanilla extract	½ ounce	1 ounce	2 ounces	2½ ounces
frozen foods				
Frozen fully cooked meatballs	1 pound	2 pounds	4 pounds	6 pounds
miscellaneous				
Bottled or filtered water for coffee	2 quarts plus 1 cup	1 gallon plus 1 pint	2 gallons plus 1 quart	3½ gallons
Sugar substitute	18 packets	36 packets	72 packets	108 packets

authentic toscana shopping list: **1 to 2 days before**

ingredients	12 people	25 people	50 people	75 people
produce				
Carrots	4 ounces	8 ounces	1 pound	1½ pounds
Fresh basil	8 ounces	16 ounces	32 ounces	48 ounces
Fresh Italian parsley	1 bunch (about 3 ounces)	1 bunch (about 3 ounces)	1 bunch (about 3 ounces)	2 bunches (about 6 ounces)
Fresh sage	⅓ ounce	¾ ounce	1½ ounces	2¼ ounces
Garlic	2 heads	4 heads	8 heads	12 heads
Heads of romaine lettuce	1½ pounds	3 pounds	6 pounds	9 pounds
Lemons	2	4	6	8
Mushrooms	4 ounces	8 ounces	1 pound	1½ pounds
Onions	8 ounces	1 pound	2 pounds	3 pounds
Zucchini	4 ounces	8 ounces	1 pound	1½ pounds
dairy, cheese, & deli				
Cheddar cheese, shredded	8 ounces	1 pound	2 pounds	3 pounds
Half-and-half	4 ounces	8 ounces	16 ounces (1 pint)	24 ounces (1½ pints)
Heavy whipping cream	28 ounces (1¾ pints)	56 ounces (3½ pints)	112 ounces (3½ quarts)	168 ounces (5¼ quarts)
Large eggs	9	18	36	54
Mascarpone cheese	12 ounces	1½ pounds	3 pounds	4½ pounds
Mozzarella cheese, shredded	8 ounces	1 pound	2 pounds	3 pounds
Parmesan cheese, grated	15 ounces	1¾ pounds	3½ pounds	5¼ pounds
Ricotta cheese	2 pounds	4 pounds	8 pounds	12 pounds
Unsalted butter	6 ounces	12 ounces	1½ pounds	2¼ pounds
Whole milk	24 ounces (1½ pints)	48 ounces (1½ quarts)	96 ounces (3 quarts)	144 ounces (1 gallon plus 1 pint)
miscellaneous				
Croutons	6 ounces	12 ounces	24 ounces	36 ounces
Ground coffee	4 ounces	8 ounces	1 pound	1½ pounds
Ladyfinger cookies	36 cookies (11 ounces)	72 cookies (21 ounces)	144 cookies (42 ounces)	216 cookies (63 ounces)
Strong brewed coffee for making tiramisu	1 ounce	2 ounces	4 ounces	6 ounces

Always take a calculator when shopping for quantity recipes to quickly and easily calculate the most appropriate package sizes for your particular needs. We have listed most items in ounces so that you are not limited to size-specific packaging if shopping in bulk. When in doubt over what amount to buy, always round up—it's far better to have a little extra of an ingredient than to run out while cooking. If your eighth-grade algebra skills have gotten rusty, remember that there are 16 ounces in a pound and 8 fluid ounces in a cup. See page 73 for additional conversions.

classic caesar salad

ingredients	12 people	25 people	50 people	75 people
Heads of romaine lettuce	1½ pounds	3 pounds	6 pounds	9 pounds
Hard-boiled eggs	3	6	12	18
Extra-virgin olive oil	½ cup	1 cup	2 cups	3 cups
Lemon juice	¼ cup (2 lemons)	½ cup (4 lemons)	1 cup (6 lemons)	1½ cups (8 lemons)
Dijon mustard	1½ teaspoons	1 tablespoon	2 tablespoons	3 tablespoons
Garlic cloves, minced	3 cloves	6 cloves	12 cloves	18 cloves
Worcestershire sauce	½ teaspoon	1 teaspoon	2 teaspoons	1 tablespoon
Salt	¾ teaspoon	1½ teaspoons	1 tablespoon	1 tablespoon plus 1½ teaspoons
Freshly ground black pepper	¼ teaspoon, plus more to taste	½ teaspoon, plus more to taste	1 teaspoon, plus more to taste	1½ teaspoons, plus more to taste
Anchovy fillets (optional)	3 anchovies	6 anchovies	12 anchovies	18 anchovies
Parmesan cheese, grated	4 ounces	8 ounces	1 pound	1½ pounds
Croutons	6 ounces	12 ounces	24 ounces	36 ounces

(fyi) helpful hint:

A plastic salad spinner makes quick work of drying lettuce, as well as herbs, greens, and many vegetables.

do it ahead:

The dressing can be made and the lettuce can be washed and dried a day in advance. Toss the salad with the dressing just before serving.

do it for less time:

• Look for bags of ready-to-use romaine lettuce in the produce section of your grocery store. You will need one-third less than the amount called for in the recipe.

• Use bottled lemon juice instead of freshly squeezed to save time.

($) do it for less money:

Make your own croutons by cutting stale bread into ½-inch cubes. Spray with vegetable cooking spray or brush with melted butter. Bake for 15 to 20 minutes in a 350-degree oven until golden brown.

directions:

1. Cut or tear the lettuce into 1-inch pieces, discarding any imperfect outer leaves. Fill a sink with cool water and wash the lettuce; repeat if necessary to remove all dirt and grit. Dry the lettuce thoroughly and store in the refrigerator until ready to serve.

2. Place the hard-boiled eggs, olive oil, lemon juice, Dijon mustard, garlic, Worcestershire sauce, salt, pepper, and anchovies (if using) in the bowl of a blender or food processor. Blend until smooth. Taste and adjust the seasonings as needed. (The salad can be made up to this point a day in advance.)

3. Just before serving, place the chilled lettuce in a large bowl. Using tongs or your hands (wearing disposable plastic gloves), gradually add the dressing, tossing well to coat.

4. Sprinkle with the Parmesan cheese and croutons, and add additional freshly ground black pepper if desired.

equipment:

• 36-inch salad bowl
• blender or food processor
• tongs or disposable plastic gloves

portion size: 1 heaped cup of salad plus 2 tablespoons dressing

chilled penne pasta with pesto and pine nuts

ingredients	12 people	25 people	50 people	75 people
Penne pasta (uncooked)	1½ pounds	3 pounds	6 pounds	9 pounds
Extra-virgin olive oil	1 cup, plus more as needed	2¼ cups, plus more as needed	4½ cups, plus more as needed	6¾ cups, plus more as needed
Fresh basil leaves	4 cups	8 cups	16 cups	24 cups
Walnuts	⅓ cup	¾ cup	1⅓ cups	2 cups
Garlic cloves, peeled	4 cloves	8 cloves	15 cloves	22 cloves
Parmesan cheese, grated	4 ounces	8 ounces	1 pound	1½ pounds
Salt	½ teaspoon	1 teaspoon	2 teaspoons	1 tablespoon
Freshly ground black pepper	¼ teaspoon	½ teaspoon	1 teaspoon	1½ teaspoons
Pine nuts, toasted	¾ cup	1½ cups	3 cups	4½ cups

equipment:

- food processor
- large mixing bowl
- large spoon
- stockpots with lids

directions:

1. Bring a large stockpot of salted water to a rolling boil. Cook the pasta in batches for 8 to 10 minutes, or until al dente (slightly firm), being careful not to over-cook. Drain and repeat with the remaining pasta. Drizzle with a little olive oil if needed to keep from sticking.

2. Place the basil leaves, olive oil, walnuts, garlic, Parmesan cheese, salt, and pepper in the bowl of a food processor. Process until the mixture forms a coarse paste. Taste and adjust the seasonings as needed.

3. Toss the cooked pasta and the pesto together in a large mixing bowl. Combine in batches if needed for manageability. Sprinkle with the toasted pine nuts.

4. Cover and chill until ready to serve.

helpful hints: (fyi)

- If you do not have large stockpots, cook the pasta in batches. Likewise, if working with a small food processor, divide the pesto ingredients in half and prepare in two batches.

- To toast the pine nuts, spread them in a single layer on a baking sheet. Bake for 10 to 15 minutes in a 350-degree oven, stirring frequently and watching carefully to keep them from burning.

do it ahead:

The entire dish can be made a day in advance. Save space in your refrigerator by storing the prepared pasta in resealable plastic storage bags. If the pasta seems dry when time to serve, toss with extra pesto or a drizzle of extra-virgin olive oil.

do it for less time:

Substitute pre-made pesto instead of making your own. It is frequently available in the refrigerated section of the grocery store alongside packaged ravioli. You will need about 16 ounces of pesto for 12 servings.

authentic toscana

portion size: 6 to 8 ounces

italian meatball lasagna

ingredients	12 people	25 people	50 people	75 people
Vegetable cooking spray	as needed	as needed	as needed	as needed
Whole milk	3 cups (24 ounces)	6 cups (48 ounces)	12 cups (96 ounces)	18 cups (144 ounces)
Unsalted butter, divided	6 tablespoons (3 ounces)	1½ sticks (6 ounces)	3 sticks (12 ounces)	4½ sticks (18 ounces)
All-purpose flour	½ cup	1 cup	2 cups	3 cups
Salt and freshly ground black pepper	to taste	to taste	to taste	to taste
Chopped onions	1½ cups	3 cups	6 cups	9 cups
Mushrooms, sliced	4 ounces	8 ounces	1 pound	1½ pounds
Marinara sauce	36 ounces	72 ounces	144 ounces	216 ounces
Cabernet Sauvignon wine	2 cups	1 (750-ml) bottle	2 (750-ml) bottles	3 (750-ml) bottles
Garlic, chopped	2 tablespoons	¼ cup	½ cup	¾ cup
Carrots, peeled and thinly sliced	4 ounces (about ¾ cup)	8 ounces (about 1½ cups)	1 pound (about 3 cups)	1½ pounds (about 4½ cups)
Zucchini, sliced into ¼-inch pieces	4 ounces (about 1 cup)	8 ounces (about 2 cups)	1 pound (about 4 cups)	1½ pounds (about 6 cups)
Fully cooked meatballs	15 (about 1 pound)	30 (about 2 pounds)	60 (about 4 pounds)	90 (about 6 pounds)
Whole milk ricotta cheese	2 pounds	4 pounds	8 pounds	12 pounds
Chopped fresh parsley	¼ cup	½ cup	1 cup	1½ cups
No-boil lasagna noodles	¾ pound	1½ pounds	3 pounds	4½ pounds
Cheddar cheese, shredded	8 ounces	1 pound	2 pounds	3 pounds
Mozzarella cheese, shredded	8 ounces	1 pound	2 pounds	3 pounds
Parmesan cheese, grated	3 ounces	6 ounces	12 ounces	18 ounces

authentic toscana

(fyi) helpful hint:

The white sauce used in this lasagna is called béchamel. It can easily be turned into different sauces by adding other ingredients such as cheese or mustard. To avoid a lumpy sauce, make sure the milk is hot before adding to the flour.

do it ahead:

The lasagna can be cooked a day in advance. Refrigerate until ready to reheat. Reheat in a 350-degree oven until the internal temperature reaches 170 degrees on an instant-read thermometer. Allow at least 1 hour to reheat each pan.

directions:

1. Preheat the oven to 375 degrees. Spray the baking pans with the vegetable cooking spray.

2. Warm the milk in a saucepan or stockpot over medium heat.

3. Melt three fourths of the butter in another stockpot over low heat. Whisk in the flour, stirring constantly for 5 minutes to make a roux.

4. Slowly pour the hot milk into the roux, whisking constantly. Bring the mixture to a boil, reduce the heat, and simmer about 10 minutes, or until the raw flour taste is gone.

5. Season with salt and pepper to taste, cover, and set aside.

6. Melt the remaining butter in a large sauté pan. Add the onions in batches and sauté for 5 minutes, or until translucent. Remove from the pan with a slotted spoon and set aside.

7. Add the mushrooms to the pan, and sauté until they've

portion size: 1 (2½ to 3-inch) square

equipment:

- 2 large stockpots
- for 12 guests, use one (13 x 9 x 2-inch) baking pan
- for 25 guests, use two (13 x 9 x 2-inch) baking pans or one (12 x 20 x 2-inch) baking pans
- for 50 guests, use two (12 x 20 x 2-inch) baking pans
- for 75 guests, use three (12 x 20 x 2-inch) baking pans
- heavy-duty aluminum foil
- instant-read thermometer
- ladle
- large sauté pan
- lasagna pans
- mixing bowl
- saucepan or stockpot for milk
- slotted spoon or spider
- whisk
- wooden spoon

released most of their liquid and are beginning to brown.

directions: (continued)

8. In a separate stockpot, combine the marinara, wine, and garlic. Bring to a boil over medium heat, and add the onions, mushrooms, carrots, and zucchini.

9. Cut the meatballs in half and add to the marinara mixture. Reduce the heat and simmer for 30 minutes.

10. In a mixing bowl, combine the ricotta cheese with half of the parsley. Season with salt and pepper to taste.

11. To assemble the lasagna, divide all the ingredients by the number of pans you're making, and place into separate bowls. Or, simply make an effort to create thin, even layers of each ingredient. Ladle a thin layer of the marinara sauce on the bottom of each baking dish. Place a layer of noodles on top. Ladle a third of the marinara sauce on top, half of the ricotta cheese, half of the cheddar cheese, half of the mozzarella cheese, half of the white sauce, and another layer of the noodles.

12. Ladle another third of the marinara sauce, and top with the remaining ricotta, cheddar, mozzarella, and white sauce.

13. Top with a final layer of noodles. Spread the remaining marinara sauce on top. Sprinkle with the Parmesan cheese and remaining parsley.

14. Bake, uncovered, for 1 hour. Cover with aluminum foil and continue to bake for 30 minutes, or until the internal temperature reaches 170 degrees on an instant-read thermometer.

do it for less time:

- Look for pre-chopped garlic in the produce section of your grocery store.

- Use fully cooked meatballs from the freezer section of your grocery or club store. Be sure to thaw ahead of time in the refrigerator.

do it for less money:

Use ground beef, pork, turkey, or sausage in place of the meatballs. Brown the meats in a little olive oil, and then drain before using.

sweet potato gnocchi with sage butter sauce

ingredients	12 people	25 people	50 people	75 people
Canned sweet potatoes, drained	6 pounds	12 pounds	24 pounds	36 pounds
All-purpose flour	1 2/3 cups	3 1/4 cups	6 1/2 cups	9 3/4 cups
Large eggs, beaten	2	4	8	12
Ground cinnamon	1/4 teaspoon	1/2 teaspoon	1 teaspoon	1 1/2 teaspoon
Ground nutmeg	pinch	1/4 teaspoon	1/2 teaspoon	3/4 teaspoon
Salt	2 1/2 teaspoons	1 tablespoon plus 2 teaspoons	3 tablespoons plus 1 teaspoon	1/4 cup plus 1 tablespoon
Freshly ground black pepper	1/2 teaspoon	1 teaspoon	2 teaspoons	1 tablespoon
Chicken stock	1/2 cup (4 ounces)	1 cup (8 ounces)	2 cups (16 ounces)	3 cups (24 ounces)
All-purpose flour	1 tablespoon	2 tablespoons	1/4 cup	1/3 cup
Heavy whipping cream	1 1/4 cups (10 ounces)	2 1/2 cups (20 ounces)	5 cups (40 ounces)	7 1/2 cups (60 ounces)
Parmesan cheese, grated	3/4 cup	1 1/2 cups	3 cups	4 1/2 cups
Unsalted butter	4 tablespoons (2 ounces)	1 stick (4 ounces)	2 sticks (8 ounces)	3 sticks (12 ounces)
Chopped fresh sage	1/4 cup	1/2 cup	1 cup	1 1/2 cups

(fyi) helpful hint:

Make this a vegetarian dish by using vegetable stock instead of chicken stock. If you cannot find fresh sage, use dried sage. You will only need one third of the amount called for in the recipe.

do it ahead:

• Gnocchi are small Italian potato dumplings that can be boiled or fried. The dough can be made up to two days in advance and refrigerated.

• The sauce can be made a day in advance. Reheat on low, and add more milk if necessary.

do it for less time:

Some grocery stores carry dry gnocchi in the pasta section. Cook it as directed and continue with the sauce in step 6.

$ do it for less money:

As an alternative to a pastry bag, use a heavy-duty plastic storage bag. Place the dough inside, then cut off about 3/4-inch from one corner and squeeze out the dough.

directions:

1. Preheat the oven to 350 degrees. Bring a stockpot of water to a boil.

2. For the gnocchi, whip the potatoes with a mixer or food processor until just smooth.

3. Stir in the flour, eggs, cinnamon, nutmeg, salt, and pepper until just combined with the potatoes. Test the gnocchi by adding 1 teaspoon of dough to the boiling water and cook until the dough floats to the surface. Cool and taste, adjusting the seasonings as needed. (The dough can be made up to 2 days in advance. Wrap tightly in plastic wrap and store in the refrigerator until ready to continue.)

4. Place the remaining dough in a piping bag. Working in batches, squeeze out the dough over boiling water, cutting the dough with kitchen scissors every half inch.

5. Cook for 2 to 3 minutes, or until the dough floats to the surface of water. Remove the gnocchi with a slotted spoon, drain, and place on baking sheet. Cover loosely with foil and keep warm in a 200-degree oven while boiling the remaining gnocchi. Repeat with the remaining dough.

6. For the sauce, whisk together the chicken stock and flour in a small saucepan. Bring to a boil, stirring constantly. (The mixture will be thick.) Set aside.

7. Place the heavy cream in a large saucepan over medium heat. Bring to a boil, and then reduce the heat to low. Add the Parmesan cheese and butter, stirring constantly until smooth.

8. Slowly whisk in the chicken stock mixture until the sauce reaches the desired thickness. (The sauce can be made up to this point a day in advance. Cover tightly and store in the refrigerator until ready to reheat.)

9. Add the chopped sage, adjust the seasonings if needed, and gently toss with the gnocchi.

portion size: 3 1/2 ounces

equipment:

• aluminum foil
• baking sheet lined with waxed paper
• electric hand or stand mixer or food processor
• kitchen scissors
• large saucepan
• large stockpot
• pastry bag fitted with a plain 1/2-inch tip
• slotted spoon or spider
• small saucepan
• whisk

ingredients	**12** people	**25** people	**50** people	**75** people
Ladyfinger cookies	36 (11 ounces)	72 (21 ounces)	144 (42 ounces)	216 (63 ounces)
Strong brewed coffee	1½ cups	3 cups	6 cups	9 cups
Mascarpone cheese	12 ounces	1½ pounds	3 pounds	4½ pounds
Granulated sugar	½ cup	1 cup	2 cups	3 cups
Coffee liqueur	3 tablespoons	⅓ cup	¾ cup	1 cup plus 2 teaspoons
Vanilla extract	1½ teaspoons	1 tablespoon	2 tablespoons	3 tablespoons
Heavy whipping cream	2¼ cups (18 ounces)	4½ cups (36 ounces)	9 cups (72 ounces)	13½ cups (108 ounces)
Dark chocolate bars, grated	4½ ounces	9 ounces	18 ounces	24 ounces

equipment:

• 2 large mixing bowls

• electric hand or stand mixer

• grater or food processor

• one (13 x 9 x 2-inch) baking pan or disposable aluminum pan per 12 guests

• spatula

directions:

1. Place half of the ladyfingers in a single layer on the bottom of each pan. Sprinkle the ladyfingers with half of the coffee.

2. Beat together the mascarpone cheese and sugar until light and fluffy. Beat in the coffee liqueur and vanilla extract.

3. In a separate bowl, beat the cream until it forms stiff peaks. Carefully fold the whipped cream into the mascarpone mixture.

3. Spoon half of the cream mixture over the ladyfingers, and spread evenly with a spatula. Sprinkle with half of the grated chocolate.

4. Layer the remaining ladyfingers over the grated chocolate. Sprinkle with the remaining coffee and spread with the remaining mascarpone mixture. Sprinkle with the remaining grated chocolate. Cover and refrigerate overnight.

helpful hints: (fyi)

• Mascarpone cheese is a double or triple cream cheese from Italy. If it's not available in your grocery store, use softened cream cheese instead.

• Buy the brewed coffee from a coffee shop; you'll have more choices of different roasts. Try espresso for a richer coffee flavor.

do it ahead:

This no-bake dessert tastes even better when refrigerated overnight.

do it for less time:

• The tiramisu can be purchased from a bakery. Add some freshly grated chocolate to the top.

• If you have a food processor with a shredding attachment, use it to grate the chocolate in a fraction of the time it takes to grate by hand. For easier grating—by hand or with the food processor—chill the chocolate for at least one hour in the refrigerator.

do it for less money: ($)

In place of the ladyfingers, use vanilla wafers or sliced pound cake. Instead of the coffee liqueur, use brandy, orange liqueur, or just extra coffee.

portion size: 1 (2½ to 3-inch) square

chocolate-almond biscotti

ingredients	**12** people: 1 pan (18 biscotti)	**25** people: 2 pans (36 biscotti)	**50** people: 4 pans (72 biscotti)	**75** people: 6 pans (108 biscotti)
Unsalted butter for greasing pans	as needed	as needed	as needed	as needed
Large eggs, room temperature	4	8	16	24
Vanilla extract	1 teaspoon	2 teaspoons	1 tablespoon plus 1 teaspoon	2 tablespoons
Almond extract	1 teaspoon	2 teaspoons	1 tablespoon plus 1 teaspoon	2 tablespoons
Granulated sugar	$1^1/_3$ cups (11 ounces)	$2^2/_3$ cups (22 ounces)	$5^1/_3$ cups (44 ounces)	8 cups (66 ounces)
Cake flour	$2^1/_2$ cups (10 ounces)	5 cups (20 ounces)	10 cups (40 ounces)	15 cups (60 ounces)
Unsweetened cocoa powder	$3/_4$ cup ($2^1/_4$ ounces)	$1^1/_2$ cups ($4^1/_2$ ounces)	3 cups (9 ounces)	$4^1/_2$ cups ($13^1/_2$ ounces)
Baking powder	2 teaspoons	1 tablespoon plus 1 teaspoon	2 tablespoons plus 2 teaspoons	$1/_4$ cup
Salt	$1/_2$ teaspoon	1 teaspoon	2 teaspoons	1 tablespoon
Semisweet chocolate chips	$1/_2$ cup ($2^1/_2$ ounces)	1 cup (5 ounces)	2 cups (10 ounces)	3 cups (15 ounces)
Slivered almonds	$3/_4$ cup (3 ounces)	$1^1/_3$ cups (5 ounces)	$2^2/_3$ cups (10 ounces)	4 cups (15 ounces)

 helpful hints:

- Biscotti get their distinctive crispness from being double-baked in the oven, making them ideal for dipping in coffee or port.
- When making 72 or more biscotti, divide the ingredients and make in batches of 18 or 36 for manageability.

do it ahead:

The biscotti can be made two days in advance if stored in an airtight container at room temperature.

directions:

1. Preheat the oven to 350 degrees and grease the baking sheets.

2. Beat the eggs until light and fluffy in a large mixing bowl. Slowly beat in the vanilla extract, almond extract, and sugar, scraping the sides of the bowl as needed.

3. In a separate mixing bowl, combine the cake flour, unsweetened cocoa powder, baking powder, and salt.

4. Carefully fold the flour mixture into the egg mixture. Fold in the chocolate chips and almonds.

5. Divide the mixture evenly among the pans. With slightly damp hands, form into free-form, 3 x 12-inch-long logs.

6. Bake for 30 minutes. Remove from the oven and let cool for 10 to 12 minutes on the pans.

7. Using a serrated knife, cut each log diagonally into 18 slices. Place the biscotti, flat-side down, on the baking sheets. Bake for 7 minutes, and then carefully turn each biscotti over and bake for an additional 5 to 7 minutes, or until crisp.

8. Remove the biscotti to racks and let cool completely. Store in an airtight container until ready to serve.

equipment:

- 1 baking sheet per 18 biscotti
- 2 large mixing bowls
- cooling racks
- electric hand or stand mixer
- serrated knife

portion size: 1 to 2 biscotti

ingredients	12 people	25 people	50 people	75 people
Ground coffee	4 ounces (1¼ cups)	8 ounces (2½ cups)	1 pound (5 cups)	1½ pounds (7½ cups)
Bottled or filtered water	2 quarts plus 1 cup	1 gallon plus 1 pint	2 gallons plus 1 quart	3½ gallons
Half-and-half or cream	½ cup (4 ounces)	1 cup (8 ounces)	2 cups (16 ounces)	3 cups (24 ounces)
Sugar	⅓ cup (3 ounces)	¾ cup (6 ounces)	1½ cups (12 ounces)	3 cups (24 ounces)
Sugar substitute	18 packets	36 packets	72 packets	108 packets

equipment:

• coffee maker or urn

directions:

1. Follow the coffee maker's manual for brewing instructions. Use bottled water and a clean coffee pot for best results.

2. Taste the coffee before serving. Coffee that is too strong can be watered down with hot water.

helpful hints: (fyi)

• For an extra taste of Italy, serve coffee with hazelnut liquor, lemon peel twists, and whipped cream.

• Recipe allows one 5-ounce cup of coffee per guest, but can be easily doubled if your guests will drink more than a cup each.

do it ahead:

• Fill the coffee maker with the ground coffee and water before your party starts. It will take about 30 minutes to brew 45 cups of coffee in a large urn and up to an hour for 100 cups.

• If you do not have a large coffee maker, divide the ingredients into halves or thirds and brew in batches.

portion size: 1 (5-ounce) cup of coffee and 2 teaspoons of cream and sugar

Creamy Herb Mushrooms

Baby Spinach, Walnut and Orange Salad
with Raspberry Vinaigrette

Brie-Stuffed Chicken Breast
with Herbed Breadcrumbs

Rosemary-Roasted Red Bliss Potatoes

Baked Asparagus in Garlic Butter

Baskets of Assorted Artisan Breads

Poached Bosc Pears in Cabernet Sauce
with Vanilla Bean Ice Cream

Chocolate Orange Truffles

starry night

An upscale five-course menu for the perfect evening wedding, anniversary party, Christmas Eve dinner, or New Year's Eve festivities.

creamy herb mushrooms
baby spinach, walnut, and orange salad
   with raspberry vinaigrette
brie-stuffed chicken breast with herbed breadcrumbs
rosemary-roasted red bliss potatoes
baked asparagus in garlic butter
baskets of assorted artisan breads*
poached bosc pears in cabernet sauce
   with vanilla bean ice cream
chocolate-orange truffles

* Choose a variety of freshly baked breads from your favorite local bakery.

decorating ideas:

colors. Midnight blues, copper, platinum, silver, or gold.

invitations. Keep them elegant and simple with white or cream card stock edged in ribbon with navy or black script. Or use a metallic ink on a dark blue card stock. If the invitations are professionally printed, use a simple line drawing of a star or several stars and a thin, simple font. If making them by hand, use deckled-edge paper and coat the edge of the paper with metallic ink for a finished look.

table linens. Use a dark blue or black tablecloth as the base. Scatter sparkly stars over the tablecloth, and then top with gossamer sheers to keep the stars in place and soften the sparkles.

decorations. Arrange a selection of all-white flowers in vases set on round mirrors. Line shallow glass bowls with black or clear marbles, fill with water, and add several floating candles or single blooms of gardenias. For a classic look, use silver and crystal candlesticks with white tapers. For a more festive approach, spray twigs, branches, or dried leaves with silver or gold paint. Stand upright in vases, place along the length of the table as a garland, or tie in bunches with matching or complementary ribbon. Purchase mass quantities of votive candles and enjoy the whole evening through candlelight. Or weave twinkle lights through chandeliers and wind around doorways with sheer or metallic fabrics. Hang clear glass ornaments or stars from the chandeliers or ceiling.

place cards and favors. Write your guests' names in silver or fancy black script on crisp white cards. Tie "falling stars" with ribbons or thin wire on the back of each guest's chair. Write guests' names on clear glass ornaments and adorn the plates for seating arrangements. For a light-hearted party, provide rhinestone tiaras, top hats, and magic wands for your guests. Prop their place cards against the tiaras and top hats, or tie onto the magic wands.

entertainment. Hire several string players from the local high school or university to play chamber music. Bring in a dance instructor to teach

menu countdown

1 week before:
- Shop for non-perishables.
- Buy beverages.
- Stuff, pan-cook, and freeze chicken breasts.
- Make and freeze truffles.

3 days before:
- Make space in refrigerator and freezer.
- Make breadcrumbs and store in airtight container.

2 days before:
- Shop for perishables.

1 day before:
- Set up tables and décor.
- Make raspberry vinaigrette.
- Wash and dry spinach for salad.
- Peel and segment oranges for salad.
- Stuff mushrooms and refrigerate.
- Assemble asparagus for baking.
- Parbake potatoes.
- Defrost chicken breasts in refrigerator.
- Poach pears and reduce the sauce.

morning of the party:
- Buy ice.
- Defrost truffles and roll in cocoa.

1 to 2 hours ahead:
- Sprinkle chicken breasts with breadcrumbs and bake.
- Bake asparagus.
- Roast potatoes.

just before serving:
- Bake stuffed mushrooms.
- Toss salad.
- Reheat bosc pear sauce.

starry night shopping list: 1 to 2 weeks before

ingredients	12 people	25 people	50 people	75 people
alcohol				
Cabernet Sauvignon or red Zinfandel	2 (750-ml) bottles	3 (750-ml) bottles	6 (750-ml) bottles	9 (750-ml) bottles
pantry items & dry goods				
Dijon mustard	1/2 ounce	1 ounce	2 ounces	3 ounces
Extra-virgin olive oil	12 ounces	24 ounces	48 ounces	70 ounces
Granulated sugar	12 ounces	1 3/4 pounds	3 1/4 pounds	5 pounds
Honey	2 ounces	4 ounces	8 ounces	12 ounces
Mayonnaise	1 ounce	2 ounces	4 ounces	6 ounces
Raspberry vinegar	1 ounce	2 ounces	4 ounces	6 ounces
Semisweet chocolate chips	12 ounces	24 ounces	48 ounces	72 ounces
Unsweetened cocoa powder	3/4 ounce	1 1/2 ounces	3 ounces	4 1/2 ounces
Vegetable cooking spray	1 can	1 can	1 can	1 can
Walnuts	8 ounces	1 pound	2 pounds	3 pounds
dried herbs, spices, & extracts				
Black peppercorns	as needed	as needed	as needed	as needed
Dried basil	1/4 ounce	1/4 ounce	1/4 ounce	1/4 ounce
Dried marjoram	1/4 ounce	1/4 ounce	1/4 ounce	1/4 ounce
Dried oregano	1/4 ounce	1/4 ounce	1/4 ounce	1/4 ounce
Dried sage	1/4 ounce	1/4 ounce	1/4 ounce	1/4 ounce
Dried thyme	1/4 ounce	1/4 ounce	1/4 ounce	1/4 ounce
Orange extract	1/2 ounce	1 ounce	2 ounces	3 ounces
Salt	as needed	as needed	as needed	as needed
Vanilla extract	1/4 ounce	1/2 ounce	1 ounce	2 ounces

starry night shopping list: 1 to 2 days before

ingredients	**12** people	**25** people	**50** people	**75** people
baked goods				
White bread	9 ounces	18 ounces	36 ounces	54 ounces
produce				
Baby spinach	12 ounces	$1\frac{1}{2}$ pounds	3 pounds	5 pounds
Bosc pears	6	13	25	38
Fresh rosemary	$\frac{1}{2}$ ounce	1 ounce	2 ounces	3 ounces
Garlic	2 heads	2 heads	4 heads	6 heads
Green onions	1 bunch	1 bunch	2 bunches	3 bunches
Medium-size asparagus	2 pounds	4 pounds	8 pounds	12 pounds
Medium-size button mushrooms	25 (about $\frac{3}{4}$ pound)	50 (about $1\frac{1}{2}$ pounds)	100 (about 3 pounds)	150 (about $4\frac{1}{2}$ pounds)
Medium-size red-bliss potatoes	$2\frac{1}{2}$ pounds	5 pounds	10 pounds	15 pounds
Oranges	$1\frac{3}{4}$ pounds	$3\frac{1}{4}$ pounds	$6\frac{1}{2}$ pounds	$9\frac{3}{4}$ pounds
Raspberries	$2\frac{3}{4}$ ounces	$5\frac{1}{2}$ ounces	11 ounces	1 pound
dairy, cheese, & deli				
Brie cheese	6 ounces	13 ounces	25 ounces	39 ounces
Gorgonzola cheese	2 ounces	4 ounces	8 ounces	12 ounces
Heavy whipping cream	6 ounces	12 ounces	26 ounces ($1\frac{3}{4}$ pints)	40 ounces ($1\frac{1}{4}$ quarts)
Unsalted butter	1 pound	$1\frac{3}{4}$ pounds	$3\frac{1}{2}$ pounds	$5\frac{3}{4}$ pounds
meat & seafood				
Boneless, skinless chicken breasts	12 (6 to 8-ounce) breasts	25 (6 to 8-ounce) breasts	50 (6 to 8-ounce) breasts	75 (6 to 8-ounce) breasts
miscellaneous				
Vanilla bean ice cream	$3\frac{1}{2}$ pints	$6\frac{1}{2}$ pints	13 pints	$2\frac{1}{2}$ gallons

Always take a calculator when shopping for quantity recipes to quickly and easily calculate the most appropriate package sizes for your particular needs. We have listed most items in ounces so that you are not limited to size-specific packaging if shopping in bulk. When in doubt over what amount to buy, always round up—it's far better to have a little extra of an ingredient than to run out while cooking. If your eighth-grade algebra skills have gotten rusty, remember that there are 16 ounces in a pound and 8 fluid ounces in a cup. See page 73 for additional conversions.

creamy herb mushrooms

ingredients	12 people	25 people	50 people	75 people
Medium-size button mushrooms	25 (about ¾ pound)	50 (about 1½ pounds)	100 (about 3 pounds)	150 (about 4½ pounds)
Unsalted butter	4 tablespoons (2 ounces)	1 stick (4 ounces)	2 sticks (8 ounces)	3 sticks (12 ounces)
Sliced green onions	¼ cup	½ cup	1 cup	1½ cups
Minced garlic	¾ teaspoon	1½ teaspoons	1 tablespoon	1½ tablespoons
Herbed breadcrumbs (page 133)	¾ cup	1¾ cups	2½ cups	4 cups
Crumbled Gorgonzola cheese	½ cup (2 ounces)	1 cup (4 ounces)	2 cups (8 ounces)	3 cups (12 ounces)
Extra-virgin olive oil	4 ounces	8 ounces	16 ounces	24 ounces

(fyi) helpful hint:

Substitute any blue cheese, sharp cheddar, feta, Boursin, or even tofu in place of the Gorgonzola in this recipe.

do it ahead:

The mushrooms can be prepared a day in advance and baked just before serving.

do it for less time:

Use store-bought seasoned breadcrumbs in place of the homemade herbed breadcrumbs to save time.

($) do it for less money:

Spray the tops of the mushrooms with vegetable cooking spray instead of drizzling with olive oil.

directions:

1. Preheat the oven to 425 degrees.

2. Clean the mushrooms and remove the stems. Place the stems in a food processor or blender and process until smooth.

3. Melt the butter over medium heat in a large sauté pan. Add the processed mushroom stems, green onions, and garlic. Sauté for 3 to 4 minutes, or until fragrant, and then remove from the heat. Stir in the breadcrumbs and the cheese, mixing well to incorporate.

4. Spoon the mixture into the mushroom caps, and arrange the filled mushrooms on baking sheets. (The mushrooms can be made up to this point a day in advance. Cover and refrigerate until ready to bake.)

5. Drizzle the mushrooms with the olive oil. Bake for 10 to 12 minutes, or until heated through.

equipment:

- baking sheets
- food processor or blender
- large sauté pan
- wooden spoon

portion size: 2 mushrooms

baby spinach, walnut, and orange salad
with raspberry vinaigrette

ingredients	12 people	25 people	50 people	75 people
Oranges	1¾ pounds	3¼ pounds	6½ pounds	9¾ pounds
Mayonnaise	2 tablespoons	¼ cup	½ cup	¾ cup
Raspberry vinegar	2 tablespoons	¼ cup	½ cup	¾ cup
Dijon mustard	1 tablespoon	2 tablespoons	¼ cup	¼ cup plus 2 tablespoons
Raspberries	2¾ ounces (¼ cup)	5½ ounces (⅓ cup)	11 ounces (⅔ cup)	1 pound (1 cup)
Honey	2 tablespoons plus 1 teaspoon	⅓ cup	⅔ cup	1 cup
Extra-virgin olive oil	¼ cup plus 2 tablespoons (3 ounces)	¾ cup (6 ounces)	1½ cups (12 ounces)	2¼ cups (18 ounces)
Salt and freshly ground black pepper	to taste	to taste	to taste	to taste
Baby spinach	12 ounces	1½ pounds	3 pounds	5 pounds
Walnut pieces	8 ounces	1 pound	2 pounds	3½ pounds

equipment:

- 36-inch salad bowl
- large mixing bowl
- tongs or disposable gloves
- whisk

directions:

1. Peel the oranges and cut into segments.

2. Combine the mayonnaise, raspberry vinegar, Dijon mustard, raspberries, and honey in a large mixing bowl. Using the back of a spoon or fork, mash the raspberries into mixture. Gradually whisk in the oil until the mixture is emulsified. Season with salt and pepper to taste.

3. Just before serving, place a third of the dry spinach, walnuts, and orange segments in a 36-inch salad bowl. Add one third of the vinaigrette. Using tongs or your hands (wearing disposable plastic gloves), toss the lettuce with the dressing until well coated.

4. Taste the salad and add more dressing as needed, being careful not to over dress the leaves.

5. Repeat with the remaining lettuce mixture and vinaigrette.

helpful hints: (fyi)

- Zest the oranges first and use in Poached Bosc Pears (page 136).

- Toss the salad in batches for manageability.

- To keep the honey from sticking, spray the measuring cup with vegetable cooking spray before measuring the honey.

do it ahead:

All the components for the salad can be prepared a day in advance. Make the vinaigrette, wash and dry the spinach, and segment the oranges. Store everything in the refrigerator until ready to combine.

do it for less time:

- Look for bags of pre-washed, ready-to-use baby spinach in the produce section of your grocery.

- Use a blender to emulsify the salad dressing quickly.

- Substitute canned and drained tangerine segments for the fresh orange segments.

do it for less money: ($)

Use frozen raspberries instead of fresh. Thaw and use as directed.

portion size: about one heaped cup of salad plus 2 tablespoons of dressing

brie-stuffed chicken breast

ingredients	12 people	25 people	50 people	75 people
Brie cheese	6 ounces	13 ounces	25 ounces	39 ounces
Boneless, skinless chicken breasts	12 (6 to 8-ounce) breasts	25 (6 to 8-ounce) breasts	50 (6 to 8-ounce) breasts	75 (6 to 8-ounce) breasts
Unsalted butter, melted and divided	1¼ sticks (5 ounces)	2½ sticks (10 ounces)	5 sticks (20 ounces)	8 sticks (32 ounces)
Herbed breadcrumbs (page 133)	6½ ounces	13 ounces	26 ounces	2½ pounds
Vegetable cooking spray	as needed	as needed	as needed	as needed

(fyi) helpful hint:

Invest in a kitchen scale to help you accurately measure and portion your ingredients.

do it ahead:

• The chicken can be prepared a day in advance if covered and refrigerated. Keep chilled unitl ready to bake.

• The chicken can also be prepared up to a week in advance if wrapped well in plastic, then in foil, and frozen. Defrost in the refrigerator the day before the party and bake just before serving.

• For very best results, do not sprinkle breadcrumbs on the chicken until right before baking. But if time demands, the chicken can be fully prepared in advance with the breadcrumbs.

do it for less time:

Use store-bought, seasoned breadcrumbs in place of the herbed breadcrumbs to save time.

($) do it for less money:

Brie is a soft, creamy French cheese sold in wedges or whole wheels. You can use chive-flavored cream cheese in lieu

directions:

1. Preheat the oven to 350 degrees.

2. Cut the Brie into 1-inch cubes about ½ ounce each. There is no need to remove the rind. (For easier cutting, place the Brie in the freezer for a few minutes before cutting.)

3. Using a paring knife, cut a slit along the thickest length of each chicken breast about 1 inch long and 1 inch deep, taking care not to puncture the outer edge of the chicken. Place a piece of Brie into the pocket. If necessary, make the pocket deeper to accommodate the Brie.

4. Pour half of the butter into a large sauté pan. Cook the chicken until the outside is golden brown, about 3 to 4 minutes. Turn the chicken, and cook for 3 to 4 more minutes. (The chicken can be prepared to this stage up to 1 week in advance. Wrap well and freeze until the day before the party, then defrost in the refrigerator before continuing. Alternatively, prepare the chicken a day in advance. Cover and refrigerate until ready to bake.)

5. Place the browned chicken on baking sheets in a single layer. Using a pastry brush, coat the top surface of the chicken breasts with the remaining melted butter. Sprinkle 2 tablespoons of the Herbed Breadcrumbs (page 133) over each chicken breast. Spray the breadcrumbs with vegetable cooking spray.

6. Bake for 20 to 30 minutes, or until the chicken is cooked through and the breadcrumbs are golden brown.

equipment:

• baking sheets
• large sauté pans
• paring knife
• pastry brush
• tongs

portion size: 1 (6 to 8-ounce) chicken breast

herbed breadcrumbs

ingredients	12 people	25 people	50 people	75 people
Day-old white bread	9 slices (9 ounces)	18 slices (18 ounces)	36 slices (36 ounces)	54 slices (54 ounces)
Dried oregano	$\frac{1}{2}$ teaspoon	1 teaspoon	2 teaspoons	1 tablespoon
Dried basil	$\frac{1}{2}$ teaspoon	1 teaspoon	2 teaspoons	1 tablespoon
Dried thyme	$\frac{1}{2}$ teaspoon	1 teaspoon	2 teaspoons	1 tablespoon
Dried marjoram	$\frac{1}{2}$ teaspoon	1 teaspoon	2 teaspoons	1 tablespoon
Dried sage	$\frac{1}{2}$ teaspoon	1 teaspoon	2 teaspoons	1 tablespoon
Salt	$1\frac{1}{4}$ teaspoons	$2\frac{1}{2}$ teaspoons	2 tablespoons plus 2 teaspoons	3 tablespoons plus $1\frac{1}{2}$ teaspoons
Freshly ground black pepper	$1\frac{1}{4}$ teaspoons	$2\frac{1}{2}$ teaspoons	2 tablespoons plus 2 teaspoons	3 tablespoons plus $1\frac{1}{2}$ teaspoons

equipment:

• food processor
• serrated knife

directions:

1. Remove the crusts from the bread and discard them. Tear the bread into 1-inch pieces.

2. Process in a food processor until the bread forms fine crumbs. Add the remaining ingredients and process until mixed.

helpful hints: (fyi)

• These homemade breadcrumbs taste great made with stale bread or bagels. Use them on chicken, fish, and shrimp, or sprinkle on top of casseroles before baking.

• Leave fresh bread uncovered overnight so that it will dry out.

do it ahead:

The breadcrumbs can be made up to three days in advance. Store in an airtight container at room temperature.

do it for less time:

Use panko—Japanese breadcrumbs—or pre-made Italian breadcrumbs if you're short on time, and add the herbs for flavor.

do it for less money: ($)

Look for the day-old rack in your bakery for discounted bread items. If you don't want to buy all the dried herbs, substitute an Italian seasoning that includes oregano, basil, thyme, and rosemary.

rosemary-roasted red bliss potatoes

ingredients	12 people	25 people	50 people	75 people
Red-bliss potatoes	2½ pounds	5 pounds	10 pounds	15 pounds
Extra-virgin olive oil	½ cup (4 ounces)	1 cup (8 ounces)	2 cups (16 ounces)	3 cups (24 ounces)
Chopped fresh rosemary	⅓ cup	⅔ cup	1⅓ cups	2 cups
Salt and freshly ground black pepper	to taste	to taste	to taste	to taste

do it ahead:

The potatoes can be washed and cut into quarters a day in advance. To prevent discoloration, place the potatoes in a large mixing bowl and just cover with water. Add enough milk to come ½-inch above the potatoes. Stir slightly to combine the water and milk. Drain and pat dry before baking. Alternatively, the potatoes can be parbaked a day in advance. Let cool, cover, and refrigerate until ready to continue baking.

do it for less time:

Instead of chopping the fresh rosemary, use dried. Use only one third of the amount called for when using dried herbs in place of fresh.

do it for less money:

You can use russet potatoes in place of the red potatoes. Cut each potato into six to eight pieces. New white potatoes will also work well in this recipe.

directions:

1. Preheat the oven to 400 degrees.

2. Scrub and dry the potatoes. Cut each potato into quarters and place in a large mixing bowl. Add the olive oil, rosemary, and salt and pepper to taste.

3. Place the potatoes in a single layer on each pan. Bake for 30 minutes. (The potatoes can be parbaked to this stage up to a day in advance. Let cool, cover, and refrigerate until ready to continue baking.)

4. Bake for an additional 30 minutes, or until the potatoes are cooked through, golden brown, and slightly crunchy. Serve immediately.

equipment:

- baking sheets
- large stainless steel bowl
- spatula
- vegetable brush

portion size: 3 ounces (about 8 pieces)

baked asparagus in garlic butter

ingredients	12 people	25 people	50 people	75 people
Medium-size asparagus	2 pounds	4 pounds	8 pounds	12 pounds
Unsalted butter	2 sticks (8 ounces)	4 sticks (16 ounces)	8 sticks (32 ounces)	12 sticks (48 ounces)
Minced garlic	¼ cup	½ cup	1 cup	1½ cups
Salt and freshly ground black pepper	to taste	to taste	to taste	to taste

equipment:

- heavy-duty aluminum foil
- ladle
- medium saucepan
- shallow baking pans

directions:

1. Preheat the oven to 450 degrees.

2. Trim the tough ends from the asparagus. Place the spears in a single layer on baking pans.

3. Melt the butter in a medium saucepan over medium heat. Add the garlic and stir to combine. Cook 3 to 4 minutes, being careful not to brown the garlic.

4. Ladle the butter evenly over the asparagus. Season with salt and pepper to taste. (The asparagus can be prepared to this stage a day in advance. Cover with foil and refrigerate until ready to bake.)

5. Bake, covered with foil, for 15 minutes, or until the asparagus is bright green and just tender. Be careful not to over-cook, as the asparagus will become soggy. Serve immediately.

helpful hint:

Look for thin to medium-size asparagus. If using thick asparagus, peel or trim the bottom half of the spears.

do it ahead:

You can assemble the asparagus and butter sauce up to a day in advance. Cover tightly with foil, and store in the refrigerator until ready to bake.

do it for less time:

Look for pre-chopped garlic in the produce section of your grocery store.

do it for less money:

This recipe will also work for baby carrots or sliced zucchini. Cook the carrots for 35 to 40 minutes and the zucchini for 15 to 20 minutes.

portion size: about 5 spears

poached bosc pears in cabernet sauce with vanilla bean ice cream

ingredients	12 people	25 people	50 people	75 people
Ripe pears	6	13	25	38
Cabernet Sauvignon or red Zinfandel	1½ (750-ml) bottles	3 (750-ml) bottles	6 (750-ml) bottles	9 (750-ml) bottles
Vanilla extract	1 teaspoon	2 teaspoons	1 tablespoon plus 1 teaspoon	2 tablespoons
Granulated sugar	¾ pound	1¾ pounds	3¼ pounds	5 pounds
Orange zest	1 tablespoon (about 1 orange)	2 tablespoons (about 2 oranges)	⅓ cup (about 4 oranges)	½ cup (about 7 oranges)
Vanilla bean ice cream	3½ pints	6½ pints	13 pints	2½ gallons

(fyi) helpful hint:

Making large quantities of ice cream can be difficult without the correct machinery and freezer storage space. As there are so many great brands on the market that are reasonably priced, we suggest you buy it ready-made.

do it ahead:

• This dish can be completely prepared a day in advance.

• Remember to remove the ice cream from the freezer at least 30 minutes before service. This will allow it to soften slightly and become more manageable for serving.

do it for less time:

• Substitute orange juice for orange zest.

• To save time, use canned pear halves. Drain the pears and place in a large stockpot or bowl. Pour the hot wine mixture over the pear halves and let steep for two to three hours or overnight. Remove the pears and cook the wine mixture as directed in step four.

(S) do it for less money:

If you do not have a melon scoop, use a teaspoon-size stainless steel measuring spoon.

directions:

1. Peel the pears and cut in half lengthwise. Remove the cores using a melon scoop.

2. Combine the wine, vanilla extract, sugar, and orange zest in a stockpot, and bring to a boil. Add the pears to the stockpot, and simmer for 1 to 1½ hours, or until tender. (The cooking time will vary according to ripeness of the fruit.) Allow the pears to cool in the stockpot, and then remove the pears from the liquid.

3. Alternatively, place the pears in shallow roasting pans. Pour the hot wine mixture over the pear halves, cover with foil, and bake at 350 degrees for 1 hour, or until soft. Allow the pears to cool in the wine mixture, and then pour the liquid into a stockpot.

4. Bring the poaching liquid to a boil. Reduce the heat and simmer until the liquid is reduced by half or is thick and syrupy. Strain the sauce through a sieve. Taste for sweetness, and add more sugar if necessary. The sauce can be served warm, at room temperature, or chilled.

5. Likewise, the pears can be served warm, at room temperature, or chilled with ¼ cup of the sauce and ½ cup of the vanilla bean ice cream. For a nice juxtaposition, serve the chilled pears with warm sauce and cold ice cream.

equipment:

• ½ cup (4-ounce) ice cream scoop

• ladle

• large stockpots or shallow roasting pans

• melon baller or small scoop

• slotted spoon

• sieve

• zester or microplane grater

portion size: ½ pear, ¼ cup (2 ounces) sauce, ½ cup ice cream

chocolate-orange truffles

ingredients	12 people (25 truffles)	25 people (50 truffles)	50 people (100 truffles)	75 people (150 truffles)
Heavy whipping cream	$3/4$ cup	$1^1/2$ cups	$3^1/4$ cups	5 cups
Semisweet chocolate chips	2 cups	4 cups	8 cups	12 cups
Orange extract	1 tablespoon, plus more if needed	2 tablespoons, plus more if needed	$1/4$ cup, plus more if needed	$1/4$ cup plus 2 tablespoons, plus more if needed
Unsweetened cocoa powder	$1/4$ cup	$1/2$ cup	1 cup	$1^1/2$ cups

equipment:

- for 12 guests, use an 8 x 8-inch baking pan
- for 25 guests or more, use 13 x 9 x 2-inch baking pans
- baking sheets
- food processor
- heavy-bottomed saucepan
- mixing bowl
- plastic wrap
- waxed or parchment paper

directions:

1. Line the baking sheets with waxed paper.

2. Heat the cream in a saucepan until hot but not boiling.

3. Place the chocolate chips in the bowl of a food processor or blender. Pour the hot cream over the chocolate, let stand for 1 minute, and then process until smooth.

4. Add the orange extract and process to combine. Taste the mixture and add more orange extract if needed.

5. Pour the mixture into the baking pan, cover with plastic wrap, and chill in the refrigerator about $2^1/2$ to 3 hours, or until firm.

6. Score each pan into $1^1/4$-inch squares. Scoop out the pre-scored squares of mixture with a spoon and form by hand into irregular ball-shaped truffles.

7. Place the truffles on the prepared baking sheet and refrigerate as you continue filling the remaining baking sheets. Refrigerate the truffles at least 30 minutes to set.

8. Place the cocoa powder in a mixing bowl.

9. With clean, dry hands, roll each truffle between your palms to make a perfect ball shape. (The truffles can be made up to this point 3 months in advance. Layer in airtight containers with waxed paper between each layer. Freeze, defrost at room temperature the day before the party, and dust in cocoa powder before serving.)

10. Drop each truffle in the cocoa powder and gently roll with your hands to coat.

11. Store in the refrigerator in airtight containers with waxed paper between each layer.

helpful hints:

- Vary the flavors of the truffles by using mint or almond extract, or substitute alcohols like rum, bourbon, or champagne for the extract.

- For added opulence, dip the chilled truffles in melted chocolate. Roll in any variety of toppings, such as finely chopped nuts, tiny silver or gold dragées (edible candy balls), edible gold leaf, colorful glitter powders, or candied mimosa blossoms, violets, and rose petals.

- Heavy whipping cream is thicker than regular whipping cream and will work better in this recipe. Look for 6 grams of fat per tablespoon on the nutrition table on the carton.

- If you find the unsweetened cocoa to be too bitter, sift together equal parts cocoa powder and powdered sugar.

do it ahead:

Truffles can be made and frozen for up to three months. Thaw in the refrigerator and roll in cocoa powder before serving.

do it for less time:

Buy an inexpensive box of plain truffles and decorate them using our "do it for less" ideas in the helpful hints listed above.

portion size: 2 truffles

Egg Rolls with Sweet and Sour Sauce

Beef Saté Skewers with
Spicy Peanut Dipping Sauce

Stir-Fried Ginger-Pineapple Chicken

Jasmine Rice with Scallions

Garlic Snow Peas and Almonds

Mango or Coconut Sorbet

Chocolate-Dipped Fortune Cookies

asian inspiration

A taste of the Orient for a perfectly Zen birthday or a rehearsal dinner of good fortune.

asian menu:

egg rolls with sweet and sour sauce*
beef saté skewers with spicy peanut dipping sauce
stir-fried ginger-pineapple chicken
jasmine rice with scallions
garlic snow peas and almonds
mango, coconut, or green tea sorbet**
chocolate-dipped fortune cookies

* Buy egg rolls from your favorite Chinese restaurant or from the freezer sections of larger grocery and club stores. Cut each egg roll in half diagonally and serve with store-bought sweet and sour sauce. Allow 1 egg roll and 1 to 2 ounces of sweet and sour sauce per guest. Serve an all-vegetable egg roll along with the jasmine rice and snow peas for your vegetarian guests.

** Serve your favorite sorbet with this menu, allowing $1/2$ cup per guest.

decorating ideas:

colors. Jade green, mandarin orange, lacquered red, jet black, and teak.

invitations. Choose a variety of patterned origami paper or Japanese book-binding paper. Use a solid color that coordinates with the patterned papers for the invitation and attach with a rustic twig or a cloisonné pin from an Asian import store. Create matching menus using the same format.

table linens. Use raw silk remnants, rich jacquards, or bamboo runners down long wooden tables, or cover folding tables with neutral base colors like chocolate brown or black.

decorations. Fill round or square glass vases with smooth black river stones, water, and floating candles. Accent a piece of driftwood or tree branch with silk or satin flowers attached with floral wire. Place bonsai trees at regular intervals along the table. Use any rectangular serving pieces with Zen-inspired shapes. Plant easy-to-grow winter grasses in small individual boxes (or one long, thin box) and place in the center of the table or along the buffet. Hang several brightly colored lanterns from the ceiling with silk butterflies for accents. Choose several delicate orchids instead of elaborate floral arrangements.

place cards and favors. Pre-plate the first course and use rice hats as a fun plate topper and name card holder combined, or make original origami pieces for each guest. Write names on small pieces of paper and slip them part-way into a fortune cookie so that the name can still be read. Buy sets of take-out style chopsticks from a local Chinese restaurant and write the guests' names on the paper holders. Or buy beautiful, enamel-coated chopsticks and ceramic or wooden chopstick rests that can double as party favors. Prop name cards in front of miniature Buddhas made of stone or jade. Place 4-inch bamboo plants in clean baby food jars or small vases. Set name cards in between the stalks, and let the guests take home their bamboo for good luck.

entertainment. Play traditional Kyoto music or use a table-top fountain for a soothing effect.

menu countdown

1 week before:
- Shop for non-perishables.
- Buy beverages.

3 days before:
- Make space in refrigerator and freezer.

2 days before:
- Shop for perishables.

1 day before:
- Set up tables and décor.
- Assemble and marinate beef saté skewers.
- Prepare peanut sauce, omitting the soy sauce and lime juice.
- Chop pineapple and red bell peppers.
- Slice chicken.
- Clean snow peas.
- Toast almonds.

morning of the party:
- Buy ice.
- Dip fortune cookies in chocolate.

1 to 2 hours ahead:
- Grill beef saté skewers.
- Prepare rice.

just before serving:
- Stir-fry chicken.
- Stir-fry snow peas.
- Stir in the soy sauce and lime juice to the peanut sauce.

asian inspiration shopping list: 1 to 2 weeks before

ingredients	12 people	25 people	50 people	75 people
alcohol				
Mirin or seasoned rice vinegar	3 ounces	6 ounces	12 ounces	18 ounces
pantry items & dry goods				
Chicken stock	3 quarts (96 ounces)	1½ gallons (192 ounces)	3 gallons (384 ounces)	4½ gallons (576 ounces)
Cornstarch	¼ cup	½ cup	1 cup	1½ cups
Granulated sugar	5 ounces	10 ounces	20 ounces	30 ounces
Honey	20 ounces	38 ounces	76 ounces	112 ounces
Jasmine rice	2 pounds	4 pounds	8 pounds	12 pounds
Lime juice	8 ounces (or 1¼ pounds limes)	1 pint (or 2½ pounds limes)	2 pints (or 5 pounds limes)	3 pints (or 7½ pounds limes)
Peanut oil	16 ounces	32 ounces	64 ounces	96 ounces
Semisweet chocolate chips or good-quality dark chocolate bars	9 ounces	18 ounces	36 ounces	54 ounces
Sliced almonds	3 ounces	6 ounces	12 ounces	18 ounces
Soy sauce	21 ounces	42 ounces	84 ounces	126 ounces
Sweet and sour sauce	3 ounces	6 ounces	12 ounces	18 ounces
Unsalted peanuts	4 ounces	8 ounces	16 ounces	24 ounces
Unsweetened coconut milk	12 ounces	24 ounces	48 ounces	72 ounces
dried herbs, spices, & extracts				
Black peppercorns	as needed	as needed	as needed	as needed
Chinese five-spice powder	¼ ounce	¼ ounce	¼ ounce	¼ ounce
Ground coriander	½ ounce	¾ ounce	1½ ounces	2¼ ounces
Red curry paste	4½ ounces	9 ounces	18 ounces	27 ounces
Salt	as needed	as needed	as needed	as needed
frozen foods				
Egg rolls	12	25	50	75
Mango, coconut, or green tea sorbet	3½ pints	6½ pints	13 pints	2½ gallons

asian inspiration shopping list: 1 to 2 days before

ingredients	**12**people	**25**people	**50**people	**75**people
produce				
Fresh ginger	1 ounce	2 ounces	3 ounces	5 ounces
Garlic	4 heads	8 heads	16 heads	24 heads
Green onions	2 bunches	3 bunches	6 bunches	9 bunches
Pineapple, medium sized	1 (2 pounds whole or 24 ounces flesh)	2 (4 pounds whole or 48 ounces flesh)	4 (8 pounds whole or 96 ounces flesh)	6 (12 pounds whole or 144 ounces flesh)
Red bell pepper	1	1	2	3
Snow peas	3 pounds	6 pounds	12 pounds	18 pounds
meat & seafood				
Boneless sirloin or flank steak	6 pounds	12 pounds	24 pounds	36 pounds
Boneless, skinless chicken breasts or tenders	4 pounds	8 pounds	16 pounds	24 pounds
miscellaneous				
Fortune cookies	12	25	50	75

Always take a calculator when shopping for quantity recipes to quickly and easily calculate the most appropriate package sizes for your particular needs. We have listed most items in ounces so that you are not limited to size-specific packaging if shopping in bulk. When in doubt over what amount to buy, always round up—it's far better to have a little extra of an ingredient than to run out while cooking. If your eighth-grade algebra skills have gotten rusty, remember that there are 16 ounces in a pound and 8 fluid ounces in a cup. See page 73 for additional conversions.

beef saté skewers

ingredients	12 people	25 people	50 people	75 people
Soy sauce	2½ cups	5 cups	10 cups	15 cups
Red curry paste	½ cup	1 cup	2 cups	3 cups
Minced garlic	¾ cup	1½ cups	3 cups	4½ cups
Lime juice	¾ cup	1½ cups	3 cups	4½ cups
Ground coriander	1 tablespoon plus 1½ teaspoons	3 tablespoons	6 tablespoons	9 tablespoons
Peanut oil	1½ cups	3 cups	6 cups	9 cups
Honey	1½ cups	3 cups	6 cups	9 cups
Boneless sirloin or flank steak	6 pounds	12 pounds	24 pounds	36 pounds

(fyi) helpful hints:

• Spray the measuring cup with vegetable cooking spray to keep the honey from sticking.

• If using wooden skewers, soak them in water for 30 minutes to prevent them from burning during cooking.

• Red curry paste can be found in the Asian section of your grocery store.

do it ahead:

Prepare the skewers a day ahead to infuse the meat with the marinade.

do it for less time:

If time is short, use bottled lime juice in place of freshly squeezed juice.

($) do it for less money:

• Use fresh or frozen chicken tenders in place of the chicken breasts. Allow enough time to defrost the frozen tenders in the refrigerator. Do not marinate overnight.

• If you do not own a meat tenderizer, you can use a small, sturdy saucepan or rolling pin.

directions:

1. Combine the soy sauce, curry paste, garlic, lime juice, coriander, peanut oil, and honey in a large bowl. Whisk until smooth.

2. Trim any excess fat from the steak and discard. Using a meat tenderizer, pound the steaks to ¼-inch thickness. Cut the steaks into ¾ x 3-inch strips.

3. Place the steak strips in shallow pans or resealable plastic storage bags. Pour the marinade equally among the pans or bags. Seal well, and marinate for at least 2 hours or overnight.

4. Preheat the grill.

5. Place one strip of the steak onto each skewer. Grill for 2 to 3 minutes on each side, or until just cooked through. Serve hot or at room temperature with the Spicy Peanut Dipping Sauce (page 143).

equipment:

• meat tenderizer

• mixing bowl

• shallow roasting pans or heavy-duty resealable plastic storage bags

• tongs

• whisk

• wooden or metal skewers

portion size: 2 to 3 skewers

spicy peanut dipping sauce

ingredients	12 people	25 people	50 people	75 people
Unsalted peanuts	³/₄ cup	1¹/₂ cups	3 cups	4¹/₂ cups
Granulated sugar	1 tablespoon	2 tablespoons	¹/₄ cup	¹/₃ cup
Peanut oil	2 tablespoons	¹/₄ cup	¹/₂ cup	³/₄ cup
Red curry paste	1 tablespoon	2 tablespoons	¹/₄ cup	¹/₃ cup
Unsweetened coconut milk	1¹/₂ cups	3 cups	6 cups	9 cups
Soy sauce	1 tablespoon	2 tablespoons	¹/₄ cup	¹/₃ cup
Lime juice	1 tablespoon plus 2 teaspoons	3 tablespoons	¹/₃ cup	¹/₂ cup

equipment:

- food processor or blender
- medium saucepan
- whisk

directions:

1. Place the peanuts and sugar in the bowl of a food processor or blender, and process until finely chopped.

2. Heat the oil in a medium saucepan. Whisk in the curry paste and coconut milk. Stir in the ground peanut mixture. Bring the mixture to a boil, stirring constantly, and then remove from the heat and allow to cool slightly.

3. Pour the mixture back into the food processor or blender and blend until smooth. (The sauce can be prepared to this point up to a day in advance. Cover tightly and refrigerate until ready to proceed.)

4. Just before serving, stir in the soy sauce and lime juice. Serve warm or at room temperature.

helpful hint: (fyi)

Red curry paste can be found in the Asian section of your grocery store.

do it ahead:

The sauce can be prepared a day in advance, adding the soy sauce and lime juice just before serving. Cover the sauce tightly and store in the refrigerator until an hour before the party. Let come to room temperature, and then stir in the soy sauce and lime juice.

do it for less time:

If pressed for time, buy pre-made peanut sauce from your local Asian food market or Thai restaurant.

do it for less money: ($)

Instead of buying curry paste, combine two parts heavy cream with one part curry powder.

stir-fried ginger-pineapple chicken

ingredients	12 people	25 people	50 people	75 people
Boneless, skinless chicken breasts	4 pounds	8 pounds	16 pounds	24 pounds
Cornstarch	1/4 cup	1/2 cup	1 cup	1 1/2 cups
Chopped fresh ginger	1 tablespoon plus 2 teaspoons	3 tablespoons	6 tablespoons	1/2 cup plus 1 tablespoon
Chinese five-spice powder	1/4 teaspoon	1/2 teaspoon	1 teaspoon	1 1/2 teaspoons
Salt	1 1/2 teaspoon	1 tablespoon	2 tablespoons	3 tablespoons
Chicken stock	3/4 cup	1 1/2 cups	3 cups	4 1/2 cups
Granulated sugar	1/3 cup	3/4 cup	1 1/2 cups	2 1/4 cups
Mirin or seasoned rice vinegar	1/3 cup	3/4 cup	1 1/2 cups	2 1/4 cups
Soy sauce	1 tablespoon	2 tablespoons	1/4 cup	1/3 cup
Peanut oil	1/3 cup	3/4 cup	1 1/2 cups	2 1/4 cups
Minced garlic	1 tablespoon plus 1 teaspoon	2 tablespoons plus 1 1/2 teaspoons	1/4 cup plus 1 tablespoon	1/2 cup
Fresh pineapple, chopped	2 pounds (about 3 cups)	4 pounds (about 6 cups)	8 pounds (about 12 cups)	12 pounds (about 18 cups)
Red bell pepper, finely diced	1/2	1	2	3
Green onions, sliced diagonally	1/2 bunch	1 bunch	2 bunches	3 bunches

(fyi) helpful hint:
Mirin is a low-alcohol wine made from rice. It adds sweetness to a variety of Asian dishes. If you cannot find it in the Asian or wine section of your grocery store, use seasoned rice vinegar.

do it ahead:
Slice the chicken a day in advance to save time before the party.

do it for less time:
• Look for pre-chopped ginger and garlic in the produce section of your local grocery store.

• Substitute drained canned pineapple chunks in place of fresh pineapple.

($) do it for less money:
Use fresh or frozen chicken tenders in place of the chicken breasts. Allow time to defrost the frozen tenders in the refrigerator.

directions:

1. Slice the chicken breasts against the grain into 1/4-inch-wide strips about 2 inches in length.

2. Combine the cornstarch, ginger, five-spice powder, salt, chicken stock, sugar, mirin, and soy sauce in a mixing bowl.

3. Heat the oil in a large sauté pan or wok over medium-high heat. Add the garlic and cook for 30 seconds. Remove the garlic from the pan.

4. Add the chicken in batches and stir-fry for 1 minute, or until cooked through. Remove the chicken from the pan.

5. Add the pineapple, red bell pepper, and green onions to the pan. Stir-fry for 2 minutes.

6. Pour the cornstarch mixture into the pan and bring to a boil. Cook for 2 minutes, or until the sauce thickens.

7. Return the garlic and the chicken to the pan. Stir until the chicken is warmed through and coated in the sauce. Serve immediately.

equipment:
• heavy-duty resealable plastic storage bags
• large sauté pans or wok
• mixing bowl
• tongs
• wooden spoon

portion size: 6 to 8 ounces

jasmine rice with scallions

ingredients	12 people	25 people	50 people	75 people
Jasmine rice	2 pounds (5 cups)	4 pounds (10 cups)	8 pounds (20 cups)	12 pounds (30 cups)
Chicken or vegetable stock	10 cups (80 ounces)	20 cups (160 ounces)	40 cups (320 ounces)	60 cups (480 ounces)
Salt	1 tablespoon	2 tablespoons	1/4 cup	1/3 cup
Green onions, sliced	1 bunch	2 bunches	4 bunches	6 bunches

equipment:

- aluminum foil
- large stockpots with lids, roasting pans, or chafing dish inserts
- wooden spoon

directions:

1. Divide the rice equally among the stockpots and fill with enough water to cover the rice. Using a wooden spoon, swirl the rice around to loosen the starch. Drain the water and repeat the rinsing process.

2. Set the stockpots over high heat, and pour the hot chicken stock over the rice in equal portions. Add the salt and half the green onions, and stir to combine.

3. Bring the rice to a boil, cover with tight-fitting lids or aluminum foil, and then reduce the heat to low.

4. Simmer for 20 to 25 minutes, or until the rice is tender and the stock is absorbed. Remove from the heat, keeping covered until ready to serve.

5. Alternatively, pour the hot stock and rice in a roasting pan covered with foil. Bake at 350 degrees for 25 to 30 minutes, or until the rice is tender. If prepared in a stainless steel chafing dish insert, the finished rice can then go directly from the oven to the chafing dish on the buffet.

6. Just before serving, add the remaining green onions. Fluff the rice with a fork to combine.

helpful hints:

- If jasmine rice is not available, use a regular long-grain rice. The cooking time will be the same.

- Scallions are commonly called green onions, but in the menu, use the more elegant term.

do it for less time:

If you have to make very large quantities of rice and are pressed for time or short on stove-top space, order cooked rice from your local Asian restaurant and add the chopped green onions before serving.

portion size: 1/3 cup

garlic snow peas and almonds

ingredients	12 people	25 people	50 people	75 people
Snow peas	3 pounds	6 pounds	12 pounds	18 pounds
Peanut oil	1/3 cup	2/3 cup	1 1/3 cups	2 cups
Minced garlic	2 tablespoons	1/4 cup	1/2 cup	3/4 cup
Sliced almonds, toasted	3/4 cup	1 1/2 cups	3 cups	4 1/2 cups
Salt and freshly ground black pepper	to taste	to taste	to taste	to taste

(fyi) helpful hint:

Look for bright green pods with no discoloration when choosing the snow peas. Use within two days of purchase. If you do not have a large wok, cook the snow peas in batches in sauté pans.

do it ahead:

• The snow peas can be trimmed the day before the party.

• The almonds can be toasted the day before the party. Store in an airtight container at room temperature.

($) do it for less money:

Use broccoli cut into small florets in lieu of the snow peas and cook until crisp-tender and bright green.

directions:

1. Remove the stem end and strings from the snow peas.

2. Heat the oil in a large wok or sauté pan. Add the garlic and sauté for 1 minute.

3. Add the snow peas to the pan and cook for an additional minute.

4. Mix in the almonds, season with salt and pepper, and serve immediately.

equipment:

• large wok or sauté pan
• wooden spoon

portion size: 4 ounces

chocolate-dipped fortune cookies

ingredients	**12**people	**25**people	**50**people	**75**people
Semisweet chocolate chips or good quality-dark chocolate bars	2 cups (9 ounces)	3¾ cups (18 ounces)	7½ cups (36 ounces)	11¼ cups (54 ounces)
Plain fortune cookies	12	25	50	75

equipment:

• baking sheets

• microwave-safe glass bowl

• parchment or waxed paper

• spatula

directions:

1. Line baking sheets with parchment or waxed paper.

2. Place the chocolate chips in bowl. If using bars, chop finely and place in a bowl.

3. Place the chocolate chips in bowl. Microwave on high for 30 seconds. Stir the chocolate, and continue to microwave in 30-second intervals, stirring until melted and smooth.

4. Dip one half of each fortune cookie in the melted chocolate and allow the excess chocolate to drip back into the bowl. Place the dipped cookies on the prepared pan and allow the chocolate to harden at least 1 hour at room temperature before storing.

5. To store, layer cookies in between waxed paper in an airtight container in a cool, dry place. Do not refrigerate, as the cookies will soften.

helpful hint:

(fyi)

Plain fortune cookies are available in the bakery section of some grocery stores. They can also be bought from your local Chinese restaurant. Prepare these the day of the party for best results; the cookies tend to go stale quickly once removed from their plastic wrappers.

portion size: 1 cookie

Tabbouleh Salad

Moroccan Lamb Tangine
with Honey and Lemon

Mint Yogurt Sauce

Curried Rice

Marrakech Chicken

Toasted Almond and Feta Zucchini

Pita Bread

Chocolate Baklava

Mint Tea

arabian nights

An exotic dining experience for a couples' supper club, small engagement party, or 40-year-old's birthday party that offers an escape from the usual.

arabian nights menu:

tabbouleh salad
moroccan lamb tagine with honey and lemon
mint yogurt sauce
curried rice
marrakech chicken
toasted almond and feta zucchini
pita bread *
chocolate baklava
iced mint tea

* Allow one pita per person.

decorating ideas:

colors. Jewel tones of royalty like purples, reds, magentas, blues, greens, and golds.

invitations. Transfer gold or copper leaf onto the back of postcards and the interior flap of matching envelopes. Or use parchment paper tied with a gold rope and tassel. Write the invitations with black, flamboyant calligraphy. For a more hip but less elegant look, typeset the invitation on a photo of sand dunes, a belly dancer's bare stomach, or a camel scene like we show on the left.

table linens. Layer rich colors of raw silks and satins. Eat on the floor with pillows and large pieces of silk spread underneath. Wrap jewel-colored ribbons around the napkins and tuck in a blown-glass swizzle stick. Try using fingerbowls of citrus or rose-scented water instead of flatware, if only for one course. Hang sheer fabrics from the ceiling around the eating area for an exotic feel.

decorations. Escape to the Kasbah by filling a tagine with exotic fruits and nuts in their shells. Arrange vases with long sprigs of fresh mint. Fill bowls with rose petals or scatter them on the tablecloth. Embellish the table with tassels, rattan mats or runners, and large urns filled with sprays of purple and red flowers. Burn candles made with high-quality essential oils like lemon, orange, ylang-ylang, and patchouli to complement the flavors of the evening's dishes. Have a magic lamp for guests to rub, but don't promise a genie.

place cards and favors. Make a folded gold leaf card with a tassel to match the invitations. Buy tiny satin pillows, place them on each plate, and top with each guest's name card. Or, if you make a photography-based invitation, use a graphic element or a portion of the image to create matching place cards. Fill miniature decorative bottles with massage oils, again using only products with high-quality essential oils. Prop the place cards against the bottles. Fill colored sheer bags with candied almonds. Attach a place card to the bag with ribbon for both name cards and favors.

entertainment. Hire a belly dancer or rent a "How to Belly Dance" instructional video. Play Moroccan music in the background.

menu countdown

1 week before:
- Shop for non-perishables.
- Buy beverages.
- Prepare chocolate baklava and store in airtight container.

3 days before:
- Make space in refrigerator and freezer.

2 days before:
- Shop for perishables.
- Prepare tea and chill.

1 day before:
- Set up tables and décor.
- Zest and juice lemons for lamb and tabbouleh salad.
- Cook lamb tagine.
- Prepare mint yogurt sauce.
- Cook Marrakech chicken.
- Chop zucchini.
- Caramelize onions for zucchini.
- Toast almonds.

morning of the party:
- Buy ice.

1 to 2 hours ahead:
- Make tabbouleh salad.
- Reheat lamb tagine.
- Make curried rice.
- Reheat Marrakech chicken.

just before serving:
- Toast almonds and sauté zucchini.

arabian nights shopping list: 1 to 2 weeks before

ingredients	12 people	25 people	50 people	75 people
✔ pantry items and dry goods				
All-purpose flour	1 ounce	2 ounces	4 ounces	6 ounces
Beef stock	1 quart (32 ounces)	2 quarts (64 ounces)	4 quarts (128 ounces)	6 quarts (192 ounces)
Bulgur wheat	2 pounds	4 pounds	8 pounds	12 pounds
Chicken stock	3 quarts (96 ounces)	6 quarts (192 ounces)	12 quarts (384 ounces)	18 quarts (576 ounces)
Extra-virgin olive oil	3 ounces	6 ounces	12 ounces	18 ounces
Granulated sugar	10 ounces	1¼ pounds	2½ pounds	3¾ pounds
Honey	14 ounces	25 ounces	50 ounces	74 ounces
Lemon juice	6 ounces	12 ounces	24 ounces	36 ounces
Light brown sugar	2 tablespoons	¼ cup	½ cup	¾ cup
Light corn syrup	1 ounce	2 ounces	3 ounces	5 ounces
Long-grain white rice	1¼ pounds	2½ pounds	5 pounds	7½ pounds
Mini semisweet chocolate chips	2 ounces	3 ounces	6 ounces	9 ounces
Olive oil	10 ounces	20 ounces	40 ounces	80 ounces
Sliced black olives	20 ounces	2½ pounds	5½ pounds	8½ pounds
Slivered almonds	4 ounces	8 ounces	1 pound	1½ pounds
Walnuts, chopped	½ pound	1 pound	2 pounds	3 pounds
dried herbs, spices, & extracts				
Black peppercorns	as needed	as needed	as needed	as needed
Curry powder	½ ounce	1 ounce	2 ounces	3 ounces
Ground allspice	¼ ounce	¼ ounce	¼ ounce	¼ ounce
Ground cardamom	¼ ounce	¼ ounce	¼ ounce	¼ ounce
Ground cinnamon	¾ ounce	1½ ounces	3 ounces	4½ ounces
Ground cumin	¾ ounce	1¼ ounces	2½ ounces	3¾ ounces
Ground ginger	¼ ounce	1/2 ounce	1 ounce	1½ ounces
Ground turmeric	½ ounce	1 ounce	2 ounces	3 ounces
Salt	as needed	as needed	as needed	as needed
frozen foods				
Frozen phyllo dough	½ pound	1 pound	2 pounds	3 pounds
miscellaneous				
Green tea bags	10	20	40	60

arabian nights shopping list: 1 to 2 days before

ingredients	**12** people	**25** people	**50** people	**75** people
baked goods				
Pita bread	12 rounds	25 rounds	50 rounds	75 rounds
produce				
English cucumber	1	2	4	6
Fresh cilantro	2 bunches (about 6 ounces)	4 bunches (about 12 ounces)	8 bunches (about 24 ounces)	12 bunches (about 36 ounces)
Fresh ginger	4½ ounces	9 ounces	18 ounces	1¾ pounds
Fresh mint	6 bunches (about 12 ounces)	12 bunches (about 24 ounces)	24 bunches (about 48 ounces)	36 bunches (72 ounces)
Fresh parsley	4 bunches (about 12 ounces)	8 bunches (about 1½ pounds)	16 bunches (about 3 pounds)	24 bunches (about 4½ pounds)
Garlic	2 heads	4 heads	8 heads	12 heads
Green onions	3 bunches	6 bunches	12 bunches	18 bunches
Lemons	8	16	32	48
Onions	7 pounds	14 pounds	28 pounds	42 pounds
Roma tomatoes	1½ pounds	3 pounds	6 pounds	9 pounds
Zucchini	3 pounds	6 pounds	12 pounds	18 pounds
dairy, cheese, & deli				
Feta cheese	12 ounces	24 ounces	48 ounces	72 ounces
Plain yogurt	16 ounces	32 ounces	64 ounces	96 ounces
Sour cream	2 ounces	3 ounces	6 ounces	8 ounces
Unsalted butter	11 ounces	1½ pounds	2¾ pounds	4 pounds
meat & seafood				
Boneless, skinless chicken breasts	12 (6 to 8-ounce) breasts	25 (6 to 8-ounce) breasts	50 (6 to 8-ounce) breasts	75 (6 to 8-ounce) breasts
Lamb stewing meat	6 pounds	12 pounds	24 pounds	36 pounds

Always take a calculator when shopping for quantity recipes to quickly and easily calculate the most appropriate package sizes for your particular needs. We have listed most items in ounces so that you are not limited to size-specific packaging if shopping in bulk. When in doubt over what amount to buy, always round up—it's far better to have a little extra of an ingredient than to run out while cooking. If your eighth-grade algebra skills have gotten rusty, remember that there are 16 ounces in a pound and 8 fluid ounces in a cup. See page 73 for additional conversions.

tabbouleh salad

arabian nights

ingredients	12 people	25 people	50 people	75 people
Chicken stock	4 cups (32 ounces)	8 cups (64 ounces)	16 cups (128 ounces)	18 cups (192 ounces)
Bulgur wheat	4 cups	8 cups	16 cups	24 cups
Hot water	as needed	as needed	as needed	as needed
Fresh parsley, chopped	2 bunches (6 ounces)	4 bunches (12 ounces)	8 bunches (24 ounces)	12 bunches (36 ounces)
Chopped fresh mint leaves	1 cup, packed	2 cups, packed	4 cups, packed	6 cups, packed
Roma tomatoes, diced	1½ pounds	3 pounds	6 pounds	9 pounds
Green onions, finely chopped	8	16	32	48
Lemons, zested and juiced	3	6	12	18
Extra-virgin olive oil	6 tablespoons (3 ounces)	¾ cup (6 ounces)	1½ cups (12 ounces)	2¼ cups (20 ounces)
Ground cumin	2 teaspoons	1 tablespoon plus 1 teaspoon	2 tablespoons plus 2 teaspoons	¼ cup plus 1 tablespoon
Salt and freshly ground black pepper	to taste	to taste	to taste	to taste

(fyi) helpful hints:

• Bulgur wheat is sometimes labeled as cracked wheat or tabbouleh in grocery stores. This recipe works just as well with couscous.

• Use vegetable stock in place of the chicken stock for a vegetarian dish.

do it ahead:

The lemons can be zested and juiced a day in advance.

do it for less time:

• You can use canned diced tomatoes, thoroughly drained.

• Omit the zest and use bottled lemon juice if you like. The lemon flavor will be less intense, so adjust the amount of juice to your liking for a stronger punch.

directions:

1. Pour the chicken stock in a stockpot and bring just to a simmer.

2. Stir in the bulgur wheat, and add enough hot water to cover the bulgur. Let the mixture stand for 15 to 20 minutes until the bulgur has softened.

3. Drain well, gently pressing on the bulgur to extract the excess water. Place the drained bulgur in a large mixing bowl.

4 Add the parsley, mint, tomatoes, green onions, lemon juice, lemon zest, olive oil, and ground cumin, stirring to combine. Season with salt and pepper to taste.

5. Cover and refrigerate for up to 3 hours. Allow the salad to come to room temperature before serving.

equipment:

• large mixing bowl
• large sieve or colander
• stockpot
• wooden spoon
• zester or microplane grater

portion size: ¾ to 1 cup

moroccan lamb tagine with honey and lemon

ingredients	12 people	25 people	50 people	75 people
Salt	1 tablespoon	2 tablespoons	1/4 cup	1/3 cup
Freshly ground black pepper	1 1/2 teaspoons	1 tablespoon	2 tablespoons	3 tablespoons
Ground cinnamon	2 teaspoons	1 tablespoon plus 1 teaspoon	2 tablespoons plus 2 teaspoons	1/4 cup
Ground allspice	3/4 teaspoon	1 1/2 teaspoons	1 tablespoon	1 tablespoon plus 2 teaspoons
Ground turmeric	3/4 teaspoon	1 1/2 teaspoons	1 tablespoon	1 tablespoon plus 2 teaspoons
Lamb stewing meat, cut into 3/4-inch pieces	6 pounds	12 pounds	24 pounds	36 pounds
Olive oil	1/2 cup	1 cup	2 cups	3 cups
Chopped onions	6 cups (about 5 large onions)	12 cups (about 10 large onions)	24 cups (about 20 large onions)	36 cups (about 30 large onions)
Minced garlic	1/4 cup	1/2 cup	1 cup	1 1/2 cups
Chopped fresh ginger	1/3 cup	2/3 cup	1 1/3 cups	2 cups
Beef or chicken stock	4 cups (32 ounces)	8 cups (64 ounces)	16 cups (128 ounces)	24 cups (192 ounces)
Lemons, zested and juiced	5	10	20	30
Honey	1/3 cup	2/3 cup	1 1/3 cups	2 cups
Chopped fresh parsley	3/4 cup	1 1/2 cups	3 cups	4 1/2 cups

equipment:

- ladle
- large sauté pans
- large stockpots with lids
- resealable plastic storage bags
- tongs
- wooden spoon
- zester or microplane grater

directions:

1. Combine the salt, pepper, cinnamon, allspice, and turmeric in a small bowl. Spread the cubed lamb on a large baking sheet and season with the spices, tossing to coat evenly.

2. Heat enough oil to cover the bottom of a large sauté pan. Add the seasoned lamb in batches and brown on all sides, about 5 minutes, and then transfer to a stockpot.

3. Sauté the onion in batches in the same sauté pan for 7 minutes, or until translucent, and then add to the stockpot.

4. Sauté the garlic and ginger for 2 minutes, or until fragrant, and then add to the stockpot.

5. Pour several ladles of the stock into the sauté pan to deglaze. Bring to a boil, scraping up any browned bits from the pan. Pour the stock from the sauté pan and the remaining stock into the stockpot.

6. Set the stockpot over high heat and bring to a boil. Reduce the heat, cover, and let simmer for 1 1/2 to 2 hours, or until the lamb is tender. (The stew can be made up to 2 days ahead at this point. Cover tightly and refrigerate until ready to reheat.)

7. Add the juice and zest from lemons. Uncover and continue to cook for 30 minutes longer, or until the lamb is very tender.

8. Just before serving, stir in the honey and parsley. Season with salt and pepper to taste.

helpful hint:

As a variation, add 2 cups of sliced olives.

do it ahead:

- A tagine is the name for both this Moroccan-style stew and the cone-shaped casserole dish traditionally used for cooking the stew. It tastes even better on day two. Store covered in the refrigerator until ready to reheat.

- The lemons can be zested and juiced a day in advance.

do it for less money:

For a less-expensive alternative, use chicken thighs and legs or stewing beef instead of lamb. Allow 1 thigh and 1 leg per guest, and reduce the cooking time to about 1 1/4 hours. You can also use stewing beef; cook for at least 2 hours.

portion size: 8 to 10 ounces

mint yogurt sauce

ingredients	12 people	25 people	50 people	75 people
Cucumber, peeled and seeded	1	2	4	6
Salt	to taste	to taste	to taste	to taste
Fresh mint leaves	¼ cup, packed	⅓ cup, packed	⅔ cup, packed	1 cup, packed
Ground cardamom	¼ teaspoon	½ teaspoon	1 teaspoon	1½ teaspoons
Plain yogurt	2 cups	4 cups	8 cups	12 cups
Sour cream	¼ cup	⅓ cup	⅔ cup	1 cup
Freshly ground black pepper	to taste	to taste	to taste	to taste

do it ahead:

This sauce acts as a cool foil to the earthy tagine. Prepare it a day in advance to allow the flavors to meld.

do it for less money:

You can use dried mint in place of fresh, but use only one third of the amount specified in the recipe. You can also use cumin or curry powder in place of the more expensive cardamom.

directions:

1. Cut the cucumber into ½-inch pieces.

2. Place the cucumber, salt, yogurt, sour cream, mint leaves, and cardamom in a blender, and blend until smooth.

3. Stir in the yogurt and sour cream. Taste and season with pepper and additional salt as needed.

4. Cover and refrigerate until ready to serve.

equipment:

• blender or food processor

• spatula

portion size: 2 tablespoons (1 ounce)

curried rice

ingredients	12 people	25 people	50 people	75 people
Water	5½ cups	11 cups	1½ gallons	2 gallons plus 1 cup
Long-grain white rice	1¼ pounds (3 cups)	2½ pounds (6 cups)	5 pounds (12 cups)	7½ pounds (18 cups)
Curry powder	1 tablespoon	2 tablespoons	¼ cup	⅓ cup
Ground turmeric	2 teaspoons	1 tablespoon plus 1 teaspoon	2 tablespoons plus 2 teaspoons	¼ cup
Thinly-sliced green onions	1½ cups	3 cups	6 cups	9 cups
Chopped fresh parsley	¾ cup	1½ cups	3 cups	4½ cups
Salt and freshly ground black pepper	to taste	to taste	to taste	to taste

equipment:

- large stockpots with lids
- wooden spoon

directions:

1. Divide the water and rice equally among the stockpots, if using more than one. Bring to a boil over high heat.

2. Stir in the curry powder and turmeric. Reduce the heat to low, cover, and simmer 25 to 35 minutes, or until the rice is tender.

3. Fluff the cooked rice with a fork. Add the green onions and parsley, and season with salt and pepper to taste. Stir to combine and serve hot.

helpful hint: fyi

Turmeric is a spice used to add both flavor and color to food. It is one of the ingredients that gives American-style mustard its bright yellow color.

do it for less money: $

If you cannot find turmeric in your local grocery store, try an ethnic Indian store where spices are often cheaper.

portion size: ½ cup

marrakech chicken

ingredients	12 people	25 people	50 people	75 people
All-purpose flour	¼ cup	½ cup	1 cup	1½ cups
Ground turmeric	1 tablespoon	2 tablespoons	¼ cup	⅓ cup
Ground ginger	1 tablespoon	2 tablespoons	¼ cup	⅓ cup
Curry powder	1 tablespoon	2 tablespoons	¼ cup	⅓ cup
Ground cinnamon	1 tablespoon	2 tablespoons	¼ cup	⅓ cup
Ground cumin	1 tablespoon	2 tablespoons	¼ cup	⅓ cup
Chicken stock	6 cups (48 ounces)	12 cups (96 ounces)	24 cups (192 ounces)	36 cups (288 ounces)
Boneless, skinless chicken breasts	12 (6 to 8-ounce) breasts	25 (6 to 8-ounce) breasts	50 (6 to 8-ounce) breasts	75 (6 to 8-ounce) breasts
Salt and freshly ground black pepper	to taste	to taste	to taste	to taste
Olive or peanut oil	½ cup, plus more as needed	1 cup, plus more as needed	2 cups, plus more as needed	3 cups, plus more as needed
Sliced onions	6 cups (about 3 large onions)	12 cups (about 6 large onions)	24 cups (about 12 large onions)	36 cups (about 24 onions)
Minced garlic	3 tablespoons	⅓ cup	⅔ cup	1 cup
Lemon juice	¾ cup	1½ cups	3 cups	4½ cups
Sliced black olives	2 cups	4 cups	8 cups	12 cups
Honey	½ cup	1 cup	2 cups	3 cups
Chopped fresh cilantro	2 cups	4 cups	8 cups	12 cups

(fyi) helpful hints:

• For a different taste, substitute dried apricots or golden raisins for the olives. Use kalamata olives for extra flavor.

• For a delectable vegetarian version, replace the chicken with 6 ounces of sliced eggplant and 2 ounces of portobello mushrooms per person.

do it ahead:

The chicken can be made through step 9 a day in advance. Reheat in a 350-degree oven until warmed through. Add additional chicken stock or water if the stew seems too thick.

($) do it for less money:

This dish will also work with chicken thighs or legs. Allow one leg and one thigh per guest, and increase the cooking time by 45 minutes to an hour.

directions:

1. Preheat the oven to 250 degrees.

2. Combine the flour, turmeric, ginger, curry powder, cinnamon, and cumin in a mixing bowl. Slowly whisk in the chicken stock until smooth.

3. Season the chicken with salt and pepper.

4. Heat the oil in a large sauté pan over medium heat. Cook the chicken in batches for 3 to 4 minutes per side, or until cooked through.

5. Reserve the juices in the pan, place the chicken on a baking sheet, and move to the oven.

6. Add the onions to the pan juices in the sauté pan and cook until the onions become translucent, about 4 minutes. Add more oil as needed.

7. Add the garlic to pan and sauté for 1 minute. Slowly whisk in the chicken stock mixture. Bring the mixture to a boil, stirring constantly.

9. Add the lemon juice. Lower the heat and simmer, stirring occasionally for 10 minutes, or until the sauce thickens. If using chicken thighs or legs, let the chicken simmer in the sauce for 45 minutes to an hour. Add more stock or water if the sauce gets too thick or starts to dry out. (The dish can be made up to this point a day in advance. Return the chicken to the pan, cover tightly, and store in the refrigerator. Reheat before continuing to the next step, and add additional chicken stock or water if the stew seems too thick.)

10. Just before serving, stir in the olives and honey. Season with salt and pepper to taste. Return the chicken to the pan and simmer until heated through.

11. Garnish with the chopped cilantro and serve immediately.

portion size: 1 (6 to 8-ounce) chicken breast

equipment:

• baking sheets
• large sauté pans
• mixing bowl
• tongs
• whisk

toasted almond and feta zucchini

ingredients	12 people	25 people	50 people	75 people
Zucchini	3 pounds	6 pounds	12 pounds	18 pounds
Unsalted butter	2 sticks (8 ounces)	4 sticks (16 ounces)	8 sticks (32 ounces)	12 sticks (48 ounces)
Olive oil	3 tablespoons	$1/3$ cup	$2/3$ cup	1 cup
Onions, thinly sliced	3 pounds	6 pounds	12 pounds	18 pounds
Feta cheese, crumbled	12 ounces	24 ounces	48 ounces	72 ounces
Slivered almonds, toasted	1 cup (4 ounces)	2 cups (8 ounces)	4 cups (1 pound)	6 cups ($1^1/2$ pounds)
Salt and freshly ground black pepper	to taste	to taste	to taste	to taste

equipment:

- baking sheet
- large sauté pans
- tongs or wooden spoon

directions:

1. Trim the ends from the zucchini, and cut in half lengthwise. Cut each half into $1/2$-inch-thick slices to make a half-moon shape.

2. Heat the butter and olive oil in a large sauté pan over medium heat. Add the onions in batches and cook, stirring frequently for 15 to 18 minutes, or until the onions have reduced and become golden brown. Remove the onions from the pan. (The dish can be prepared a day in advance up to this point. Store the onions in an airtight container in the refrigerator until ready to continue cooking. Reheat the onions before sautéing the zucchini.)

3. Add the zucchini to the pan and sauté for 2 to 3 minutes, or until crisp-tender. Stir in the caramelized onions.

4. Remove from the heat and toss with the feta and almonds. Season with salt and pepper to taste, and serve immediately.

helpful hints:

- To toast the almonds, place in a single layer on a baking sheet. Bake for 10 minutes in a 350-degree oven, or until light golden. Shake pan frequently and watch carefully to prevent burning.

- The recipe calls for both butter and olive oil to help raise the low smoke point of butter. Many Middle-Eastern dishes also rely on ghee, a form of clarified butter, with a higher smoke point. To make ghee, melt butter over low heat and skim the froth from the top. Continue cooking the milk solids until they start to brown and give off a nutty aroma. Pour off the clear butter into a container, leaving behind any milk solids, and store in the refrigerator for up to 6 months or in the freezer for up to a year. Use as needed for high-heat sautéing.

do it ahead:

The onions can be caramelized a day in advance and refrigerated. Reheat before adding the zucchini.

do it for less time:

Don't overload the pans when cooking the onions. The more onions in the sauté pan, the longer it will take for them to caramelize. It is far more time-efficient to divide the onions among several pans or cook them in batches.

portion size: 6 ounces

chocolate baklava

ingredients	12 people	25 people	50 people	75 people
Granulated sugar	¼ cup	¾ cup	1½ cups	2¼ cups
Honey	3 tablespoons	⅓ cup	⅔ cup	1 cup
Water	¼ cup	½ cup	1 cup	1½ cups
Light corn syrup	1 tablespoon plus 1½ teaspoons	3 tablespoons	6 tablespoons	9 tablespoons
Unsalted butter for greasing pans	1 tablespoon (½ ounce)	2 tablespoons (1 ounce)	4 tablespoons (2 ounces)	6 tablespoons (3 ounces)
Frozen phyllo dough, thawed	½ pound (about 10 sheets)	1 pound (about 20 sheets)	2 pounds (about 40 sheets)	3 pounds (about 60 sheets)
Light brown sugar	2 tablespoons	¼ cup	½ cup	¾ cup
Walnuts, finely chopped	½ pound	1 pound	2 pounds	3 pounds
Ground cinnamon	½ teaspoon	1 teaspoon	2 teaspoons	1 tablespoon
Mini semisweet chocolate chips	¼ cup	½ cup	1 cup	1½ cups
Unsalted butter, melted	4 tablespoons (2 ounces)	1 stick (4 ounces)	2 sticks (8 ounces)	3 sticks (12 ounces)

(fyi) helpful hints:

• Baklava is a delicious Mediterranean dessert combining layers of pastry, nuts, and honey. We've added chocolate for an extra element of decadence.

• Phyllo dough is sometimes labeled as "filo" dough. A 1-pound box contains about twenty 13 x 9-inch sheets. Defrost it in the refrigerator for best results.

• As an alternative to brushing butter on each sheet of phyllo, fill an oil-misting bottle with walnut oil and spray each sheet.

• To keep the phyllo dough from curling during baking, sprinkle or spray the pastry with cold water before placing in the oven.

do it ahead:

The baklava can be made up to a week in advance if covered and stored at room temperature.

do it for less time:

• You can use 1 cup of warm honey for each 13 x 9 x 2-inch pan in lieu of the sugar syrup.

• If you're intimidated by phyllo dough, buy the baklava from a Greek restaurant and drizzle with warm chocolate sauce.

directions:

1. Combine the sugar, honey, water, and light corn syrup in a medium saucepan over low heat. Stir until the sugar has dissolved, and then increase the heat to medium.

2. Without stirring, heat the mixture until it reaches a temperature of 225 degrees on an instant-read thermometer, or until it becomes syrupy, about 6 to 10 minutes.

3. Remove from the heat and allow to cool.

4. Preheat the oven to 350 degrees. Grease a 13 x 9 x 2-inch baking pan. Unroll the thawed phyllo dough and cover with a damp towel to keep it from drying out while assembling the baklava.

5. Combine the brown sugar, walnuts, cinnamon, and mini chocolate chips in a bowl.

6. Lay a sheet of phyllo in the prepared pan. Brush with the melted butter. Top with another sheet of phyllo. Brush with more butter. Continue this process until one third of the phyllo sheets have been used, about 3 to 4 sheets per pan.

7. Spread half of the nut mixture equally over the pastry. Top with one-third more buttered sheets of the phyllo, about 3 to 4 sheets per pan.

8. Spread with the remaining nut mixture. Place the remaining buttered sheets of the phyllo on top, and trim any overhanging pastry.

9. Using a sharp knife, score the top layer of the pastry in to 30 equal-sized squares.

10. Bake for 20 minutes. Reduce the heat to 300 degrees, and bake for an additional 15 to 20 minutes, or until golden brown.

11. Remove the baklava from the oven. While it is still hot, cut through all the layers of the pastry and filling using the scored lines as a guide. Cut each square on the diagonal for a triangular presentation.

12. Drizzle the cooled sugar syrup over the hot baklava.

13. Cover tightly and store at room temperature to allow the baklava to absorb the syrup for at least 6 hours, or preferably overnight.

portion size: 1 to 2 pieces

equipment:

• 13 x 9 x 2-inch baking pans
• candy thermometer
• medium saucepan
• mixing bowl
• pastry brush
• wooden spoon

iced mint tea

ingredients	12 people	25 people	50 people	75 people
Water	8 cups	16 cups (1 gallon)	32 cups (2 gallons)	48 cups (3 gallons)
Chopped fresh mint	3 cups	6 cups	9 cups	12 cups
Green tea bags	10	20	40	60
Granulated sugar	³/₄ cup	1¹/₂ cups	3 cups	4¹/₂ cups
Fresh mint sprigs	12	25	50	75

equipment:

• large sieve
• large stockpots
• pitchers

directions:

1. Divide the water equally among stockpots. Bring to a boil.

2. Turn off the heat. Add the chopped mint, green tea bags, and sugar, stirring until the sugar has dissolved.

3. Let steep 20 minutes, and then remove the tea bags and strain the mixture. Taste for sweetness, and add more sugar if needed.

4. Cool to room temperature and refrigerate. Serve in chilled glasses with sprigs of fresh mint.

helpful hint:

Serve this refreshing after-dinner drink in decorative jewel-colored glasses as the Moroccans do.

do it ahead:

The tea can be made up to two days in advance and refrigerated.

do it for less time:

Save yourself the trouble of straining the tea by wrapping the loose mint in cheesecoth and tying with some kitchen twine.

do it for less money:

If the fresh mint is not available, use half green tea bags and half mint or peppermint tea bags.

portion size: 5 ounces

Roasted Potato Salad
with Dijon Mustard and Chives

Kentucky Sweet-Talkin'
Barbecued Chicken

Five-Alarm Chili

Coleslaw with a Kick

Buckaroo Beans

Fresh Corn on the Cob with Sage Butter

Double-Fudge Brownies
with Creamy Fudge Frosting

Ice-Cold Lemonade

down-home barbecue

A backyard bonanza to kick off summertime, celebrate Father's Day, or tame a posse of hungry kids.

down-home barbecue menu:

roasted potato salad with dijon mustard and chives
kentucky sweet-talkin' barbecued chicken
five-alarm chili
coleslaw with a kick
buckaroo beans
fresh corn on the cob with sage butter
double-fudge brownies with creamy fudge frosting
ice-cold lemonade*

* Make the lemonade from concentrate or a mix. For a bright, fresh-squeezed presentation, serve in clear pitchers with slices of lemon and sprigs of fresh mint. For a colorful array of choices, mix the lemon juice with a variety of other juices. Make orange lemonade with orange juice and orange slices, grape lemonade with grape juice and small bunches of grapes, or pink lemonade with a strawberry juice drink or red food coloring.

decorating ideas:

colors. Natural homey colors like blueberry blue, apple red, burlap brown, and sunflower yellow.

invitations. Handwrite rustic invitations on brown butcher paper or make postcards cut from cardboard boxes. For a prettier look, glue the invitations onto gingham or calico fabric and trim with pinking shears.

table linens. Go for ginghams in classic red and white checks and top with denim remnants for placemats. Use striped kitchen towels as bibs and hold in place with twine and clothes pins. Roll up cheap bandanas from the dollar store and tie with twine for a rustic napkin. (Wash and dry them first so they'll be able to soak up all that barbecue sauce!) Choose calico prints and flowered cottons for napkins and tablecloths for a more country feel. For a splash of bright color with a '50s bent, use oil cloth (a laminated fabric that wipes clean in a jiffy) to cover the tables.

decorations. Fill a cast-iron skillet with sunflower blossoms or bottles of extra barbecue sauce and other condiments. Use galvanized buckets to hold rolled napkins, flatware, and bunches of daisies or sunflowers. Even the clear pitchers of icy lemonade garnished with lemon rounds and fresh mint can act as practical centerpieces. Use bundles of hay for extra seating and up-turned cowboy hats lined with colorful napkins or dishtowels to serve corn chips. Look for tin ware from the local junk store. Dig out your old Radio Flyer wagon and arrange condiments in it next to the serving area. Use a wheel barrow to ice down drinks. Hang iron stars of Texas or rustic kitchen utensils from the trees above the table.

entertainment. Organize an afternoon of old-time games like a potato sack race or an egg toss. (Use partially filled water balloons for easier clean-up.) Play country music with fiddles or ask friends to bring their guitars and lead a sing-along. Dress like Dolly Parton or Hank Williams.

menu countdown

1 week before:
- Shop for non-perishables.
- Buy beverages.
- Bake and freeze unfrosted brownies. Prepare frosting and refrigerate.
- Make barbecue sauce.

3 days before:
- Make space in refrigerator and freezer.

2 days before:
- Shop for perishables.
- Make sage butter.

1 day before:
- Set up tables and décor.
- Bake potatoes for potato salad.
- Prep corn, but do not cook.
- Parboil chicken breasts.
- Make chili.
- Shred cabbages and carrots, chop jalapeños, and juice lemon for the coleslaw.
- Make beans.
- Make lemonade and chill.

morning of the party:
- Buy ice.
- Defrost brownies and bring frosting to room temperature.
- Prepare potato salad.

1 to 2 hours ahead:
- Reheat chili.
- Reheat beans.
- Frost brownies.
- Toss coleslaw.

just before serving:
- Grill corn on the cob.
- Grill chicken.

down-home barbeque shopping list: **1 to 2 weeks before**

ingredients	**12** people	**25** people	**50** people	**75** people
✓ alcohol				
Dark beer	8 ounces	16 ounces	32 ounces	48 ounces
Kentucky bourbon	8 ounces	16 ounces	32 ounces	48 ounces
Light beer	10 ounces	20 ounces	40 ounces	60 ounces
pantry items & dry goods				
All-purpose flour	6 ounces	12 ounces	24 ounces	36 ounces
Baking powder	¼ teaspoon	½ teaspoon	1 teaspoon	1½ teaspoons
Barbecue sauce	14 ounces	28 ounces	56 ounces	84 ounces
Beef stock	20 ounces	1¼ quarts (40 ounces)	2½ quarts (80 ounces)	3¾ quarts (120 ounces)
Canned great Northern or white beans	60 ounces	120 ounces	240 ounces	360 ounces
Canned red kidney beans	60 ounces	120 ounces	240 ounces	360 ounces
Canola or vegetable oil	2½ ounces	6 ounces	12 ounces	18 ounces
Cider vinegar	4 ounces	8 ounces	16 ounces	24 ounces
Corn syrup	¾ ounce	1½ ounces	3 ounces	4½ ounces
Dark brown sugar	12 ounces	24 ounces	46 ounces	70 ounces
Dark molasses	6 ounces	12 ounces	24 ounces	32 ounces
Diced tomatoes	52 ounces	104 ounces	208 ounces	312 ounces
Dijon mustard	4 ounces	8 ounces	16 ounces	24 ounces
Extra-virgin olive oil	4 ounces	8 ounces	16 ounces	24 ounces
Granulated sugar	8 ounces	1 pound	2 pounds	3 pounds
Lemon juice	1 ounce (or 1 lemon)	2 ounces (or 2 lemons)	4 ounces (or 4 lemons)	6 ounces (or 6 lemons)
Mayonnaise	26 ounces	52 ounces	104 ounces	156 ounces
Mini chocolate chips	6 ounces	12 ounces	24 ounces	36 ounces
Olive oil	2 ounces	3 ounces	6 ounces	8 ounces
Powdered sugar	8 ounces	1 pound	2 pounds	3 pounds
Tabasco sauce	to taste	to taste	to taste	to taste
Tomato paste	6 ounces	12 ounces	24 ounces	36 ounces
Tomato sauce	24 ounces	48 ounces	96 ounces	144 ounces
Unsweetened cocoa powder	3 ounces	6 ounces	12 ounces	18 ounces
Vegetable cooking spray	1 can	1 can	1 can	1 can
Worcestershire sauce	5 ounces	10 ounces	20 ounces	30 ounces
dried herbs, spices, & extracts				
Black peppercorns	as needed	as needed	as needed	as needed
Cayenne pepper	½ ounce	¾ ounce	1½ ounces	2¼ ounces
Chile powder	2 ounces	4 ounces	8 ounces	12 ounces
Dry mustard	½ ounce	1 ounce	2 ounces	3 ounces
Ground cumin	½ ounce	1 ounce	2 ounces	3 ounces
Salt	as needed	as needed	as needed	as needed
Vanilla extract	¼ ounce	½ ounce	1 ounce	2 ounces

down-home barbeque shopping list: **1 to 2 days before**

✓ ingredients	12 people	25 people	50 people	75 people
produce				
Carrots	8 ounces	1 pound	2 pounds	3 pounds
Corn on cob	12 ears	25 ears	50 ears	75 ears
Fresh chives	1 ounce	1 ounce	1 ounce	1½ ounces
Fresh sage	1 ounce	2 ounces	4 ounces	6 ounces
Garlic	2 heads	3 heads	5 heads	7 heads
Green bell pepper	12 ounces	1½ pounds	3 pounds	4½ pounds
Green cabbage	1 pound	2 pounds	4 pounds	6 pounds
Jalapeño peppers	3	5	10	15
Red cabbage	1 pound	2 pounds	4 pounds	6 pounds
Small red or new potatoes	2½ pounds	5 pounds	10 pounds	15 pounds
Yellow onions	2¾ pounds	5½ pounds	11 pounds	17 pounds
dairy, cheese, & deli				
Heavy whipping cream	2 ounces	4 ounces	8 ounces	12 ounces
Large eggs	4	8	16	24
Unsalted butter	1 pound	2 pounds	4 pounds	5½ pounds
meat & seafood				
Bacon	4 ounces	8 ounces	1 pound	1½ pounds
Bone-in, skin-on chicken breasts	12 (8-ounce) breasts (6 pounds)	25 (8-ounce) breasts (12½ pounds)	50 (8-ounce) breasts (25 pounds)	75 (8-ounce) breasts (37½ pounds)
Chicken legs	12 (3-ounce) legs (2¼ pounds)	25 (3-ounce) legs (4½ pounds)	50 (3-ounce) legs (9½ pounds)	75 (3-ounce) legs (14 pounds)
Ground beef	2½ pounds	5 pounds	10 pounds	15 pounds

Always take a calculator when shopping for quantity recipes to quickly and easily calculate the most appropriate package sizes for your particular needs. We have listed most items in ounces so that you are not limited to size-specific packaging if shopping in bulk. When in doubt over what amount to buy, always round up—it's far better to have a little extra of an ingredient than to run out while cooking. If your eighth-grade algebra skills have gotten rusty, remember that there are 16 ounces in a pound and 8 fluid ounces in a cup. See page 73 for additional conversions.

dining in the great outdoors

- **Shade.** Set up the food buffet in a shaded area. If the party site doesn't have any shade, invest in or rent large umbrellas or an easy-to-assemble canopy (sometimes called an "EZ Up").

- **Timing.** To keep the food looking and tasting fresh, place on the buffet just before guests are ready to eat. Do not let the food sit out on the buffet for more than an hour, even less time if the weather is very hot. If guests will be arriving at different times, put out smaller platters of food that can be easily replaced every hour.

- **Protection.** Keep the food covered with mesh domes to keep out any visiting insects.

- **Trash management.** If you are using disposable plates, cups, and flatware, make sure to have trash cans available. Line with plastic liners and empty often to prevent overfilling and keep bugs at bay.

- **Terminator.** Spray the buffet area and seating areas with bug spray the morning of the event. Do not be tempted to spray the buffet during the party. Burn citronella candles a half hour before the party starts to help keep unwanted guests away. If you have yellow jacket traps, set them up away from the buffet area, preferably at the perimeter of the party site.

- **Helpful extras.** On each table, set up care-baskets filled with disposable moist towelettes, extra napkins, sunscreen, and insect repellent.

- **Grilling reminders.** Always have a fire extinguisher on hand. Familiarize yourself with how it works before the party. Keep it close (but not too close) to the heat source. Check the use-by date and replace it if necessary. Never spray hot coals with lighter fluid to try relighting them. This causes the gases to ignite and can result in serious injuries. Let the coals smolder until they are covered in gray ash. This is the best indication that they are ready to use. For best results, use a chimney starter for your charcoal and avoid lighter fluid altogether. To build a portable barbecue, add charcoal and a grate to a clean metal wheelbarrow.

roasted red potato salad with dijon mustard and chives

ingredients	12 people	25 people	50 people	75 people
Small red or new potatoes	2½ pounds	5 pounds	10 pounds	15 pounds
Extra-virgin olive oil	½ cup	1 cup	2 cups	3 cups
Salt and freshly ground black pepper	to taste	to taste	to taste	to taste
Chopped fresh chives	½ cup	1 cup	2 cups	3 cups
Mayonnaise	¾ cup	1½ cups	3 cups	4½ cups
Dijon mustard	¼ cup	½ cup	1 cup	1½ cups

equipment:

• baking sheets
• large mixing bowls
• spatula
• vegetable brush
• wooden spoon or disposable gloves

directions:

1. Preheat the oven to 400 degrees.

2. Scrub and dry the potatoes. Cut each potato into quarters, and place in a large mixing bowl. Add the oil, and toss to coat evenly.

3. Place the potatoes in a single layer on baking sheets. Season generously with salt and pepper, and bake for 30 minutes.

4. Using a spatula, turn the potatoes over. Bake for an additional 30 minutes, or until the potatoes are cooked through, golden brown, and slightly crunchy.

5. Remove from the oven and let cool completely. (The dish can be made up to a day in advance to this point. Store the potatoes in an airtight container and refrigerate until ready to complete.)

6. Combine the chives, mayonnaise, and Dijon mustard in large mixing bowl. Add to the cooled potatoes, and toss until coated using a wooden spoon or your hands (wearing disposable plastic gloves). Season with additional salt and pepper to taste. Serve immediately, or refrigerate and serve within 3 hours.

helpful hint: (fyi)

You can divide the ingredients evenly among mixing bowls and toss in batches for manageability.

do it ahead:

The potatoes can be baked a day in advance. Cool and refrigerate until ready to combine with the remaining ingredients.

do it for less time:

Save time by buying pre-roasted potatoes from the hot food counter of your local grocery or deli. For an even faster alternative, just add Dijon mustard and chopped chives to a store-bought potato salad.

portion size: 3 ounces

kentucky sweet-talkin' barbecued chicken

ingredients	12 people	25 people	50 people	75 people
Olive oil	2 tablespoons plus 1½ teaspoons	⅓ cup	⅔ cup	1 cup
Finely chopped yellow onions	2 cups	4 cups	8 cups	12 cups
Minced garlic	¼ cup	½ cup	1 cup	1½ cups
Salt and freshly ground black pepper	to taste	to taste	to taste	to taste
Dry mustard	2 tablespoons	¼ cup	½ cup	¾ cup
Chile powder	2 tablespoons	¼ cup	½ cup	¾ cup
Cayenne pepper	2 teaspoons	4 teaspoons	3 tablespoons plus 2 teaspoons	¼ cup
Tomato sauce	3 cups	6 cups	12 cups	18 cups
Cider vinegar	½ cup	1 cup	2 cups	3 cups
Worcestershire sauce	½ cup	1 cup	2 cups	3 cups
Dark beer	1 cup	2 cups	4 cups	6 cups
Kentucky bourbon	1 cup	2 cups	4 cups	6 cups
Ground cumin	2 teaspoons	1 tablespoon plus 1 teaspoon	3 tablespoons plus 2 teaspoons	¼ cup
Dark brown sugar	½ cup	1 cup	2 cups	3 cups
Dark molasses	2 tablespoons	¼ cup	½ cup	¾ cup
Tabasco sauce	to taste	to taste	to taste	to taste
Chicken legs	12 (3-ounce) legs	25 (3-ounce) legs	50 (3-ounce) legs	75 (3-ounce) legs
Bone-in, skin-on chicken breasts	12 (8-ounce) breasts	25 (8-ounce) breasts	50 (8-ounce) breasts	75 (8-ounce) breasts

(fyi) helpful hints:

• Take the guesswork out of cooking chicken by investing in an instant-read thermometer. Available at grocery and cookware stores, it is the most accurate way to determine if meat and poultry are properly cooked.

• For safety, boil any sauce that has come into contact with the uncooked meat before serving.

• You can also prepare this recipe in the oven. Cover a baking pan with foil, and place the legs in a single layer in one pan and the breasts in a single layer in another pan. Brush the legs and breasts liberally with the barbecue sauce on both sides. Cover with additional foil.

directions:

1. Heat the olive oil in large, heavy-bottomed saucepan over medium heat.

2. Add the onions and garlic, season with several pinches of salt and pepper, and stir to combine. Cover and let the onions sweat for about 10 minutes, stirring occassionally. Turn down the heat if the onions or garlic seem to be browning too fast.

3. Add the dry mustard, chile powder, and cayenne, stirring well to coat the onions.

4. Add the tomato sauce, cider vinegar, Worcestershire sauce, beer, bourbon, cumin, brown sugar, and molasses. Stir well to combine.

5. Bring to a boil, reduce the heat, and simmer for 35 to 40 minutes, or until the sauce has thickened, but can still be poured. (If the sauce thickens too much, add several drops of water until it reaches the desired consistency.)

6. Season with salt, pepper, and Tabasco to taste. (The sauce can be made up to a month in advance. Refrigerate until ready to use.)

portion size: 1 (8-ounce) chicken breast and 1 (3-ounce) chicken leg

equipment:

- brush
- instant-read thermometer
- large saucepan
- tongs
- wooden spoon

directions: (continued)

7. While the sauce is simmering, preheat the grill.

8. Place the chicken legs over direct medium heat, and grill for 7 to 8 minutes per side.

9. Add the chicken breasts to the grill with the legs. Grill for 10 minutes per side.

10. Baste the legs and breasts liberally with the barbecue sauce, and turn. Grill another 1 to 2 minutes, or until the meat is cooked through and an instant-read thermometer registers 175 degrees.

11. Baste again with the barbecue sauce. Serve any extra sauce that has not come in contact with the raw chicken in squeeze bottles on the side.

Refrigerate the breasts, and bake the legs for 35 minutes in a 350-degree oven. Add the breasts to the oven and continue baking both pans for 25 to 30 minutes, or until the meat is just cooked through and an instant-read thermometer registers 175 degrees. Brush the chicken with additional sauce before serving.

do it ahead:

• To cut down the cooking time on the grill, parboil the chicken pieces in simmering water for 10 to 12 minutes. Drain and cool. (This can be done a day in advance; wrap the chicken well and refrigerate until ready to grill.) Baste liberally with the barbecue sauce, and grill as normal until cooked through.

• The sauce can be made up to a month in advance. Cover well and store in the refrigerator until ready to use.

do it for less time:

• Buy a store-bought barbecue sauce instead of making your own. For extra punch, dress up the sauce by adding ingredients such as hot sauce, Dijon mustard, onions, honey, teriyaki sauce, pineapple juice, or orange juice.

• As an alternative to grilling, buy rotisserie chicken, cut into eight pieces, and smother with sauce before heating. Or, buy chicken already cooked and sauced in the deli section of the grocery store. Add your own seasoning ideas with extra barbecue sauce and reheat in the oven.

down-home barbecue

five-alarm chili

ingredients	12 people	25 people	50 people	75 people
Canola or vegetable oil	1/3 cup	3/4 cup	1 1/2 cups	2 1/4 cups
Yellow onions, chopped	1 1/2 pounds	3 pounds	6 pounds	9 pounds
Green bell pepper, chopped	12 ounces	1 1/2 pounds	3 pounds	4 1/2 pounds
Minced garlic	1 tablespoon plus 1 1/2 teaspoons	3 tablespoons	1/4 cup plus 2 tablespoons	1/2 cup plus 1 tablespoon
Ground beef	2 1/2 pounds	5 pounds	10 pounds	15 pounds
Canned diced tomatoes, undrained	52 ounces (6 1/2 cups)	104 ounces (13 cups)	208 ounces (25 cups)	312 ounces (40 cups)
Tomato paste	3/4 cup	1 1/2 cups	3 cups	4 1/2 cups
Beef stock	2 1/2 cups	5 cups	10 cups	15 cups
Chile powder	1/3 cup	3/4 cup	1 1/2 cups	2 1/4 cups
Ground cumin	1 tablespoon	2 tablespoons	1/4 cup	1/3 cup
Cayenne pepper	1 1/2 teaspoons	1 tablespoon	2 tablespoons	3 tablespoons
Canned red kidney beans, drained	60 ounces	120 ounces	240 ounces	360 ounces
Salt and freshly ground black pepper	to taste	to taste	to taste	to taste

(fyi) helpful hints:

• Divide the ingredients in half and cook in two stockpots for manageability.

• Customize the flavor by adding your favorite "secret" ingredient such as coffee, beer, or cocoa powder. Add more cayenne pepper if desired, but remember that not all guests will like very spicy chili—especially children.

• Serve with a condiment bar of chopped onions, Tabasco sauce, grated cheddar cheese, sour cream, and corn chips.

do it ahead:

Chili tastes even better on the second day. Make it a day in advance and reheat slowly, stirring occasionally, until it reaches a temperature of 165 degrees on an instant-read thermometer.

directions:

1. Pour the oil in the stockpot and set over medium heat.

2. Sauté the onions in the oil for 5 minutes, or until translucent.

3. Add the green bell peppers and garlic. Sauté for 2 minutes, stirring constantly.

4. Add the ground beef and cook until browned. Drain the grease from the meat with a sieve and return the meat to the pan.

5. Add the diced tomatoes, tomato paste, beef stock, chile powder, cumin, and cayenne pepper.

6. Bring to a boil, stirring frequently. Cover, reduce the heat, and simmer for 45 minutes, stirring occasionally.

7. Add the beans and cook for 15 minutes longer. Season with salt and pepper to taste.

equipment:

• ladle
• large sieve or colander
• large stockpots with lids
• wooden spoon

portion size: 8 ounces (about 1 cup)

coleslaw with a kick

ingredients	**12** people	**25** people	**50** people	**75** people
Mayonnaise	2½ cups (20 ounces)	5 cups (40 ounces)	10 cups (80 ounces)	15 cups (120 ounces)
Lemon juice	2 tablespoons (1 lemon)	¼ cup (2 lemons)	½ cup (4 lemons)	¾ cup (6 lemons)
Granulated sugar	1 tablespoon	2 tablespoons	¼ cup	⅓ cup
Green cabbage, shredded	1 pound	2 pounds	4 pounds	6 pounds
Red cabbage, shredded	1 pound	2 pounds	4 pounds	6 pounds
Carrots, shredded	½ pound	1 pound	2 pounds	3 pounds
Jalapeño peppers, minced	3	5	10	15
Salt and freshly ground black pepper	to taste	to taste	to taste	to taste

equipment:

- large mixing bowl
- wooden spoon

directions:

1. Combine the mayonnaise, lemon juice, and sugar in a large mixing bowl.

2. Add the green cabbage, red cabbage, carrots, and jalapeños, and toss well to coat.

3. Season with salt and pepper to taste, and refrigerate for at least 1 hour before serving.

helpful hints: (fyi)

- Divide the ingredients evenly and mix in batches for manageability.

- This coleslaw also works well with a balsamic vinaigrette in place of the mayonnaise-based dressing.

- For a more traditional coleslaw, omit the jalapeños.

- For a variation, replace half of the carrots with thinly sliced jicama or fennel.

do it ahead:

- The cabbages and carrots can be shredded and the jalapeños can be chopped a day in advance.

- The lemons can be juiced a day in advance. Store in the refrigerator.

do it for less time:

- Use pre-shredded cabbage and carrots available in the produce section of grocery and club stores.

- Use canned and drained jalapeños in place of fresh jalapeños.

- Use bottled lemon juice in place of freshly-squeezed juice.

portion size: 3 ounces

buckaroo beans

ingredients	12 people	25 people	50 people	75 people
Bacon	4 ounces	8 ounces	1 pound	1½ pounds
Yellow onions, chopped	¾ pound	1½ pounds	3 pounds	4½ pounds
Barbecue sauce	1¾ cups (14 ounces)	3/2 cups (28 ounces)	7 cups (56 ounces)	10½ cups (84 ounces)
Light beer	1¼ cups (10 ounces)	2½ cups (20 ounces)	5 cups (40 ounces)	7½ cups (60 ounces)
Dark molasses	½ cup plus 2 tablespoons	1¼ cups	2½ cups	3¾ cups
Dijon mustard	¼ cup	½ cup	1 cup	1½ cups
Dark brown sugar	¼ cup, packed	½ cup, packed	1 cup, packed	1½ cups, packed
Worcestershire sauce	2 tablespoons	¼ cup	½ cup	¾ cup
Canned great Northern beans	60 ounces	120 ounces	158 ounces	360 ounces

helpful hint:

Any canned white beans can be used in place of the great Northern beans.

do it ahead:

Make the beans a day in advance to allow the flavors to meld.

do it for less time:

• When preparing a pound or more of bacon, cook it in bulk by placing the individual strips on baking trays. Bake in a 400-degree oven for 20 minutes, turning halfway through, or until crispy. Drain on paper towels.

• To save time opening cans, look for larger sizes in club and warehouse stores.

directions:

1. Cook the bacon in batches in a sauté pan over medium heat until crispy. Remove the bacon, leaving the pan drippings. Cut the bacon into ¼-inch pieces.

2. Return the pan drippings to the heat, and add the onions. Cook for 5 minutes, or until translucent.

3. Place the cooked onions in a stockpot and add the barbecue sauce, beer, molasses, Dijon mustard, dark brown sugar, and Worcestershire sauce. Stir until smooth. Add the beans to the stockpot, and gently stir to combine.

4. Bring the mixture to a boil, and then reduce the heat to low. Simmer for 1 hour, or until slightly thickened, stirring occasionally.

equipment:

• large saucepan or stockpot
• large sauté pan
• tongs or fork
• wooden spoon

portion size: 5 to 6 ounces

fresh corn on the cob with sage butter

ingredients	**12** people	**25** people	**50** people	**75** people
Corn on the cob	12	25	50	75
Fresh sage, chopped	1/4 cup	1/2 cup	1 cup	1 1/2 cups
Unsalted butter, softened	2 sticks (8 ounces)	4 sticks (16 ounces)	8 sticks (32 ounces)	12 sticks (48 ounces)
Salt and freshly ground black pepper	to taste	to taste	to taste	to taste

equipment:

• aluminum foil
• mixing bowl
• spreading knife
• wooden spoon

directions:

1. Preheat the grill.

2. Remove the husks, the silk, and the bottom stump from the corn.

3. Combine the sage and butter until light and creamy. (The butter can be made up to 2 days in advance and refrigerated until ready to use.) Spread each ear of corn with about 1 tablespoon of butter.

4. Place each ear of corn in the center of a piece of aluminum foil about 13 x 9 inches in size. Wrap the corn completely in the foil. (The corn can be prepared a day in advance up to this point. Refrigerate until ready to grill.)

5. Grill for 20 minutes, or until the kernels are soft. Allow the corn to cool slightly before serving. Serve with salt and pepper to season.

helpful hints:

• You can replace the sage with basil, rosemary, parsley, thyme, oregano, or chopped garlic.

• If you don't have a grill, bake the corn in a 350 degree oven for 20 to 30 minutes, or until crisp-tender.

• For a rustic look, peel down the corn husks and leave intact. Remove the silks, and wash the corn. Spread the kernels with the herbed butter and pull the husks back into their original position. To serve, pull down the husks and use as a handle for easier eating.

do it ahead:

• The herbed butter can be made up to two days in advance and refrigerated.

• The corn can be prepped a day in advance. Refrigerate until ready to grill.

portion size: 1 ear of corn

double-fudge brownies

ingredients	12 people (1 pan, 25 brownies)	25 people (2 pans, 50 brownies)	50 people (4 pans, 100 brownies)	75 people (6 pans, 150 brownies)
Vegetable cooking spray	as needed	as needed	as needed	as needed
Unsalted butter, melted	1 stick (4 ounces)	2 sticks (8 ounces)	4 sticks (16 ounces)	6 sticks (24 ounces)
Unsweetened cocoa powder	1/2 cup	1 cup	2 cups	3 cups
Granulated sugar	1 cup	2 cups	4 cups	6 cups
Dark brown sugar	1 cup	2 cups	4 cups	6 cups
Large eggs, beaten	4	8	16	24
Vanilla extract	2 teaspoons	1 tablespoon plus 1 teaspoon	2 tablespoons plus 2 teaspoons	1/4 cup
All-purpose flour	1 1/2 cups	3 cups	6 cups	9 cups
Baking powder	1/4 teaspoon	1/2 teaspoon	1 teaspoon	1 1/2 teaspoons
Salt	1/4 teaspoon	1/2 teaspoon	1 teaspoon	1 1/2 teaspoons
Mini chocolate chips	1 1/4 cups (6 ounces)	2 1/2 cups (12 ounces)	5 cups (24 ounces)	7 1/2 cups (36 ounces)

do it ahead:

These brownies can be made ahead of time and frozen for up to one week. Defrost the morning of the party at room temperature and frost with Creamy Fudge Frosting (p. 173).

do it for less time:

Start with a brownie mix or buy pre-made brownies from a local bakery and spread with the Creamy Fudge Frosting (on the opposite page) to save time.

directions:

1. Preheat the oven to 350 degrees and spray the baking pans with vegetable cooking spray.

2. Combine the melted butter, cocoa powder, sugar, and brown sugar in a large mixing bowl. Gradually add the eggs, beating constantly until smooth. Stir in the vanilla.

3. In a separate bowl, sift together the flour, baking powder, and salt.

4. Gradually add the flour mixture to the egg mixture, stirring well. Add the chocolate chips, and stir until all the ingredients are combined.

5. Divide the batter among the baking pans. Bake for 35 to 45 minutes, or until a toothpick inserted into the center of the pan comes out with a few moist crumbs attached.

6. Set the pans on the cooling racks, and allow the brownies to cool completely in the pans before frosting.

7. Spread the cooled brownies with the Creamy Fudge Frosting (opposite page). Cut each pan into 25 brownies about 1 1/2 x 1 1/2-inches square.

equipment:

- 1 (8 x 8-inch) baking pan per 12 guests
- cooling racks
- electric hand or stand mixer
- large mixing bowls
- spatula

portion size: 2 (1 1/2 x 1 1/2-inch) brownies

creamy fudge frosting

ingredients	12 people	25 people	50 people	75 people
Unsalted butter, softened	5 tablespoons (2½ ounces)	1¼ sticks (5 ounces)	2½ sticks (10 ounces)	3¾ sticks (15 ounces)
Vanilla extract	¾ teaspoon	1½ teaspoons	1 tablespoon	1 tablespoon plus 1½ teaspoons
Unsweetened cocoa powder	3 tablespoons	¼ cup plus 2 tablespoons	¾ cup	1 cup plus 2 tablespoons
Corn syrup	1 tablespoon plus ½ teaspoon	3 tablespoons	¼ cup plus 2 tablespoons	½ cup plus 1 tablespoon
Heavy whipping cream	¼ cup	½ cup	1 cup	1½ cups
Sifted powdered sugar	1½ cups (6 ounces)	3 cups (12 ounces)	6 cups (1½ pounds)	9 cups (2¼ pounds)

equipment:

- electric hand or stand mixer
- large mixing bowl
- spatula
- spreading knife

directions:

1. Beat the butter in a mixing bowl until light and fluffy. Add the vanilla, cocoa powder, corn syrup, and heavy whipping cream, and mix until smooth.

2. Gradually add the powdered sugar, stirring constantly until the mixture is a spreading consistency. (Add more cream if necessary.)

3. Pour into an airtight container and store in the refrigerator.

4. Bring to room temperature and stir before frosting the brownies (recipe on the opposite page).

helpful hints:

- Before measuring the corn syrup, spray the measuring cup with vegetable oil spray to make clean-up easy.

- Remember to sift the powdered sugar first before measuring.

do it ahead:

The frosting can be made a week in advance. Cover well and store in the refrigerator. Bring to room temperature before frosting the brownies.

Baby Greens Salad
with Champagne Vinaigrette

Pecan-Crusted Halibut Fillet
with Dijon Cream Sauce

Lemon Rice Pilaf

Garden-Fresh Green Beans

Strawberries and Chantilly Cream

Mini Chocolate-Almond Tartlets

Peach Bellinis

garden elegance

Jump into springtime with the easy elegance of a delightful garden wedding, Mother's Day brunch, or engagement party.

garden menu:

baby greens with champagne vinaigrette
pecan-crusted halibut fillet with dijon cream sauce
lemon rice pilaf
garden-fresh green beans
strawberries and chantilly cream
mini chocolate-almond tartlets
peach bellinis

decorating ideas:

colors. Lavender and violet, pearl gray, Tiffany blue, peony pink, and pale gold.

invitations. Use floral or iridescent papers or rich cotton stocks that match the theme. Print or write the invitations on vellum paper and attach to the base card with an elegant ribbon.

table linens. For a clean and simple look, choose crisp, scalloped cloths with dainty napkins. If you prefer shabby chic, choose vintage laces and fabrics with mismatched (but complementary) napkins.

decorations. Arrange bundles of beautiful flowers like peonies, gerber daisies, or tulips in simple vases and bowls, or use several vintage pieces with clean white tableware for a balance. Don't be afraid to mix and match different patterns of china, silver trays, and platters. If serving near Eastertime, dye eggs to match your color theme. Fill white ceramic or glass bowls with the eggs, or plant winter grasses in white boxes and nestle the colored eggs in the bright green blades of grass.

place cards and favors. Plant johnny jump-ups, pansies, or lilies of the valley in tiny porcelain bowls from a local consignment shop. Prop the name cards against the bowls, with care instructions for the plant on the back. Tie satin or sheer wire ribbons to the backs of chairs with name tags attached. Buy boxes of dainty pocket handkerchiefs, and fluff inside different teacups for each guest. Place the name cards in the handkerchiefs, serve tea after the meal, and send the guests home with their antique teacups and a sheer bag of special-blend tea as a party favor.

entertainment. Keep the background music subtle but pretty, with classical guitar or quiet jazz.

menu countdown

1 week before:
- Shop for non-perishables.
- Buy beverages.
- Make tartlets and freeze.

3 days before:
- Make space in refrigerator and freezer.

2 days before:
- Shop for perishables.

1 day before:
- Set up tables and décor.
- Make champagne vinaigrette.
- Prep salad greens.
- Grind pecans for halibut crust.
- Chop onions, and juice and zest lemons for rice.
- Trim and blanch green beans, and slice mushrooms.

morning of the party:
- Buy ice.
- Clean strawberries.
- Defrost tartlets.

1 to 2 hours ahead:
- Make Dijon cream sauce.
- Cook rice pilaf.

just before serving:
- Cook halibut.
- Whip cream.
- Toast almonds, and sauté green beans.
- Toss salad.
- Make bellinis.

garden elegance shopping list: 1 to 2 weeks before

ingredients	12 people	25 people	50 people	75 people
alcohol				
Champagne	2 (750-ml) bottles	4 (750-ml) bottles	8 (750-ml) bottles	12 (750-ml) bottles
Orange liqueur	2 ounces	4 ounces	8 ounces	12 ounces
pantry items & dry goods				
All-purpose flour	12 ounces	1½ pounds	3 pounds	4½ pounds
Breadcrumbs	7 ounces	12½ ounces	24½ ounces	37 ounces
Champagne vinegar	2¼ ounces	4½ ounces	9 ounces	13½ ounces
Chicken or vegetable stock	1¼ quarts (36 ounces)	2¼ quarts (72 ounces)	4½ quarts (144 ounces)	6¾ quarts (216 ounces)
Dijon mustard	9 ounces	18 ounces	36 ounces	54 ounces
Extra-virgin olive oil	9 ounces	18 ounces	36 ounces	54 ounces
Granulated sugar	7½ ounces	15 ounces	30 ounces	45 ounces
Ground almonds	2 ounces	4 ounces	8 ounces	12 ounces
Long-grain white rice	1 pound	2 pounds	4 pounds	6 pounds
Mayonnaise	1½ ounces	3 ounces	6 ounces	9 ounces
Peach nectar	32 ounces	80 ounces	160 ounces	224 ounces
Pecans	7 ounces	14 ounces	28 ounces	42 ounces
Semisweet chocolate chips	3 ounces	6 ounces	12 ounces	24 ounces
Sliced almonds	4 ounces	8 ounces	16 ounces	24 ounces
Unsweetened chocolate	1 ounce	2 ounces	4 ounces	6 ounces
Unsweetened cocoa powder	1 ounce	1¾ ounces	3½ ounces	5½ ounces
Vegetable cooking spray	1	1	1	1
Whole almonds	25 (1¼ ounces)	50 (2½ ounces)	100 (5 ounces)	150 (7½ ounces)
dried herbs, spices, & extracts				
Almond extract	¼ ounce	¼ ounce	½ ounce	½ ounce
Bay leaves	3 leaves	5 leaves	10 leaves	15 leaves
Black peppercorns	as needed	as needed	as needed	as needed
Salt	as needed	as needed	as needed	as needed
Vanilla extract	¼ ounce	½ ounce	1 ounce	2 ounces

garden elegance shopping list: 1 to 2 days before

ingredients	12 people	25 people	50 people	75 people
produce				
Green beans	3 pounds	6 pounds	12 pounds	18 pounds
Large strawberries	3 pints	6 pints	12 pints	18 pints
Lemons	2	4	8	12
Mixed baby greens	1 pound	1¾ pounds	3½ pounds	5¼ pounds
Mushrooms, sliced	6 ounces	12 ounces	1½ pounds	2¼ pounds
Onions	6 ounces	12 ounces	24 ounces	36 ounces
dairy, cheese, & deli				
Heavy whipping cream	18 ounces (1¼ pints)	36 ounces (1¼ quarts)	72 ounces (2¼ quarts)	100 ounces (3¼ quarts)
Large eggs	5	10	20	30
Unsalted butter	1 pound	2 pounds	4 pounds	6 pounds
meat & seafood				
Skinless halibut fillets	12 (4-ounce) fillets (3 pounds)	25 (4-ounce) fillets (6¼ pounds)	50 (4-ounce) fillets (12½ pounds)	75 (4-ounce) fillets (25 pounds)

Always take a calculator when shopping for quantity recipes to quickly and easily calculate the most appropriate package sizes for your particular needs. We have listed most items in ounces so that you are not limited to size-specific packaging if shopping in bulk. When in doubt over what amount to buy, always round up—it's far better to have a little extra of an ingredient than to run out while cooking. If your eighth-grade algebra skills have gotten rusty, remember that there are 16 ounces in a pound and 8 fluid ounces in a cup. See page 73 for additional conversions.

baby greens with champagne vinaigrette

ingredients	12 people	25 people	50 people	75 people
Champagne vinegar	2¼ ounces	4½ ounces	9 ounces	13½ ounces
Dijon mustard	2 tablespoons	¼ cup	½ cup	¾ cup
Mayonnaise	2 tablespoons	¼ cup	½ cup	¾ cup
Salt	1 teaspoon, plus more to taste	2 teaspoons, plus more to taste	1 tablespoon plus 2 teaspoons, and more to taste	2 tablespoons, plus more to taste
Extra-virgin olive oil	1⅛ cups (9 ounces)	2¼ cups (18 ounces)	4½ cups (36 ounces)	6½ cups (54 ounces)
Freshly ground black pepper	to taste	to taste	to taste	to taste
Mixed baby greens salad	1 pound	1¾ pounds	3½ pounds	5¼ pounds

(fyi) helpful hints:

• Baby greens, sometimes called mesclun mix, is a combination of young salad greens, including arugula, frisée, oak leaf, radicchio, sorrel, and baby spinach. You can find it in bulk or pre-bagged in the produce section of your grocery store.

• A plastic salad spinner makes quick work of drying lettuce, as well as herbs, greens, and many vegetables.

do it ahead:

The dressing can be made and the baby greens can be washed and dried a day in advance. Toss the salad with the dressing just before serving.

($) do it for less money:

Serve spinach leaves instead of baby mixed greens, and use a balsamic vinaigrette in lieu of the champagne vinaigrette.

directions:

1. Combine the champagne vinegar, Dijon mustard, mayonnaise, and salt in a mixing bowl.

2. Slowly whisk in the olive oil in a steady stream until the mixture has emulsified. Season with black pepper to taste and additional salt if needed. (The dressing can be made a day in advance and stored in the refrigerator.)

3. Just before serving, place the baby greens in a 36-inch salad bowl and drizzle with the vinaigrette. (Do this in batches for manageability, if necessary.)

4. Using tongs or your hands (wearing disposable plastic gloves), toss the salad until well coated. Taste the salad and add more dressing as needed, being careful not to over-dress the leaves.

5. Repeat with the remaining baby greens and vinaigrette.

equipment:

• 36-inch salad bowl
• mixing bowl
• tongs or disposable gloves
• whisk

portion size: 1 heaped cup of salad plus 2 tablespoons of dressing

pecan-crusted halibut fillet

ingredients	12 people	25 people	50 people	75 people
Halibut fillets, skinned	12 (4-ounce) fillets (3 pounds)	25 (4-ounce) fillets (6$\frac{1}{4}$ pounds)	50 (4-ounce) fillets (12$\frac{1}{2}$ pounds)	75 (4-ounce) fillets (18$\frac{3}{4}$ pounds)
All-purpose flour	1$\frac{3}{4}$ cups (7 ounces)	3$\frac{1}{2}$ cups (14 ounces)	7 cups (28 ounces)	10$\frac{1}{2}$ cups (42 ounces)
Salt	$\frac{3}{4}$ teaspoon	1$\frac{1}{2}$ teaspoons	1 tablespoons	1 tablespoon plus 1$\frac{1}{2}$ teaspoon
Freshly ground black pepper	1 teaspoon	2$\frac{1}{4}$ teaspoons	1 tablespoon plus 1$\frac{1}{2}$ teaspoons	2 tablespoons plus 1 teaspoon
Large eggs	3	6	12	18
Dijon mustard	1 tablespoon	2 tablespoons	$\frac{1}{4}$ cup	$\frac{1}{3}$ cup
Finely chopped pecans	1$\frac{3}{4}$ cups	3$\frac{1}{2}$ cups	7 cups	10$\frac{1}{2}$ cups
Plain breadcrumbs	1$\frac{3}{4}$ cups	3$\frac{1}{2}$ cups	7 cups	10$\frac{1}{2}$ cups
Unsalted butter	6 tablespoons (3 ounces)	1$\frac{1}{2}$ sticks (6 ounces)	3 sticks (12 ounces)	4$\frac{1}{2}$ sticks (18 ounces)

equipment:

- 3 large mixing bowls
- baking pans
- large sauté pans
- spatula
- tongs
- whisk
- wooden spoon

directions:

1. Preheat the oven to 350 degrees.

2. Cut the halibut into 4-ounce fillets.

3. Combine the flour, salt, and pepper in a mixing bowl.

4. In another bowl, whisk the eggs and mustard.

5. In a third bowl, combine the chopped pecans and breadcrumbs. (See pages 110 and 133 for information on making breadcrumbs.)

6. Set the three bowls in a row, with a baking pan at the end for placing the fillets. Dredge each fillet in the flour, shaking off any excess flour back into the bowl. Dip the halibut in the egg mixture to coat, and then place in the pecan mixture. Press lightly to coat both sides of the fillet and place on the baking sheet. Repeat with the remaining fillets. (The fillets can be refrigerated for up to 2 hours at this point before sautéing.)

7. Melt 2 tablespoons of the butter in a large sauté pan over medium heat. Add as many fillets as will comfortably fit in the pan. Cook for about 3 minutes per side, or until light brown. (The fillets can be drained on paper towels and refrigerated at this point for up to 6 hours before baking.)

8. Arrange the sautéed fillets on the baking sheets and bake for 10 to 15 minutes, or until cooked through. Serve with the Dijon Cream Sauce on page 180.

helpful hint:

To make chopping the nuts easier, add a little sugar to your food processor. Pulse the processor to keep from grinding the nuts too finely.

do it ahead:

To minimize a fish smell throughout the house, bread and sauté the fish the morning of your party and refrigerate until the party. (The halibut can also be coated and dipped in the crust up to 2 hours before sautéing. Refrigerate until ready to use.) Bake the sautéed fish in the oven for 15 to 20 minutes before serving.

do it for less time:

Ask your fishmonger to skin the fillets and cut them into 4-ounce portions for you.

do it for less money:

- You can substitute 4 to 6-ounce boneless and skinless chicken breasts or turkey cutlets for the halibut.

- A less-expensive white fish such as cod will also work for this recipe.

dijon cream sauce

ingredients	**12** people	**25** people	**50** people	**75** people
Heavy whipping cream	1⅓ cups (11 ounces)	2⅔ cups (22 ounces)	5¼ cups (42 ounces)	8 cups (64 ounces)
Dijon mustard	¾ cup plus 2 tablespoons	1¾ cups	3½ cups	5¼ cups
Salt and freshly ground black pepper	to taste	to taste	to taste	to taste

(fyi) helpful hints:

• This easy-to-make sauce can be ready in minutes and tastes just as delicious on chicken and pork as it does on the pecan-crusted halibut that we're pairing it with.

• For extra texture, use a country-grain mustard in place of the Dijon.

directions:

1. Combine the heavy whipping cream and Dijon mustard in a large saucepan. Whisk constantly over low heat until warm.

2. Season with salt and pepper to taste, and ladle over the halibut fillets (page 179).

equipment:

• 1-ounce ladle
• large saucepan
• whisk

portion size: 1 ounce (2 tablespoons)

lemon rice pilaf

ingredients	12 people	25 people	50 people	75 people
Chicken or vegetable stock	4½ cups (36 ounces)	9 cups (72 ounces)	18 cups (144 ounces)	27 cups (216 ounces)
Unsalted butter	3 tablespoons (1½ ounces)	6 tablespoons (3 ounces)	1½ sticks (6 ounces)	2 sticks (8 ounces)
Finely diced onion	1 cup	2 cups	4 cups	6 cups
Long-grain white rice	1 pound (2½ cups)	2 pounds (5 cups)	4 pounds (10 cups)	6 pounds (15 cups)
Lemons, finely zested and juiced	2	4	8	12
Bay leaves	3	5	10	15
Salt	¾ teaspoon	1½ teaspoons	1 tablespoon	1 tablespoon plus 2 teaspoons
Freshly ground black pepper	½ teaspoon	1 teaspoon	2 teaspoons	1 tablespoon

equipment:

- heavy-duty aluminum foil
- large sauté pans
- roasting pans
- stockpot
- zester or microplane grater

directions:

1. Preheat the oven to 350 degrees. Place the stock in a stockpot over high heat and bring to a simmer.

2. Melt the butter in a large sauté pan over medium heat. Add the onions and cook for 2 minutes, or until softened. Add the rice and stir to coat with the butter. Cook for 2 to 3 minutes, or just until the rice becomes fragrant. (Be careful not to burn.)

3. Transfer the rice to a large roasting pan. Pour in the hot stock. Stir in the lemon juice, lemon zest, bay leaves, salt, and pepper.

4. Cover the pan tightly with aluminum foil and bake for 25 to 30 minutes, or until the liquid is absorbed and the rice is tender.

5. Fluff the rice with a fork before serving and garnish with lemon rounds.

helpful hint:

This can also be made on the stovetop in 6 to 8-quart stockpots. Instead of transferring the rice to a roasting pan, just keep in the stockpot. Pour in the hot stock and remaining ingredients. Bring to a boil, and reduce the heat. Cover and cook over low until the liquid is absorbed and the rice is tender.

do it ahead:

Chop the onions the day before the party.

do it for less time:

If time is precious, omit the zest and use only bottled lemon juice. The lemon flavor will be less intense without the zest, so adjust the amount of juice to your liking for a stronger punch.

portion size: about ⅓ cup

garden fresh green beans

ingredients	**12** people	**25** people	**50** people	**75** people
Green beans	3 pounds	6 pounds	12 pounds	18 pounds
Unsalted butter, melted	1 stick (4 ounces)	2 sticks (8 ounces)	4 sticks (16 ounces)	6 sticks (24 ounces)
Mushrooms, sliced	6 ounces	12 ounces	1½ pounds	2¼ pounds
Sliced almonds, toasted	1 cup	2 cups	4 cups	6 cups
Salt and freshly ground black pepper	to taste	to taste	to taste	to taste

do it ahead:

• The green beans can be prepped a day in advance: Trim the ends and remove any strings from the beans. Blanch in boiling water for 2 minutes, and then shock in ice water to stop the cooking and preserve their bright green color. Drain and refrigerate for up to a day. Reheat in the sauté pan with the melted butter.

• Clean and slice the mushrooms a day in advance. Refrigerate until ready to sauté.

do it for less time:

Look for pre-sliced mushrooms in your produce department.

directions:

1. Trim the ends from the green beans and cut into 2-inch pieces.

2. Fill the stockpots with salted water and bring to a boil. Add the green beans to the boiling water. Reduce the heat and simmer for 5 to 6 minutes, or until the beans turn bright green and are still slightly crunchy. Drain the beans and reserve in a large mixing bowl. (If preparing a day in advance, shock in ice water, drain, and refrigerate until ready to sauté.)

3. While the green beans are cooking, melt one fourth of the butter in a large sauté pan. Add the mushrooms and sauté until soft, about 5 minutes.

4. Add the cooked mushrooms to the reserved green beans. Pour in the remaining melted butter, sprinkle with the toasted almonds, and season with salt and pepper to taste. Toss to coat the beans evenly.

5. Serve immediately, or hold for up to 10 minutes in a warm oven.

equipment:

• 2 large stockpots
• large mixing bowl
• large sauté pan
• tongs
• wooden spoon

portion size: about 3 ounces

strawberries and chantilly cream

ingredients	12 people	25 people	50 people	75 people
Heavy whipping cream	³/₄ cup (6 ounces)	1¹/₂ cups (12 ounces)	3 cups (24 ounces)	4¹/₂ cups (36 ounces)
Granulated sugar	2 tablespoons	¹/₄ cup	¹/₂ cup	1 cup
Vanilla extract	¹/₂ teaspoon	1 teaspoon	2 teaspoons	1 tablespoon
Large strawberries, cleaned, hulled, and sliced	3 pints	6 pints	12 pints	18 pints

equipment:

- electric hand or stand mixer
- large stainless steel mixing bowl
- spatula

directions:

1. Place the cream, sugar, and vanilla in a chilled stainless steel mixing bowl. Beat on low speed until the sugar is dissolved.

2. Increase the speed to high and beat until the cream forms soft peaks. Serve with the strawberries.

helpful hints:

- Chantilly cream is a lightly sweetened whipped cream flavored with vanilla or liqueur. For the best volume, chill the bowl and beater in the refrigerator or freezer for at least 30 minutes before whipping the cream.

- One pint of strawberries contains about 12 to 14 large berries or 20 to 25 smaller berries.

- To dress up the strawberries, place them in a bowl and drizzle with your favorite liqueur. Gently toss to coat, then refrigerate them for up to 2 hours before serving. You will need about 2 tablespoons of liqueur for each pint of strawberries.

do it ahead:

The whipped cream can be made up to an hour in advance.

do it for less time:

If you don't have the time to clean and hull fresh strawberries, use frozen whole strawberries. Thaw them in a large colander at room temperature for an hour as close to dessert time as possible to prevent them from becoming too mushy.

portion size: 3 strawberries and 1 ounce of cream

mini chocolate-almond tartlets

ingredients	12 people (25 tartlets)	25 people (50 tartlets)	50 people (100 tartlets)	75 people (150 tartlets)
for the pastry:				
Vegetable cooking spray	as needed	as needed	as needed	as needed
All-purpose flour	1 cup plus 2 tablespoons (5 ounces), plus more for flouring surface	2¼ cups (10 ounces), plus more for flouring surface	5 cups (20 ounces), plus more for flouring surface	7¼ cups (30 ounces), plus more for flouring surface
Granulated sugar	⅓ cup plus 1 tablespoon	¾ cup	1½ cups	2¼ cups
Unsweetened cocoa powder	¼ cup	½ cup	1 cup	1½ cups
Unsalted butter, cut into ½-inch pieces	1 stick (4 ounces)	2 sticks (8 ounces)	4 sticks (16 ounces)	6 sticks (24 ounces)
Large eggs	1	2	4	6
Vanilla extract	¾ teaspoon	1½ teaspoons	1 tablespoon	1 tablespoon plus 1½ teaspoons
for the filling:				
Unsalted butter, cut into ½-inch pieces	6 tablespoons (3 ounces)	1½ sticks (6 ounces)	3 sticks (12 ounces)	4½ sticks (18 ounces)
Granulated sugar	¼ cup	½ cup	1 cup	1½ cups
Large eggs	1	2	4	6
Almond extract	½ teaspoon	1 teaspoon	2 teaspoons	1 tablespoon
Ground almonds	⅓ cup (2 ounces)	¾ cup (4 ounces)	1½ cups (8 ounces)	2¼ cups (12 ounces)
Unsweetened chocolate, grated	1 ounce	2 ounces	4 ounces	6 ounces
Whole almonds	25 (1¼ ounces)	50 (2½ ounces)	100 (5 ounces)	150 (7½ ounces)
for the topping:				
Semisweet chocolate chips	¾ cups (3 ounces)	1¼ cups (6 ounces)	2½ cups (12 ounces)	5 cups (24 ounces)

(fyi) helpful hint:

Mini tartlet shells or tins can be found at cookware and restaurant supply stores. As an alternative, you can use mini muffin pans.

do it ahead:

The completed tartlets can be frozen in plastic containers up to a week in advance or stored at room temperature up to a day in advance.

directions:

for the pastry:

1. Preheat the oven to 350 degrees. Spray the tartlet shells with vegetable cooking spray.

2. Place the flour, sugar, and cocoa powder into the bowl of a food processor. Add the butter, and pulse the ingredients until the mixture has the consistency of cornmeal.

3. Whisk the eggs and vanilla together in a small bowl. With food processor running, slowly pour in the egg mixture until the ingredients form a ball. (It the mixture is too dry, add a little cold milk or water, one teaspoon at a time, until the dough comes together.)

4. Place the dough onto a floured work surface and knead lightly until smooth. Form the dough into balls about ¾-inch in diameter.

5. Place one ball into each tartlet shell. Using damp fingers, press the dough evenly into the bottom and sides of the shells. Place the shells on the baking sheets.

portion size: 2 tartlets

equipment:

- 1½-inch mini tartlet shells or mini muffin pans
- baking sheets
- cooling racks
- food processor
- heavy-duty resealable plastic storage bag
- kitchen scissors
- microwave-safe glass bowl
- mixing bowl
- whisk

for the filling:

1. Place the butter, sugar, eggs, almond extract, ground almonds, and grated chocolate in the bowl of a food processor. Process all the ingredients until the mixture is smooth.

2. Spoon 1 teaspoon of the filling into each prepared shell, and place one whole almond into the center of each tartlet.

3. Bake for 15 minutes, or until the filling is firm to the touch.

4. Cool on wire racks for 10 minutes, or until cool enough to touch. Gently squeeze the tartlet shells and invert the tartlet into the palm of your hand.

for the topping:

1. Place the chocolate chips in bowl. Microwave on high for 30 seconds. Stir the chocolate, and continue to microwave in 30-second intervals and stir until melted and smooth.

2. Pour the melted chocolate into a plastic storage bag. With scissors, cut off a very small corner section of the bag.

3. Squeeze the chocolate out of the bag and drizzle over the tartlets in a zigzag pattern. Allow the chocolate to harden, and then serve the tartlets alone or with the Strawberries and Chantilly Cream on page 183.

do it for less time:
• Look for pre-cooked tartlet shells in the frozen food section of club and specialty food stores.

• In lieu of making the pastry yourself, you can buy the unfold-and-bake pastry crust, usually found near the refrigerated cookie dough in the grocery store. Unfold the dough and cut out small circles with a cookie cutter or the rim of a glass. Press the dough into tartlet shells or mini muffin pans. One 15-ounce box of dough should yield about 30 shells.

do it for less money:
If you cannot find ground almonds, make your own by grinding slivered almonds and a little sugar in a food processor until fine.

peach bellinis

ingredients	12 people	25 people	50 people	75 people
Orange liqueur, chilled	¼ cup (2 ounces)	½ cup (4 ounces)	1 cup (8 ounces)	1½ cups (12 ounces)
Peach nectar, chilled	4 cups (32 ounces)	10 cups (80 ounces)	1¼ gallons (160 ounces)	1¾ gallons (224 ounces)
Champagne, chilled	2 (750-ml) bottles	4 (750-ml) bottles	8 (750 ml) bottles	12 (750-ml) bottles

equipment:
• large glass pitchers
• wooden spoon

directions:

1. Pour the orange liqueur and peach nectar into large glass pitchers, and stir well to combine.

2. Just before serving, add the champagne. Pour into champagne flutes.

do it for less time:
Traditional bellinis are made with fresh peach purée. To save time, use peach nectar available in the juice aisle of your grocery store.

do it for less money:
You can use sparkling apple juice or ginger ale in place of the champagne, frozen orange juice concentrate in place of the orange liqueur, and fresh orange juice in place of the peach nectar.

portion size: about 5 ounces

Butternut Squash Soup

Oven-Roasted Turkey
with Herb Gravy and Cornbread Stuffing

Creamy Mashed Potatoes

Candied Yams

Lemon Broccoli

Fresh Cranberry Relish

Pecan Pie
with Spiced Whipped Cream

bountiful harvest

An autumnal feast for Thanksgiving* or Christmas dinner.

butternut squash soup
oven-roasted turkey with herb gravy
  and cornbread dressing
creamy mashed potatoes
candied yams
lemon broccoli
fresh cranberry relish
pecan pie with spiced whipped cream

* Sooner or later, you will find yourself preparing your first Thanksgiving dinner. This menu covers all the basics. Feel free to substitute your own favorite holiday recipes for any listed. You can cut this menu in half for a smaller crowd.

decorating ideas:

colors. Pumpkin orange, butternut yellow, cranberry red, and cinnamon brown.

invitations. Collect autumn-colored leaves and glue them onto card stock. Write on the back of the card with copper-colored ink. For a rustic flair, attach pheasant feathers onto note cards printed with the invitation details.

table linens. Use white or off-white tablecloths with long, rich-colored runners. Or purchase large swaths of autumn-colored burlap and fringe the edges; spread flat to use as a tablecloth or arrange in a gentle bunch in the middle of the table to supplement the centerpiece.

centerpieces. Arrange five perfect pumpkins on a bed of autumn leaves set in the center, or place the pumpkins in even intervals down the length of the table. Arrange ornamental corn and squash in wooden bowls, natural baskets, or copper trays accented with dried floral arrangements in yellow, red, and brown tones. Group pillar candles in rich colors with tapers of the same shades. Lean small shocks of wheat against cornucopias filled with gourds and fruits. Fill an oversized wooden bowl with giant red apples or miniature pumpkins. Add vases of yellow and rust-red daisies to the table for a fall accent.

place cards and favors. Make slits in the tops of miniature pumpkins, gourds, or pears, and slice off the bottom portion of each to make them sit flat. Insert place cards in the slits. For a more casual affair, make hand-shaped turkeys reminiscent of children's crafts (or let your children make them). Fill small bags with mulling spices. Tie a name card around the mulling bag to use as both a place card and a Thanksgiving memory.

entertainment. Play classic folk music from the Amish country with mandolins, flutes, and violins.

menu countdown

1 week before:
- Shop for non-perishables.
- Buy beverages.
- Buy frozen turkey or order fresh turkey. Start defrosting (page 188).
- Make pie crusts and freeze.

3 days before:
- Make space in refrigerator and freezer.

2 days before:
- Shop for perishables.
- Pick up fresh turkey.
- Make cranberry relish.
- Defrost pie crust.

1 day before:
- Set up tables and décor.
- Make soup, but do not add cream.
- Chop vegetables for turkey.
- Prepare cornbread dressing, but do not bake.
- Squeeze lemon juice, and prep broccoli for cooking.
- Make mashed potatoes.
- Prep thyme for gravy.
- Make candied yams.
- Make pecan pies.

morning of the party:
- Buy ice.
- Cook turkey.

1 to 2 hours ahead:
- Bake cornbread dressing.
- Reheat mashed potatoes.
- Reheat yams.
- Reheat soup, and add cream.
- Make lemon broccoli.

just before serving:
- Make gravy.
- Make spiced whipped cream.

TALKING TURKEY

Thanksgiving just wouldn't be complete without the quintessential holiday turkey. As it emerges from the oven, plump and aromatic with crispy golden skin, all eyes widen with anticipation for that deliciously moist meat. If only it always happened that way.

Some Thanksgiving turkey stories have almost become urban legends—from the lady that stayed awake the night before Thanksgiving trying to defrost a 24-pound frozen turkey with a hairdryer to the man that was convinced that if he placed his turkey in the dishwasher and ran it through the pots and pans cycle several times, it would eventually cook. Please, please, please do not attempt any of these ideas at home. The holidays are stressful enough without having to deal with turkey trauma, too. You can depend on our "do it for less" tips for a terrific turkey.

- **fresh or frozen?** Most turkeys eaten today are frozen. Frozen turkeys are readily available in any supermarket and very affordable. Some specialty stores sell fresh turkeys. Usually they are corn-fed and sometimes organic, making them more expensive than frozen. So now for the big question: Is there a difference in taste? Unequivocally, yes.

  If budget allows, try a fresh turkey at your next Thanksgiving. You will be pleasantly surprised. The meat tastes, somehow, meatier. Its texture is chewier and less mushy than that of frozen birds.

- **size matters.** Just how big should the turkey be? As a rule, allow $1\frac{1}{2}$ pounds of turkey per person. For fifteen people, then, you would need a $22\frac{1}{2}$-pound turkey. The exception to the rule is for turkeys weighing less than 14 pounds. These have a smaller meat-to-bone ratio and require 2 pounds per person. These figures give everyone a fair portion. If you want to enjoy leftovers, order a larger turkey than calculated.

- **defrosting.** To inhibit the growth of bacteria, always defrost the turkey in its unopened wrapper and set in a roasting pan or rimmed baking pan to catch any juices. It should be defrosted in a refrigerator set at 40 degrees or less. Allow about 5 hours of refrigerated defrosting time for every pound. Make your calculations carefully—a 20-pound turkey will take about 100 hours, or just over 4 days, to defrost. For a quicker but more labor-intensive method, immerse the still-wrapped turkey breast-side down in cold water. Change the water every 30 minutes. Allow 30 minutes per pound to thaw.

- **that bag of "stuff."** Once the turkey has defrosted, you can remove the mystery plastic bag from the cavity. The bag contains the giblets, which can be used to make gravy. Also remove the neck from the front of the turkey; it may be in a plastic bag as well.

- **the right stuff.** Should you stuff the bird or cook the dressing separately? The dressing will be more flavorful if cooked in the turkey, but it may not reach a temperature hot enough to kill possible bacteria. For safety's sake, we recommend that you avoid stuffing the turkey and serve any dressing alongside. Bake the dressing separately in a casserole for 35 to 40 minutes at 375 degrees. If you love the turkey-basted taste of true stuffing, cut the turkey into eight pieces like a chicken. Place skin-side up on a casserole of dressing. Roast the turkey and dressing together. All of the flavors, none of the risk, and easier carving.

oven-roasted turkey

There are many good ways to prepare the turkey for cooking—stuffing herbs under the skin, laying a butter-soaked layer of cheesecloth over the surface of the skin, or even soaking the bird in a brine solution for a day. For our tried and trusted method, brush the skin with a mixture of melted butter and olive oil, then season with salt and pepper.

Place the prepared turkey in a preheated 325-degree oven. Baste every 30 to 40 minutes with the pan drippings, taking care not to allow too much heat to escape from the oven. (Butterball-brand turkeys are the exception, as they are self-basting and require no attention during cooking.) Cover the turkey breast with foil when it is two-thirds done to prevent the meat from drying out. Check for doneness 1 hour before the estimated end time by placing an instant-read thermometer deep in the lower part of the thigh without touching the bone. The thermometer should read 180 degrees at the thigh and in the stuffing. For a moist bird, allow the turkey to rest for 20 to 30 minutes, loosely covered with foil, before carving. Sometimes we cook two small turkeys—one for Thanksgiving and the other for leftovers. Cook the second turkey while you're eating Thanksgiving dinner.

deep-fried turkey

approximate cooking times

weight	unstuffed turkey	stuffed turkey
10 to 12 pounds	$3\frac{1}{2}$ hours	4 hours
12 to 15 pounds	4 hours	$4\frac{1}{2}$ hours
15 to 18 pounds	$4\frac{1}{4}$ hours	$4\frac{3}{4}$ hours
18 to 21 pounds	$4\frac{3}{4}$ hours	$5\frac{1}{4}$ hours
22 to 25 pounds	$5\frac{1}{4}$ hours	$5\frac{3}{4}$ hours

More and more people are enjoying Southern-inspired deep-fat fried turkeys on Thanksgiving. The whole turkey is immersed in a special turkey fryer of hot oil. The result is a tender and crispy turkey that cooks in a fraction of the time, about 3 minutes per pound.

With a bit of common sense, you can enjoy a perfectly cooked turkey this next Thanksgiving. Keep the following guidelines in mind if you plan on frying your turkey.

- **Safety.** When working with large amounts of oil, exercise extreme caution. The oil will stay hot long after cooking is completed, and a serious oil burn can be devastating. Do not allow children or animals near the cooking area. Never leave the fryer unattended. Place the fryer on a flat surface. Avoid wooden decks that could catch fire or concrete that may stain. Follow the fryer directions carefully.

- **Types of oil.** Use only oils with a high smoke point such as peanut, canola, and sunflower. The smoke point is the point at which an oil becomes too hot and starts to smoke and smell burnt. The next stop after the smoking point is the burning point, and a grease fire can be difficult to put out. (Always use a fire extinguisher—never water!—to put out a grease fire.) Fats and oils have different smoke points and, therefore, are suited to different temperatures of frying.

  Butter, for example, has a fairly low smoke point at 350 degrees and contains milk solids that burn very easily. While you would never want to deep-fry anything in butter, it works well for low-temperature sautéing.

  Olive oil, like butter, has a low smoke point, about 410 degrees. Extra-virgin olive oil has an even lower smoke point. We recommend regular olive oil for low-temperature sautéing and extra-virgin olive oil for salads and dressings. For high-temperature, deep-fat frying, rely on high-smoke-point vegetable oils (around 440 to 450 degrees) like peanut, corn, canola, and sunflower oils.

- **Amount of oil.** You will need at least 5 gallons of oil. Keep the original oil container and pour the used and cooled oil back into the container for easy disposal. To estimate the amount of oil needed, place the unopened turkey in the fryer and fill with enough water until completely covered. Remove the turkey and measure the water. This is how much oil you will need. Make sure the fryer and turkey are completely dry before using, as water will cause the grease to splatter.

carving your turkey

1. Have a serving platter nearby. Use a meat-slicing knife with a long, flexible, and sturdy blade—not a butcher knife. Electric knives work well for carving as well.

2. Remove the leg and wing by cutting through the skin between the drumstick and breast to find the thigh joint. Cut down through the joint to remove the thigh and drumstick.

3. Cut through the joint between the thigh and drumstick. Slice the leg and thigh meat by holding them upright and slicing down along the bone.

4. Cut through the shoulder joint where it meets the breast to remove the wing. The wings are generally served whole.

5. To carve the breast, make a base cut (a deep horizontal cut just above the wing). Starting up near the breastbone, carve thin slices parallel to the ribcage, cutting all the way down to your base cut.

6. Arrange turkey slices on platter. Cover with foil to keep warm.

bountiful harvest shopping list: 1 to 2 weeks before

ingredients	12 people	25 people	50 people	75 people
pantry items & dry goods				
All-purpose flour	12 ounces	24 ounces	48 ounces	72 ounces
Canned yams	11 pounds	22 pounds	43 pounds	64 pounds
Chicken stock	3 quarts (96 ounces)	6 quarts (192 ounces)	12 quarts (384 ounces)	18 quarts (576 ounces)
Chopped pecans or walnuts	1 cup (6 ounces)	2 cups (12 ounces)	4 cups (1½ pounds)	6 cups (36 ounces)
Corn syrup	20 ounces	30 ounces	42 ounces	62 ounces
Dark brown sugar	1¼ pounds	2½ pounds	5 pounds	7½ pounds
Extra-virgin olive oil for turkey	as needed	as needed	as needed	as needed
Granulated sugar	1 pound	2 pounds	4 pounds	6 pounds
Light brown sugar	7 ounces	14 ounces	1¾ pounds	2½ pounds
Maple syrup	2 ounces	4 ounces	8 ounces	12 ounces
Pecan halves	12 ounces	18 ounces	36 ounces	54 ounces
dried herbs, spices, & extracts				
Black peppercorns	as needed	as needed	as needed	as needed
Dried parsley	¼ ounce	¼ ounce	½ ounce	½ ounce
Dried sage	¼ ounce	¼ ounce	½ ounce	½ ounce
Dried thyme	¼ ounce	¼ ounce	½ ounce	½ ounce
Ground allspice	¼ ounce	¼ ounce	¼ ounce	¼ ounce
Ground cinnamon	¼ ounce	¼ ounce	¼ ounce	¼ ounce
Ground nutmeg	⅛ ounce	⅛ ounce	¼ ounce	¼ ounce
Salt	as needed	as needed	as needed	as needed
Vanilla extract	¼ ounce	¼ ounce	½ ounce	½ ounce
frozen foods				
1 (16 to 20-pound) frozen turkey (or order fresh)	1	2	4	6

bountiful harvest shopping list: 1 to 2 days before

ingredients	12 people	25 people	50 people	75 people
baked goods				
Prepared cornbread	1 pound	2 pounds	4 pounds	6 pounds
produce				
Butternut squash	5 pounds	10 pounds	20 pounds	30 pounds
Carrots	4 ounces	8 ounces	1 pound	1½ pounds
Celery	1½ pounds	2½ pounds	5 pounds	7½ pounds
Cranberries	6 ounces	12 ounces	1½ pounds	2¼ pounds
Fresh thyme	1½ ounces	3 ounces	6 ounces	9 ounces
Garlic	1 head	1 head	2 heads	3 heads
Lemon juice	2 ounces (or 2 lemons)	4 ounces (or 3 lemons)	8 ounces (or 6 lemons)	12 ounces (or 9 lemons)
Onions	2 pounds	3½ pounds	8 pounds	12 pounds
Oranges, large	2	4	7	11
Russet potatoes	10 pounds	20 pounds	40 pounds	60 pounds
Whole heads of broccoli	4½ pounds	9 pounds	18 pounds	27 pounds
dairy, cheese, & deli				
Heavy whipping cream	28 ounces (1¾ pints)	56 ounces (1¾ quarts)	112 ounces (3½ quarts)	168 ounces (5¼ quarts)
Large eggs	10	16	26	39
Milk	½ ounce	1 ounce	2 ounces	3 ounces
Unsalted butter	4 pounds	7 pounds	13 pounds	20 pounds
meat & seafood				
1 (16 to 20-pound) fresh turkey	1	2	4	6

Always take a calculator when shopping for quantity recipes to quickly and easily calculate the most appropriate package sizes for your particular needs. We have listed most items in ounces so that you are not limited to size-specific packaging if shopping in bulk. When in doubt over what amount to buy, always round up–it's far better to have a little extra of an ingredient than to run out while cooking. If your eighth-grade algebra skills have gotten rusty, remember that there are 16 ounces in a pound and 8 fluid ounces in a cup. See page 73 for additional conversions.

butternut squash soup

ingredients	**12** people	**25** people	**50** people	**75** people
Butternut squash	5 pounds	10 pounds	20 pounds	30 pounds
Unsalted butter	2 tablespoons ($\frac{1}{2}$ ounce)	4 tablespoons (2 ounces)	1 stick (4 ounces)	1$\frac{1}{2}$ sticks (6 ounces)
Finely diced onion	1 cup	2 cups	4 cups	6 cups
Finely diced celery	1 cup	2 cups	4 cups	6 cups
Minced garlic	1$\frac{1}{2}$ teaspoons	1 tablespoon	2 tablespoons	3 tablespoons
Chicken stock	6 cups (48 ounces)	12 cups (96 ounces)	24 cups (192 ounces)	36 cups (288 ounces)
Ground nutmeg	$\frac{1}{2}$ teaspoon	1 teaspoon	2 teaspoons	1 tablespoon
Maple syrup	$\frac{1}{4}$ cup	$\frac{1}{2}$ cup	1 cup	1$\frac{1}{2}$ cups
Salt	1$\frac{1}{2}$ teaspoons, plus more to taste	1 tablespoon, plus more to taste	2 tablespoons, plus more to taste	3 tablespoons, plus more to taste
Heavy whipping cream	2 cups (16 ounces)	4 cups (32 ounces)	8 cups (64 ounces)	12 cups (96 ounces)
Freshly ground black pepper	to taste	to taste	to taste	to taste

do it ahead:

This soup can be prepared a day in advance if the cream is omitted. Just before serving, reheat the soup, add the cream, and simmer for 5 minutes.

do it for less time:

You can cook the squash in the microwave.

directions:

1. Preheat the oven to 350 degrees.

2. Using a fork, prick the skin of the butternut squash all over. Slice in half, and place cut-side down on baking pans. Bake for 1 to 1$\frac{1}{2}$ hours, or until tender.

3. Allow to cool slightly. Scoop out the flesh from the squash. Discard the skins.

4. Place the butter in a large stockpot and set over medium heat. Add the onions and celery, and cook until the onions are translucent.

5. Add the garlic to the stockpot. Cook, stirring constantly, for 2 minutes.

6. Add the squash and the stock to the pot. Bring to a boil, reduce the heat, and simmer. Stir in the nutmeg, maple syrup, and salt, and simmer for 20 minutes.

7. Let the soup cool slightly, and then purée with an emulsion blender or in batches in a food processor until smooth. (The soup can be made up to this point a day in advance. Store covered in the refrigerator. Reheat before adding the cream.)

8. Return the puréed soup to the stockpot and add the cream. Reheat the soup until just hot, and season with salt and pepper to taste.

9. Keep warm for up to 1 hour over low heat until ready to serve. Ladle into warm soup bowls and serve.

equipment:

- baking pans
- emulsion blender or food processor
- ladle
- large stockpot

portion size: 1 cup

oven-roasted turkey

ingredients	12 people	25 people	50 people	75 people
1 (16 to 20-pound) turkey, thawed or fresh	1	2	4	6
Salt and freshly ground black pepper	to taste	to taste	to taste	to taste
Extra-virgin olive oil	as needed	as needed	as needed	as needed
Onions, chopped	8 ounces (1½ cups)	1 pound (3 cups)	2 pounds (6 cups)	3 pounds (9 cups)
Carrots, chopped	4 ounces (½ cup)	8 ounces (1 cup)	1 pound (2 cups)	1½ pounds (3 cups)
Celery, chopped	4 ounces (½ cup)	8 ounces (1 cup)	1 pound (2 cups)	1½ pounds (3 cups)

equipment:

- aluminum foil
- baster or long-handled spoon
- carving knife
- instant-read thermometer
- large roasting pan
- paper towels

directions:

1. Preheat the oven to 325 degrees.

2. Remove the giblets from the turkey and reserve for the gravy.

3. Rinse the cavity and dry well with paper towels. Heavily season the cavity with salt and pepper.

4. Rub the turkey well with olive oil, massaging the oil into the skin.

5. Lock the wings in place by twisting the wing tips behind and under the back of the turkey.

6. Place the turkey on its side in the roasting pan. Roast for 1 hour, basting every 30 minutes with the drippings.

7. Remove the pan from the oven, turn the turkey over on its other side, and roast for another hour, basting every 30 minutes.

9. Remove the pan from the oven, and turn the turkey so it is breast side up. Add the onions, carrots, and celery to the bottom of the roasting pan. Return to the oven and roast another 2 to 3 hours, basting occasionally, or until an instant-read thermometer inserted into the thickest part of the thigh registers 180 degrees. If the turkey is beginning to brown too quickly, cover with foil until fully cooked.

10. Remove the turkey from the roasting pan, and cover loosely with aluminum foil. Reserve the pan drippings and vegetables for the gravy.

11. Let the turkey rest in a warm place for 20 to 30 minutes before carving. While the turkey rests, finish the Herb Gravy (page 196).

helpful hint: (fyi)

Turning a turkey is no easy feat. For best results, use oven mitts covered with plastic freezer bags to keep them clean, or use silicone waterproof oven mitts, which are safe up to 500 degrees.

do it for less time:

• If oven space is tight and you are roasting more than two turkeys, carve all except one prior to cooking. You'll have a "hero" turkey for a centerpiece and maximize oven space with the carved birds.

• You can skip the turkey centerpiece altogether and pre-carve all the birds. Carve the turkey into legs, thighs, breasts, and wings. Place the legs and thighs on separate roasting pans from the breast and wings. Roast in a 325-degree oven until an instant-read thermometer registers 180 degrees and the juices run clear. The breast and wing meat will cook more quickly than the legs and thighs.

do it for less money: ($)

Use frozen turkeys instead of fresh or free-range.

portion size: 6 to 8 ounces

herb gravy

ingredients	**12** people	**25** people	**50** people	**75** people
Giblets from turkey, optional	amount varies	amount varies	amount varies	amount varies
Chicken or turkey stock	3½ cups (28 ounces)	7 cups (56 ounces)	14 cups (112 ounces)	21 cups (168 ounces)
Pan drippings from turkey	3 tablespoons (1½ ounces)	⅓ cup (3 ounces)	⅔ cup (6 ounces)	1 cup (8 ounces)
Reserved vegetables from turkey	amount varies	amount varies	amount varies	amount varies
All-purpose flour	⅓ cup	¾ cup	1½ cups	2¼ cups
Fresh thyme, chopped	1½ ounces	3 ounces	6 ounces	9 ounces
Salt and freshly ground black pepper	to taste	to taste	to taste	to taste

helpful hint:
If you have more drippings than the recipe calls for, don't throw them out. Use all the drippings created from the turkey, but use less of the stock.

do it ahead:
Chop the fresh thyme the day before the party.

do it for less time:
Cook the giblets while the turkey is roasting.

do it for less money:
You can use dried thyme in this recipe. Use one third of the amount called for in place of fresh thyme, and add it to the chicken stock in step 2 of the recipe.

directions:

1. If using the giblets, remove the liver from the giblets and discard or save for another use. Place the giblets in a saucepan and cover with cold water. Bring to a boil, lower the heat, and simmer 2 to 3 hours, or until tender.

2. In a separate stockpot, pour in the chicken stock and bring to a simmer over high heat.

3. When the turkey has cooked, remove the turkey and vegetables from the roasting pan. Reserve the drippings in the pan, and place on a burner over medium heat. Add the reserved vegetables from the pan and sauté for 2 to 3 minutes.

4. Ladle in just enough hot stock to cover the bottom of the pan, scraping up any browned bits with a wooden spoon. Sprinkle the drippings with the flour. Stir continuously over medium heat to make a roux. Cook until golden brown to remove any raw flour taste.

5. Ladle more stock into the roux, whisking to form a smooth liquid. Then whisk the roux back into the chicken stock, whisking well to remove any lumps.

6. Strain the giblet broth into the chicken stock mixture. Bring to a boil to thicken, reduce the heat to low, and season to taste with salt and pepper.

7. While the gravy is simmering, chop the giblets into bite-size pieces and add to the gravy, if desired. For a smoother gravy, omit the giblets.

8. Stir in the fresh thyme and continue simmering for at least 15 minutes, or until the gravy is thickened and smooth. Season with salt and pepper to taste.

equipment:
- ladle
- large sieve
- large stockpot
- medium saucepan
- roasting pan (used for the turkey)
- whisk
- wooden spoon

portion size: about ⅓ cup

cornbread dressing

ingredients	12 people	25 people	50 people	75 people
Unsalted butter for greasing pan	as needed	as needed	as needed	as needed
Unsalted butter	4 sticks (16 ounces)	8 sticks (32 ounces)	16 sticks (64 ounces)	24 sticks (96 ounces)
Diced onions	1½ cups (8 ounces)	3 cups (1 pound)	6 cups (2 pounds)	9 cups (3 pounds)
Celery, diced	4 stalks (8 ounces)	8 stalks (1 pound)	16 stalks (2 pounds)	24 stalks (3 pounds)
Prepared cornbread	1 pound	2 pounds	4 pounds	6 pounds
Dried parsley	2 teaspoons	1 tablespoon plus 1 teaspoon	3 tablespoons	⅓ cup
Dried sage	2 teaspoons	1 tablespoon plus 1 teaspoon	3 tablespoons	⅓ cup
Dried thyme	2 teaspoons	1 tablespoon plus 1 teaspoon	3 tablespoons	⅓ cup
Freshly ground black pepper	1 teaspoon	2 teaspoons	1 tablespoon plus 1 teaspoon	2 tablespoons
Salt	1 teaspoon	2 teaspoons	1 tablespoon plus 1 teaspoon	2 tablespoons
Chicken or vegetable stock	2 cups (16 ounces)	4 cups (32 ounces)	8 cups (64 ounces)	12 cups (96 ounces)
Chopped pecans or walnuts	1 cup (6 ounces)	2 cups (12 ounces)	4 cups (1½ pounds)	6 cups (36 ounces)

equipment:

- aluminum foil
- for 12 guests, use a 13 x 9 x 2-inch baking dish
- for 25 guests or more, use 3½-quart casseroles
- large mixing bowl
- large saute pan
- wooden spoon

directions:

1. Preheat the oven to 375 degrees and grease the baking dishes.

2. Heat half of the butter in a large sauté pan over medium heat. Add the onions and celery. Sauté until soft but not browned.

3. Cut the cornbread into small cubes. Combine the cornbread and sautéed vegetables in a large mixing bowl.

4. Add the parsley, sage, thyme, pepper, and salt to the cornbread mixture. Slowly add the stock until the dressing is just moist. Stir in the nuts, and spoon into the greased pan.

5. Chop the remaining butter into ¼-inch pieces and sprinkle over the top of the dressing. Cover with foil. (The dressing can be made up to this point a day in advance. Cover tightly and refrigerate until ready to bake.)

6. Bake, covered, for 35 minutes. Uncover and bake for 15 minutes longer, or until the top starts to brown.

do it ahead:

The dressing can be prepared for baking a day in advance. Cover tightly and store in the refrigerator until ready to bake. Alternatively, the dressing can be prepared completely a day in advance and reheated in a 300-degree oven just before serving.

do it for less time:

Prepare a packaged dressing mix as directed and add chopped nuts. Sprinkle the top with diced butter and bake according to the package directions.

do it for less money:

Use day-old white bread in place of fresh cornbread.

portion size: 2 ounces (one 2-inch square)

creamy mashed potatoes

ingredients	12 people	25 people	50 people	75 people
Milk	1 tablespoon	2 tablespoons	¼ cup	¼ cup plus 2 tablespoons
Russel potatoes	10 pounds	20 pounds	40 pounds	60 pounds
Heavy whipping cream	½ cup (4 ounces)	1 cup (8 ounces)	2 cups (16 ounces)	3 cups (24 ounces)
Unsalted butter, room temperature	2 sticks (8 ounces)	4 sticks (16 ounces)	8 sticks (32 ounces)	12 sticks (48 ounces)
Salt and freshly ground black pepper	to taste	to taste	to taste	to taste

do it ahead:

This dish can be made a day in advance. Cool and place in a buttered ovenproof casserole. Cover with plastic wrap, pressing the wrap directly onto the potatoes to keep a skin from forming. Remove the plastic wrap and reheat in a 250-degree oven, stirring occasionally until

directions:

1. Fill a large stockpot with cold water, and add the milk. Scrub and peel the potatoes and cut into 1-inch pieces. Place in the cold water as you go to keep them from discoloring.

2. Pour off any excess water so that the potatoes are just covered. Bring to a boil, lower the heat, and simmer until the potatoes are fork-tender.

3. Drain well. Let the potatoes air-dry for 5 minutes. Warm the cream in a saucepan over medium heat.

5. Mash the potatoes by hand or pulse in a food processor in batches. Do not over-process, as they will become gluey.

6. Stir in the butter until it has completely melted. Then stir in the warm cream, and season with salt and pepper to taste. For a smoother consistency, add more butter and cream.

portion size: 8 ounces (about 1 cup)

equipment:

- colander
- large stockpot
- medium saucepan
- potato masher, electric hand or stand mixer, or food processor
- vegetable brush
- vegetable peeler

candied yams

ingredients	12 people	25 people	50 people	75 people
Unsalted butter for greasing pans	as needed	as needed	as needed	as needed
Unsalted butter	1½ sticks (6 ounces)	3 sticks (12 ounces)	6 sticks (24 ounces)	9 sticks (36 ounces)
Canned yams, drained	11 pounds	22 pounds	43 pounds	64 pounds
Dark brown sugar	2¼ cups, packed	4½ cups, packed	9 cups, packed	13½ cups, packed

do it ahead:

This dish can be made a day in advance. Cool and refrigerate, and then reheat in a 350-degree oven before serving.

directions:

1. Preheat the oven to 350 degrees, and grease the baking pans.

2. Cut the remaining butter into ¼-inch pieces.

3. Distribute the yams evenly among the prepared pans to allow for even cooking. Sprinkle with the brown sugar, and distribute the butter evenly over the yams.

4. Cover with foil, and bake for 30 minutes. Uncover and bake for an additional 15 to 20 minutes, or until the yams are tender and slightly caramelized.

portion size: ½ cup

equipment:

- 13 x 9 x 2-inch casseroles or baking dishes
- aluminum foil

lemon broccoli

ingredients	12 people	25 people	50 people	75 people
Whole heads of broccoli	4½ pounds	9 pounds	18 pounds	27 pounds
Unsalted butter	2 sticks (8 ounces)	4 sticks (16 ounces)	8 sticks (32 ounces)	12 sticks (48 ounces)
Lemon juice	¼ cup (1½ lemons)	½ cup (3 lemons)	1 cup (6 lemons)	1½ cups (9 lemons)
Salt and freshly ground black pepper	to taste	to taste	to taste	to taste

equipment:

- colander
- large bowl or serving dish
- large saucepan
- small saucepan or microwaveable dish

directions:

1. Remove the stems from the broccoli and cut the heads into small florets.

2. Bring a large saucepan of water to a boil. Add the florets and cook until bright green and crisp-tender. Drain in a colander, and transfer the cooked broccoli to a large bowl.

3. Melt the butter in a small saucepan or in the microwave. Stir in the lemon juice.

4. Add the butter mixture to the broccoli and toss to coat. Season with salt and pepper to taste.

helpful hint: (fyi)

Look for heads of broccoli that are firm and evenly green without any yellow or brown spots.

do it ahead:

Clean and stem the broccoli and juice the lemons a day in advance.

do it for less time:

- Look for bags of ready-to-use broccoli florets in the produce section of your grocery store. You will need one-fourth less than amount called for in the recipe.

- Microwave the broccoli for quick and easy cooking.

- Use bottled lemon juice in place of freshly squeezed juice if you're short on time.

do it for less money: ($)

Save the broccoli stems. They can be chopped and frozen to use later in a soup.

portion size: about ¾ cup (3 to 4 ounces)

fresh cranberry relish

ingredients	12 people	25 people	50 people	75 people
Fresh cranberries	1½ cups	3 cups	6 cups	9 cups
Orange juice	¼ cup (1 large orange)	½ cup (1 to 2 large oranges)	1 cup (2 to 3 large oranges)	1½ cups (4 to 5 large oranges)
Chopped orange segments	¼ cup (1 large orange)	½ cup (2 large oranges)	1 cup (4 large oranges)	1½ cups (6 large oranges)
Granulated sugar	½ cup	1 cup	2 cups	3 cups
Orange zest	1½ teaspoons (½ large orange)	1 tablespoon (1 large orange)	2 tablespoons (1 to 2 large oranges)	3 tablespoons (2 to 3 large oranges)
Salt and freshly ground black pepper	to taste	to taste	to taste	to taste

(fyi) helpful hint:

If you can't find fresh cranberries, use frozen cranberries. They'll thaw as you cook them.

do it ahead:

This can be made up to two days in advance. Store covered in the refrigerator.

do it for less time:

• As an alternative to the orange segments, substitute canned and drained mandarin orange segments.

• You can also use store-bought orange juice instead of freshly squeezed.

directions:

1. Combine the cranberries, orange juice, orange segments, and sugar in a medium saucepan. Bring to a boil. Cover, lower the heat, and simmer for 15 minutes.

2. Stir in the orange zest. Simmer, uncovered, for 10 minutes, or until the cranberries are tender.

3. Season with salt and pepper, and let cool. Serve chilled or at room temperature.

equipment:

• medium saucepan with lid
• wooden
• zester or microplane grater

portion size: 1 ounce (2 tablespoons)

spiced whipped cream

ingredients	12 people	25 people	50 people	75 people
Heavy whipping cream	1 cup (8 ounces)	2 cups (16 ounces)	4 cups (32 ounces)	6 cups (48 ounces)
Granulated sugar	2 tablespoons	$\frac{1}{4}$ cup	$\frac{1}{2}$ cup	$\frac{3}{4}$ cup
Vanilla extract	1 teaspoon	2 teaspoons	1 tablespoon plus 1 teaspoon	2 tablespoons
Ground cinnamon	$\frac{1}{4}$ teaspoon	$\frac{1}{2}$ teaspoon	1 teaspoon	$1\frac{1}{2}$ teaspoons
Ground nutmeg	$\frac{1}{4}$ teaspoon	$\frac{1}{2}$ teaspoon	1 teaspoon	$1\frac{1}{2}$ teaspoons
Ground allspice	pinch	$\frac{1}{4}$ teaspoon	$\frac{1}{2}$ teaspoon	$\frac{3}{4}$ teaspoon

equipment:

- electric stand or hand mixer or large balloon whisk
- large, stainless steel mixing bowl

directions:

1. Pour the cream into a chilled, stainless steel mixing bowl. Beat on medium speed until frothy.

2. Gradually add the sugar, vanilla extract, cinnamon, nutmeg, and allspice. Beat at high speed until the cream forms soft peaks.

3. Store covered in the refrigerator and serve on the pecan pie (page 202) within an hour.

helpful hint: (fyi)

For the best volume, chill the bowl and beater in the refrigerator or freezer for at least 30 minutes before whipping the cream.

do it ahead:

The whipped cream can be made up to an hour in advance.

portion size: 1 tablespoon

pecan pie

ingredients	12 people (2 pies)	25 people (3 pies)	50 people (6 pies)	75 people (9 pies)
Granulated sugar	1 cup (7 ounces)	1½ cups (10½ ounces)	3 cups (21 ounces)	4½ cups (2 pounds)
Light brown sugar	1 cup (7 ounces)	1½ cup (10½ ounces)	3 cups (21 ounces)	4½ cups (2 pounds)
Unsalted butter	7 tablespoons (3½ ounces)	1¼ sticks (5 ounces)	2½ sticks (10 ounces)	4 sticks (16 ounces)
Salt	½ teaspoon	¾ teaspoon	1½ teaspoons	2¼ teaspoons
Large eggs, beaten	8	12	18	27
Corn syrup	2⅓ cups	3½ cups	5 cups	7½ cups
Vanilla extract	½ teaspoon	1 teaspoon	2 teaspoons	1 tablespoon
Pecans halves	12 ounces	18 ounces	36 ounces	54 ounces
Unbaked pie shells (page 203)	2	3	6	9

(fyi) helpful hint:

As an alternative to the pecans, try walnuts, hazelnuts, or Brazil nuts.

do it ahead:

The whole pie can be made a day in advance. Cool, and then store in an airtight container at room temperature.

directions:

1. Preheat the oven to 350 degrees.

2. Place the sugar, brown sugar, butter, and salt in a mixing bowl or food processor. Mix until all the ingredients are evenly blended.

3. Gradually add the eggs, mixing constantly until absorbed.

4. Add the corn syrup and vanilla. Mix well.

5. Fill each pie shell (see opposite page), with the egg mixture. Arrange the pecan halves in a circular pattern on the surface of the filling, starting on the outside edge and filling in toward the middle.

6. Bake for 40 to 50 minutes, or until the edge of the crust is lightly browned and the filling is set. If the crust begins to brown too quickly, cover with aluminum foil for the remainder of the baking.

equipment:

- aluminum foil
- electric stand mixer or food processor
- spatula

portion size: ⅛ to ⅒ of a pie

pie crust

ingredients	12 people (2 crusts)	25 people (3 crusts)	50 people (6 crusts)	75 people (9 crusts)
Unsalted butter for greasing pans	as needed	as needed	as needed	as needed
Unsalted butter, chilled	2½ sticks (10 ounces)	4 sticks (18 ounces)	9 sticks (36 ounces)	13½ sticks (54 ounces)
All-purpose flour	2½ cups (10 ounces)	5 cups (20 ounces)	10 cups (40 ounces)	15 cups (60 ounces)
Granulated sugar	⅓ cup	⅔ cup	1½ cups	2 cups plus 2 tablespoons
Salt	1 teaspoon	2 teaspoons	1 tablespoon plus 1 teaspoon	2 tablespoons
Egg yolks	2	4	8	12

equipment:

- 9-inch pie pans
- plastic wrap
- electric hand or stand mixer or food processor

directions:

1. Grease the pie pans.

2. Cut the remaining butter into ¼-inch pieces.

3. If using an electric mixer, combine the flour, sugar, and salt in the mixing bowl. Add the chilled butter, and blend just until the mixture resembles small peas.

4. Add the egg yolks, one at a time, until absorbed. Continue mixing on low speed until smooth and evenly blended.

5. Alternatively, if using a food processor, place the flour, butter, sugar, and salt, in the bowl of the food processor. Pulse until the mixture resembles small peas. With the motor running, add the egg yolks through the pour tube. Continue running until the mixture comes together and forms a dough. Add a little water or milk if necessary.

6. Cut the dough into equal-sized pieces—2 pieces for 2 crusts, 3 pieces for 3 crusts, and so forth.

7. Flatten each portion of dough into a disk, and cover tightly with plastic wrap. Chill for at least 1 hour. (You can prepare the dough to this point up to 2 days in advance and refrigerate until ready to proceed.)

8. On a floured surface, roll out each disk into 14-inch circles. Lay the dough over the pie plate, gently press into the pan, crimp the edges with your fingers, and trim the edges with a knife.

9. Cover with plastic wrap and chill for at least 30 minutes before filling. (The pie dough can be frozen for up to 1 week before filling. Thaw in the refrigerator for at least 3 hours before using.)

helpful hint:

This pie bakes up so rich in flavor that we recommend small slices for your guests.

do it ahead:

The dough can be made up to a week in advance and frozen, or up to two days in advance and refrigerated.

do it for less time:

Though homemade tastes decidedly better, you can use store-bought frozen pie crusts or the unfold-and-bake pie crust dough found in the same section as refrigerated cookie dough.

portion size: 1 pie crust per 8 to 10 guests

Walnut, Spinach, and Asparagus Strudel

Sesame Honey-Baked Chicken Wings

Muffuletta Sandwiches

Lemon-Caper Potato Salad

Marinated Cherry Tomato Salad

Apple-Pecan Coffee Cake
with Apple Cider Glaze

Fresh Seasonal Fruit Salad

Sangria

spring on the terrace

Enjoy the fresh air with this al fresco menu for an outdoor concert, family outing to the country, or bridal shower on the patio or in the sunroom.

spring menu:

walnut, spinach, and asparagus strudel
sesame honey-baked chicken wings
muffuletta sandwiches
lemon-caper potato salad
marinated cherry tomato salad
apple-pecan coffee cake with apple cider glaze
fresh seasonal fruit salad*
sangria

* See page 62 for instructions on preparing a seasonal fruit salad.

decorating ideas:

colors. Natural garden colors like grassy green, bark, violet, sky blue, honeysuckle white, and bursts of bright yellow.

invitations. Cut hand-drawn daisies out of white card stock and watercolor a yellow interior. Write the invitation along the outline of the back petals, or paste the daisies onto note cards. Attach an invitation to a small packet of seeds with raffia, and mail in a homemade butcher-paper envelope. For a party that will last into evening, tie a few sparklers onto the invitation for use after dark. Use clear stickers with pressed violets on mint green note cards. Seal the matching envelope with another sticker.

table linens. Use unexpected gingham colors like blue, pink, or yellow, or colorful striped or polka-dotted fabrics. Mix with solid or gossamer linens and simple plates.

decorations. Choose flowers that evoke summer such as sunflowers, daisies, or buttercups. Fill pitchers or galvanized florist buckets with fresh-cut flowers or meandering ivy. Buy pre-made cupcakes with white icing and sprinkle with edible colored beads. Pile them high on a colored-glass cake pedestal to serve as both the centerpiece and an extra dessert. Use clean terracotta pots, colored metal buckets, or picnic hampers for napkins, rolls, or flatware. Tie raffia or gingham ribbon around the napkins. Use old paned window frames to create a rustic backdrop for the buffet.

place cards and favors. Write the guests' names on small cards and attach to helium-filled balloons. Tie the balloons on the back of each chair with ribbon. Plant miniature violets or assorted herbs in small white bowls and prop the name cards against the bowls. Send the violets home with the guests as party favors.

entertainment. Play country classics like Patsy Cline or bluegrass for a bit of hillbilly chic.

menu countdown

1 week before:
- Shop for non-perishables.
- Buy beverages.
- Make coffee cake and freeze, but do not glaze.

3 days before:
- Make space in refrigerator and freezer.

2 days before:
- Shop for perishables.
- Marinate chicken wings.

1 day before:
- Set up tables and décor.
- Prepare strudel, but do not bake.
- Cook chicken wings.
- Assemble muffulettas.
- Make potato salad.
- Slice tomatoes and make the dressing, but do not toss.
- Slice fruit for sangria and chill.

morning of the party:
- Buy ice.
- Defrost and glaze coffee cake.
- Make sangria, omitting chilled wine and orange juice.

1 to 2 hours ahead:
- Bake strudel.
- Dress and toss the tomato salad.
- Bring chicken wings to room temperature or reheat in oven.

just before serving:
- Slice strudel.
- Add chilled wine and orange juice to sangria.

spring on the terrace shopping list: 1 to 2 weeks before

ingredients	12 people	25 people	50 people	75 people
alcohol				
Dry red wine	2 (750-ml) bottles	4 (750-ml) bottles	8 (750-ml) bottles	12 (750-ml) bottles
Mirin or seasoned rice vinegar	6 ounces	12 ounces	24 ounces	36 ounces
Orange liqueur	4 ounces	8 ounces	16 ounces	24 ounces
Rum	24 ounces	48 ounces	96 ounces	144 ounces
pantry items & dry goods				
All-purpose flour	9 ounces	18 ounces	36 ounces	56 ounces
Apple cider	1$\frac{1}{2}$ ounces	3 ounces	6 ounces	9 ounces
Baking powder	$\frac{1}{4}$ ounce	$\frac{1}{2}$ ounce	1 ounce	2 ounces
Baking soda	$\frac{1}{4}$ ounce	$\frac{1}{4}$ ounce	$\frac{1}{2}$ ounce	1 ounce
Balsamic vinegar	3 ounces	6 ounces	12 ounces	18 ounces
Capers	2 ounces	3 ounces	6 ounces	9 ounces
Dijon mustard	$\frac{1}{2}$ ounce	1 ounce	2 ounces	3 ounces
Extra-virgin olive oil	12 ounces	24 ounces	48 ounces	72 ounces
Granulated sugar	1$\frac{1}{2}$ pounds	3 pounds	5 pounds	8$\frac{1}{2}$ pounds
Honey	3 ounces	6 ounces	12 ounces	18 ounces
Honey-mustard dressing	16 ounces	32 ounces	64 ounces	96 ounces
Kalamata olives	1$\frac{1}{4}$ pounds	2$\frac{1}{2}$ pounds	5 pounds	7$\frac{1}{2}$ pounds
Light brown sugar	8 ounces	1 pound	2 pounds	3 pounds
Pecans, chopped	12 ounces	1$\frac{1}{2}$ pounds	3 pounds	4$\frac{1}{2}$ pounds
Powdered sugar	8 ounces	1 pound	2 pounds	3 pounds
Sesame seeds	1 ounce	2 ounces	4 ounces	6 ounces
Soy sauce	8 ounces	16 ounces	32 ounces	48 ounces
Toasted sesame oil	1$\frac{1}{2}$ ounces	3 ounces	6 ounces	9 ounces
Walnut pieces	2$\frac{1}{2}$ ounces	5 ounces	10 ounces	14 ounces
dried herbs, spices, & extracts				
Black peppercorns	as needed	as needed	as needed	as needed
Dried basil	$\frac{1}{4}$ ounce	$\frac{1}{4}$ ounce	$\frac{1}{2}$ ounce	$\frac{1}{2}$ ounce
Ground cinnamon	$\frac{1}{4}$ ounce	$\frac{1}{4}$ ounce	$\frac{1}{2}$ ounce	$\frac{1}{2}$ ounce
Ground nutmeg	$\frac{1}{4}$ ounce	$\frac{1}{4}$ ounce	$\frac{1}{2}$ ounce	$\frac{1}{2}$ ounce
Salt	as needed	as needed	as needed	as needed
Vanilla extract	$\frac{1}{4}$ ounce	$\frac{1}{4}$ ounce	$\frac{1}{2}$ ounce	$\frac{1}{2}$ ounce
frozen foods				
Frozen chopped spinach	10 ounces	1$\frac{1}{4}$ pounds	2$\frac{1}{2}$ pounds	3$\frac{3}{4}$ pounds
Frozen puff pastry	1 pound	2 pounds	4 pounds	6 pounds

ingredients	12 people	25 people	50 people	75 people
baked goods				
French baguette	2 loaves	4 loaves	8 loaves	12 loaves
produce				
Asparagus	12 ounces	1½ pounds	3 pounds	4½ pounds
Cherry tomatoes	5 pints (or 3 pounds regular tomatoes)	10 pints (or 6 pounds regular tomatoes)	20 pints (or 12 pounds regular tomatoes)	30 pints (or 18 pounds regular tomatoes)
Fresh basil	4 ounces	8 ounces	16 ounces	24 ounces
Fresh dill	½ ounce	¾ ounce	1½ ounces	2¼ ounces
Fresh ginger	3 ounces	6 ounces	12 ounces	18 ounces
Fresh oregano	¼ ounce	¼ ounce	½ ounce	½ ounce
Fresh parsley	½ ounce	¾ ounce	1½ ounces	2¼ ounces
Garlic	2 heads	4 heads	8 heads	12 heads
Green onions	3 bunches	6 bunches	12 bunches	18 bunches
Large Granny Smith apples	3	6	12	18
Lemons	5	10	20	30
Limes	4	8	16	24
Oranges	2	4	8	12
Shallots	1½ ounces	3 ounces	6 ounces	9 ounces
Small red or white potatoes	3½ pounds	7 pounds	14 pounds	21 pounds
dairy, cheese, & deli				
Assorted deli cheeses, thinly sliced	12 ounces	1½ pounds	3 pounds	4½ pounds
Assorted deli meats, thinly sliced	12 ounces	1½ pounds	3 pounds	4½ pounds
Cream cheese	1 pound	2 pounds	4 pounds	6 pounds
Large eggs	6	12	24	26
Unsalted butter	10 ounces	1¼ pounds	2¼ pounds	3½ pounds
meat & seafood				
Chicken wings	36 (4 to 5 pounds)	75 (8 to 10 pounds)	144 (16 to 20 pounds)	225 (24 to 30 pounds)
miscellaneous				
Orange juice	1 pint	1 quart	2 quart	3 quarts

Always take a calculator when shopping for quantity recipes to quickly and easily calculate the most appropriate package sizes for your particular needs. We have listed most items in ounces so that you are not limited to size-specific packaging if shopping in bulk. When in doubt over what amount to buy, always round up—it's far better to have a little extra of an ingredient than to run out while cooking. If your eighth-grade algebra skills have gotten rusty, remember that there are 16 ounces in a pound and 8 fluid ounces in a cup. See page 73 for additional conversions.

walnut, spinach, and asparagus strudel

ingredients	12 people	25 people	50 people	75 people
Asparagus, trimmed	¾ pound	1½ pounds	3 pounds	4½ pounds
Frozen chopped spinach, thawed and drained very well	10 ounces	20 ounces (1¼ pounds)	40 ounces (2½ pounds)	60 ounces (3¾ pounds)
Cream cheese, softened	1 pound (16 ounces)	2 pounds (32 ounces)	4 pounds (64 ounces)	6 pounds (96 ounces)
Chopped green onion	¼ cup	½ cup	1 cup	1½ cups
Minced garlic	2 teaspoons	1 tablespoon plus 1 teaspoon	2 tablespoons plus 2 teaspoons	3 tablespoons
Salt	¾ teaspoon	1½ teaspoons	1 tablespoon	1 tablespoon plus 1½ teaspoons
Freshly ground black pepper	¼ teaspoon	½ teaspoon	1 teaspoon	1½ teaspoons
Egg yolks, beaten and divided	4	8	16	24
Chopped walnuts	½ cup	1 cup	2 cups	3 cups
All-purpose flour for dusting	as needed	as needed	as needed	as needed
Frozen puff pastry, thawed	2 sheets (1 pound)	4 sheets (2 pounds)	8 sheets (4 pounds)	12 sheets (6 pounds)
Honey-mustard dressing	2 cups	4 cups	8 cups	12 cups

(fyi) helpful hints:

• To dry the thawed spinach, place it in the center of a clean kitchen towel. Twist the towel tightly around the spinach, squeezing the towel to extract all the liquid. Repeat if necessary.

• For best results with this recipe, use pencil-thin asparagus. If using regular or thick asparagus, peel the ends.

do it ahead:

The strudel can be prepared a day in advance through step 7. Cover tightly with plastic wrap and refrigerate until ready to brush with the egg yolk and bake.

($) do it for less money:

Omit the asparagus and double the spinach for a less-expensive version of this recipe.

directions:

1. Preheat the oven to 375 degrees. Fill the stockpots with water and bring to a boil over medium heat. Divide the asparagus among the stockpots, and boil for 30 seconds, or until bright green. Drain the blanched asparagus in a colander.

2. Place the spinach, cream cheese, green onions, and garlic in a large bowl, and mix until thoroughly combined. Season with the salt and pepper. Stir in half the beaten egg yolks and all the walnuts. (Save the remaining yolks to brush on the strudel before baking.)

3. Dust a work surface with flour. Place the puff pastry on the work surface and roll out each piece into a 9 x 12-inch rectangle.

4. Divide the spinach mixture in half. Spread the mixture 2 to 3 inches in width along the center length of the pastry, to within 1 inch of the ends.

5. Lay the asparagus, 2 to 3 pieces wide and end-to-end, in the spinach mixture. (The asparagus may need to be trimmed to fit properly.)

6. Fold the ends over the filling. Bring the upper edge of the pastry over the filling. Lightly brush the lower edge of the pastry with the beaten egg, then fold the lower edge of the pastry over the filling. The filling should be completely covered.

7. Gently pinch the seams together. Place the strudels, seam-sides down, on ungreased baking sheets. (The strudel can be prepared up to this point a day in advance. Cover tightly and refrigerate until ready to bake.)

8. Brush with the remaining beaten egg yolks. Bake for 30 to 40 minutes, or until the pastry is puffed and golden.

9. Remove from the oven and let the strudels cool for 10 minutes. Using a spatula, gently loosen the strudels from the baking sheets, and transfer to cooling racks.

10. Just before serving and when completely cooled, cut each strudel into 12 equal pieces using a serrated knife. Serve with the honey-mustard dressing.

portion size: 1 piece

equipment:

• baking sheets
• cooling racks
• colander
• large stockpots with lids
• mixing bowl
• pastry brush
• rolling pin
• serrated knife
• spatula

sesame honey-baked chicken wings

ingredients	12 people	25 people	50 people	75 people
Chicken wings	36 (4 to 5 pounds)	75 (8 to 10 pounds)	150 (16 to 20 pounds)	225 (24 to 30 pounds)
Soy sauce	1 cup	2 cups	3 cups	5 cups
Mirin or seasoned rice vinegar	3/4 cup	1 1/2 cups	3 cups	4 1/2 cups
Honey	1/4 cup	1/2 cup	1 cup	1 1/2 cups
Minced fresh ginger	2 tablespoons	1/4 cup	1/2 cup	3/4 cup
Minced garlic	2 tablespoons	1/4 cup	1/2 cup	3/4 cup
Sliced green onions	1 cup	2 cups	3 cups	5 cups
Toasted sesame oil	3 tablespoons	1/4 cup plus 2 tablespoons	3/4 cup	1 cup plus 2 tablespoons
Sesame seeds	3 tablespoons	1/4 cup plus 2 tablespoons	3/4 cup	1 cup plus 2 tablespoons

equipment:

- baking sheets
- large mixing bowl

directions:

1. Cut the end joints from the chicken wings.

2. Combine the soy sauce, mirin, honey, ginger, garlic, green onions, and sesame oil in a large mixing bowl. Add the chicken wings, and stir to coat.

3. Cover and refrigerate overnight or up to a day to marinate.

4. Preheat the oven to 350 degrees, and arrange the marinated chicken on baking sheets. Bake for about 1 hour, or until the chicken is cooked through.

5. Sprinkle with the sesame seeds, and serve warm or at room temperature.

helpful hints:

- Substitute chicken breasts or thighs and serve as an entrée.

- Mirin is a low-alcohol wine made from rice. It adds sweetness to a variety of Asian dishes. If you cannot find it in the specialty or wine section of your grocery store, use seasoned rice vinegar.

do it ahead:

The wings can be prepared a day in advance and stored in the refrigerator. Bring to room temperature or reheat in the oven before serving.

do it for less time:

As a time-saver, look for pre-chopped garlic and ginger in the produce section of your grocery store.

portion size: 3 chicken wings

muffuletta sandwiches

ingredients	12 people	25 people	50 people	75 people
Pitted kalamata olives	3 cups (20 ounces)	6 cups (40 ounces)	12 cups (80 ounces)	20 cups (160 ounces)
Extra-virgin olive oil	1/3 cup	2/3 cup	1 1/3 cups	2 cups
Coarsely chopped garlic	1 tablespoon	2 tablespoons	1/4 cup	1/3 cup
Rinsed and drained capers	3 tablespoons	1/4 cup plus 2 tablespoons	3/4 cup	1 cup plus 1 tablespoon
Balsamic vinegar	2 tablespoons	1/4 cup	1/2 cup	3/4 cup
Chopped fresh basil	1/2 cup	1 cup	2 cups	3 cups
Chopped fresh oregano	1 tablespoon	2 tablespoons	1/4 cup	1/3 cup
Salt and freshly ground black pepper	to taste	to taste	to taste	to taste
French baguette	2 loaves	4 loaves	8 loaves	12 loaves
Assorted deli cheeses, thinly sliced	12 ounces	24 ounces (1 1/2 pounds)	48 ounces (3 pounds)	72 ounces (4 1/2 pounds)
Assorted deli meats, thinly sliced	12 ounces	24 ounces (1 1/2 pounds)	48 ounces (3 pounds)	72 ounces (4 1/2 pounds)

(fyi) helpful hint:

The traditional meats and cheese used are salami, ham, and provolone, but you can use any of your favorite deli selections.

do it ahead:

These delicious New Orleans-style sandwiches can be made the night before the party if wrapped well in plastic wrap and refrigerated.

do it for less time:

Instead of making the olive spread from scratch, look for jars of pre-made tapenade in your local grocery store. Or, use a mixture of mayonnaise and store-bought pesto as an alternative to the olive spread.

($) do it for less money:

Use small black olives if you are unable to find kalamata olives.

directions:

1. Place the olives, olive oil, garlic, capers, balsamic vinegar, basil, and oregano in the bowl of a food processor. Process until the mixture is finely chopped and forms a slightly chunky paste. Taste and season with salt and pepper, and allow the mixture to stand for 30 minutes.

2. Remove the rounded ends from the loaves of bread. Cut the bread in half horizontally, and spread each half of the bread with the olive spread.

3. Layer the meats and cheeses on the bottom halves of the bread. Replace the top halves of the bread. (The sandwiches can be wrapped tightly in plastic and refrigerated overnight at this point.)

4. Cut each loaf of bread into eight 2-inch sandwiches. Secure the portion with toothpicks to keep the sandwiches intact.

equipment:

- cocktail spears or toothpicks
- food processor
- serrated knife
- spatula or knife spreader

portion size: 1 sandwich

lemon-caper potato salad

ingredients	12 people	25 people	50 people	75 people
Small red or white potatoes	3½ pounds	7 pounds	14 pounds	21 pounds
Extra-virgin olive oil	½ cup	1 cup	2 cups	3 cups
Lemons, juiced and zested	3	6	12	18
Minced shallots	3 tablespoons	¼ cup plus 2 tablespoons	¾ cup	1 cup plus 1 tablespoon
Chopped fresh parsley	2 tablespoons	¼ cup	½ cup	¾ cup
Chopped fresh dill	3 tablespoons	¼ cup plus 2 tablespoons	¾ cup	1 cup plus 1 tablespoon
Salt and freshly ground black pepper	to taste	to taste	to taste	to taste
Rinsed and drained capers	2 tablespoons	¼ cup	¼ cup plus 2 tablespoons	½ cup plus 1 tablespoon

equipment:

- colander
- large mixing bowl
- stockpot
- vegetable brush
- whisk
- wooden spoon or disposable gloves
- zester or microplane grater

directions:

1. Scrub the potatoes and cut into quarters.

2. Place in the stockpot and fill with enough water to completely cover the potatoes by 1 inch. Bring the water to a boil, reduce the heat, and simmer until the potatoes are just tender. Drain in a colander.

3. In a bowl large enough to hold the potatoes, whisk together the olive oil, lemon juice, lemon zest, shallots, parsley, and dill until well combined. Season with salt and pepper to taste.

4. Add the warm potatoes and the capers to the bowl. Toss gently with a wooden spoon or your hands (wearing disposable plastic gloves) to coat with the dressing. Serve warm, or refrigerate and serve chilled.

do it ahead:

This dish can be prepared up to a day in advance. Cover and refrigerate until ready to serve.

do it for less time:

- Buy a regular potato salad from the deli section of your grocery store and spice it up by adding capers, fresh dill, and lemon zest.

- If time is short, use bottled lemon juice in place of freshly squeezed juice, or use a combination of fresh and bottled juice. If time is really precious, omit the zest and use only bottled lemon juice. The lemon flavor will be less intense, so adjust the amount of juice to your liking for a stronger punch.

portion size: 6 ounces

marinated cherry tomato salad

ingredients	12 people	25 people	50 people	75 people
Cherry tomatoes	5 pints (or 3 pounds regular tomatoes)	10 pints (or 6 pounds regular tomatoes)	20 pints (or 12 pounds regular tomatoes)	30 pints (or 18 pounds regular tomatoes)
Green onions, thinly sliced	1 bunch	2 bunches	4 bunches	6 bunches
Dijon mustard	2 teaspoons	1 tablespoon plus 1½ teaspoons	3 tablespoons	¼ cup plus 2 tablespoons
Minced garlic	1 teaspoon	2 teaspoons	1 tablespoon plus 1 teaspoon	2 tablespoons
Dried basil	1 teaspoon	2 teaspoons	1 tablespoon plus 1 teaspoon	2 tablespoons
Salt and freshly ground black pepper	to taste	to taste	to taste	to taste
Balsamic vinegar	⅓ cup	⅔ cup	1⅓ cups	2 cups
Extra-virgin olive oil	⅔ cup	1⅓ cups	2⅔ cups	4 cups
Fresh basil, chopped	1 bunch (about 3 ounces)	2 bunches (about 6 ounces)	4 bunches (about 12 ounces)	6 bunches (about 18 ounces)

(fyi) helpful hints:

• In the heat of the summer, home-grown tomatoes create an outstanding salad. If available, use a mixture of teardrop or heirloom tomatoes in red, yellow, and orange for a colorful salad. Look for them at your local farmers' market. For the rest of the year, cherry and Roma tomatoes have the most consistent flavor.

• For the roasted tomato version, buy double the amount of tomatoes to allow for reduction during roasting.

do it for less time:

For the chilled salad version, the tomatoes can be prepped and the dressing can be made a day in advance. Toss the tomatoes with the dressing 2 hours before serving to allow the flavors to meld.

($) do it for less money:

You can stretch this recipe by adding peeled and diced cucumber or thinly sliced red onions to the chilled salad. Look for end-of-day bargains just before closing time at farmers' markets.

directions:

1. Cut the cherry tomatoes in half (or seed and roughly chop the regular tomatoes). Place in a mixing bowl, and toss in the green onions.

2. In another mixing bowl, whisk the mustard, garlic, dried basil, salt, pepper, and balsamic vinegar until smooth.

3. Slowly drizzle in the oil while whisking constantly until mixture emulsifies. Taste and adjust the seasonings as needed. (The salad can be prepared up to this point a day in advance.)

4. Pour the marinade over the tomato mixture. Add the fresh basil and toss well.

5. Cover well, and refrigerate the salad for 1½ hours.

6. Remove the salad from the refrigerator and allow to stand at room temperature for 30 minutes before serving.

7. Alternatively, you can serve a warmed roasted tomato side dish. Preheat the oven to 250 degrees. Cut the cherry tomatoes in half and squeeze to remove the seeds. (Or roughly chop and seed the regular tomatoes.) Spread the tomatoes on large baking pans.

8. Whisk the mustard, garlic, dried basil, salt, pepper, and balsamic vinegar together in a mixing bowl until smooth. Slowly drizzle in the olive oil in a steady stream, whisking constantly until the mixture has emulsified. Taste and adjust the seasonings as needed. Drizzle the sauce over the tomatoes and roast for 2 to 3 hours.

9. Stir the green onions and fresh basil into the roasted tomatoes, and serve immediately.

equipment:

• 2 mixing bowls
• whisk

portion size: about ½ cup

apple-pecan coffee cake

ingredients	12 people (1 cake)	25 people (2 cakes)	50 people (4 cakes)	75 people (6 cakes)
Unsalted butter for greasing pans	1 tablespoon (½ ounce)	2 tablespoons (1 ounce)	4 tablespoons (2 ounces)	6 tablespoons (3 ounces)
Unsalted butter, softened	2 sticks (8 ounces)	4 sticks (16 ounces)	8 sticks (32 ounces)	12 sticks (48 ounces)
Granulated sugar	1¼ cups	2½ cups	5 cups	7½ cups
Light brown sugar	1 cup	2 cups	4 cups	6 cups
Large eggs, room temperature	2	4	8	12
All-purpose flour	2 cups	4 cups	8 cups	12 cups
Baking powder	1 teaspoon	2 teaspoons	1 tablespoon	1 tablespoon plus 1½ teaspoons
Baking soda	¾ teaspoon	1½ teaspoons	1 tablespoon	1 tablespoon plus 1½ teaspoons
Salt	½ teaspoon	1 teaspoon	2 teaspoons	3 teaspoons
Ground nutmeg	½ teaspoon	1 teaspoon	2 teaspoons	3 teaspoons
Ground cinnamon	½ teaspoon	1 teaspoon	2 teaspoons	3 teaspoons
Chopped pecans	1½ cups	3 cups	6 cups	9 cups
Peeled, cored, and diced Granny Smith apples	3 cups (3 large apples)	6 cups (6 large apples)	12 cups (12 large apples)	20 cups (20 large apples)

equipment:

- cooling rack
- electric hand or stand mixer
- mixing bowls
- spatula
- tube or Bundt pan
- wooden spoon

directions:

1. Preheat the oven to 350 degrees and grease the tube pan well.

2. Place the remaining butter, granulated sugar, and brown sugar in a mixing bowl. Beat for 2 minutes, or until the mixture is light and creamy.

3. Add the eggs, one at a time, and continue to beat until well combined.

4. In a separate bowl, sift together the flour, baking powder, baking soda, salt, nutmeg, and cinnamon.

5. Gradually add the flour mixture in batches, stirring well until thoroughly combined and smooth.

6. Stir in the pecans and apples.

7. Scrape the mixture into the prepared pan. Bake for 50 to 60 minutes, or until a toothpick or skewer inserted into the center of the cake comes out clean.

8. Remove from the oven, allow to cool for 15 minutes in the pan, and invert the cake onto a cooling rack. (The cake can be made up to this point a week in advance and frozen.)

9. Drizzle the warm cake with the Apple Cider Glaze (page 215). Serve warm or at room temperature.

helpful hints: fyi

- As an alternative to the apples, try peaches or fresh blueberries.

- For 25 guests or fewer, slice this cake into 12 pieces. For more than 25 guests, slice into 16 pieces.

- You can use any firm green apple that will hold up for baking.

do it ahead:

This cake can be made a week in advance and frozen. Thaw the morning of the party at room temperature, and then warm slightly in 350-degree oven before glazing. Or, bake and glaze a day in advance and store in an airtight container at room temperature.

do it for less time:

Look for bags of pre-diced apples in the produce or freezer section of your grocery store. Thaw if frozen, and then use as directed for fresh apples. If you're really short on time, purchase a coffee cake from a bakery and arrange the slices on a platter.

portion size: 1/12 or 1/16 slices of cake

apple cider glaze

ingredients	12 people	25 people	50 people	75 people
Powdered sugar	2 cups	4 cups	8 cups	12 cups
Vanilla extract	1/2 teaspoon	1 teaspoon	2 teaspoons	1 tablespoon
Apple cider	3 tablespoons	1/4 cup plus 2 tablespoons	3/4 cup	1 cup

(fyi) helpful hint:

You can use apple juice, whole milk, or even water supplemented with extra vanilla in place of the apple cider.

do it for less time:

If you don't have time to make the glaze, pour a can of store-bought vanilla frosting in a small saucepan. Heat on low, stirring constantly until liquid enough to pour. Drizzle over cake and serve.

directions:

1. Sift the powdered sugar into a mixing bowl.

2. Add the vanilla extract and apple cider, and stir until the mixture forms a thick glaze. Add more apple cider as needed to make the glaze easy to pour.

3. Drizzle the glaze over the warm, baked coffee cake (page 213) the morning of the party.

equipment:

- mixing bowl
- sifter or sieve
- wooden spoon

sangria

ingredients	**12** people	**25** people	**50** people	**75** people
Rum, chilled	3 cups (24 ounces)	6 cups (48 ounces)	12 cups (96 ounces)	18 cups (144 ounces)
Orange liqueur, chilled	$\frac{1}{2}$ cup	1 cup	2 cups	3 cups
Granulated sugar	1 cup	2 cups	4 cups	6 cups
Oranges, thinly sliced and chilled	2	4	8	12
Lemons, thinly sliced and chilled	2	4	8	12
Limes, thinly sliced and chilled	4	8	16	24
Dry red wine, chilled	2 (750-ml) bottles	4 (750-ml) bottles	8 (750-ml) bottles	12 (750-ml) bottles
Orange juice, chilled	2 cups (16 ounces)	4 cups (32 ounces)	8 cups (64 ounces)	12 cups (96 ounces)

equipment:

- ladle
- large pitcher or punch bowl

directions:

1. Place the chilled rum, orange liqueur, and sugar in a large glass pitcher or punch bowl. Stir well until the sugar has dissolved. Add the sliced fruit.

2. Cover and refrigerate for 3 hours to allow the flavors to develop.

3. To serve, add the chilled wine and orange juice to sangria. Stir, pressing lightly on the fruit to extract their juices.

4. Taste and add additional sugar if needed.

helpful hint: (fyi)

Sangria takes its name from the Spanish word for "blood." The characteristic red color comes from the red wine that serves as a base for the drink. However, sangria is every bit as delicious with white wine substituted for the red. Use the same amount of white wine as the recipe dictates for the red for an equally refreshing variation.

do it ahead:

The day before the party, chill the alcohol and the juice, and slice the fruit and freeze in resealable plastic storage bags.

do it for less time:

Serve from a punch bowl and let guests help themselves.

do it for less money: ($)

Substitute an inexpensive vodka for the rum; the flavors of the fruit will enhance either alcohol.

portion size: 6 ounces ($\frac{3}{4}$ cup)

215

Coconut Shrimp

Island-Style Chicken
with Mango Salsa

Hawaiian Baked Beans

Honey-Barbecued Pork Ribs

Pineapple and Golden Raisin
Rice Salad

Macademia and
White Chocolate Chunk Cookies

Passion Fruit Iced Tea

on the beach luau

Embrace the spirit of the islands with your next company picnic, Hawaiian-style wedding reception, or 21st birthday.

coconut shrimp
island-style chicken with mango salsa
hawaiian baked beans
honey-barbecued pork ribs
pineapple and golden raisin rice salad
macadamia and white chocolate chunk cookies*
passion fruit iced tea**

* Skip the cookies, and arrange an exotic fruit display with whole papaya, pomegranate, star fruit, kiwi, coconut, mango, and pineapple. Cut the papayas and pomegranate in half; do not remove the seeds. Arrange them, seed-side up, on a bed of shredded coconut on a large platter. Nestle lime wedges between the papayas. After dinner, turn the display into fruit salad and serve it for dessert with ice cream or sorbet.

** Passion fruit iced tea is available in tea-bag form.

decorating ideas:

colors. All shades of sea blue, ocean green, mimosa orange, pineapple yellow, sunset red, or hibiscus pink.

Invitations. Use one of the many new colored vellum papers to create a beautiful invitation. Layer blue with green, orange with red, red with pink, or yellow with orange; push the color envelope. Mix and match for a striking combination. If you prefer a more subtle effect, go for a white-on-white theme, combining the colors of starfish, sand, linen, milk glass, and orchids.

table linens. Match the table to the invitations, choosing a base color tablecloth and covering it with fishnets or a contrasting sheer color. Use different colored sarongs on multiple tables or straw mats as placemats. Wrap napkins in banana leaves and tie with raffia. Attach paper grass skirts around the table or the base of each chair for an island feel.

decorations. Create exotic island flower arrangements with orchids, birds of paradise, and ginger root. Use feathery ferns and pineapples for an inexpensive centerpiece.

For a more casual affair, use a surf board on a long table as the centerpiece. Fill longneck beer bottles with sand and tiny shells. Line the front walkway with tiki torches. Hang a swinging hammock on the back porch. Use island instruments like xylophones and drums to supplement the decorations.

place cards and favors. Place a lei and name card at each table setting. Slick paper umbrellas into the skins of whole fruits, and prop the place cards against the umbrellas. Crack coconuts and drain their juice. Make a slit in the back of the coconut meat, and insert name cards for each place. Serve the first course of coconut shrimp in the coconut, as we did in the cover photograph. Purchase dashboard-dancing hula girls, and use them to hold the name cards. Give each guest a set of flip-flops to wear at the party and take home.

entertainment. Hire a hula dancer for the evening. Download tracks of traditional Hawaiian slack-string guitar or ukulele music.

menu countdown

1 week before:
• Shop for non-perishables.
• Buy beverages.
• Bake and freeze cookies.

3 days before:
• Make space in refrigerator and freezer.

2 days before:
• Shop for perishables.

1 day before:
• Set up tables and décor.
• Chop onion and juice the limes for salsa.
• Peel and devein the shrimp.
• Cook barbecued pork.
• Make sauce for chicken.
• Cook baked beans.
• Prepare rice salad and dressing, but do not toss together.
• Make and chill passion fruit tea.

morning of the party:
• Buy ice.
• Defrost cookies.

1 to 2 hours ahead:
• Reheat pork.
• Cook chicken.
• Reheat baked beans.
• Toss rice salad.
• Make salsa.

just before serving:
• Cook coconut shrimp.

on the beach luau shopping list: 1 to 2 weeks before

ingredients	12 people	25 people	50 people	75 people
alcohol				
Beer	8 ounces	16 ounces	32 ounces	48 ounces
pantry items & dry goods				
All-purpose flour	10½ ounces	21 ounces	42 ounces	63 ounces
Apple cider vinegar	24 ounces	48 ounces	96 ounces	144 ounces
Baking powder	¼ ounce	¼ ounce	½ ounce	¾ ounce
Baking soda	¼ ounce	¼ ounce	½ ounce	1 ounce
Barbecue sauce	14 ounces	32 ounces	64 ounces	96 ounces
Canned great Northern or white beans	60 ounces	120 ounces	240 ounces	360 ounces
Cornstarch	1½ ounces	3 ounces	6 ounces	9 ounces
Dark brown sugar	1¾ pounds	3½ pounds	7 pounds	10 pounds
Dijon mustard	1¼ ounces	3 ounces	6 ounces	9 ounces
Extra-virgin olive oil	3 ounces	6 ounces	12 ounces	16 ounces
Golden raisins	8 ounces	1 pound	2 pounds	3 pounds
Granulated sugar	2 ounces	4 ounces	8 ounces	12 ounces
Honey	18 ounces	36 ounces	72 ounces	108 ounces
Ketchup	24 ounces	48 ounces	96 ounces	144 ounces
Long-grain white rice	1¼ pounds	2½ pounds	5 pounds	7½ pounds
Macadamia nuts, chopped	5 ounces	10 ounces	20 ounces	30 ounces
Molasses	3 ounces	6 ounces	10 ounces	16 ounces
Soy sauce	13 ounces	26 ounces	52 ounces	78 ounces
Unsweetened shredded coconut	10 ounces	18 ounces	36 ounces	54 ounces
Vegetable or canola oil	32 ounces	64 ounces	128 ounces	192 ounces
White chocolate or chocolate chips	6 ounces	12 ounces	24 ounces	36 ounces
Worcestershire sauce	½ ounce	1 ounce	2 ounces	3 ounces
dried herbs, spices, & extracts				
Black peppercorns	as needed	as needed	as needed	as needed
Cayenne pepper	¼ ounce	¼ ounce	¼ ounce	½ ounce
Salt	as needed	as needed	as needed	as needed
Vanilla extract	¼ ounce	¼ ounce	½ ounce	¾ ounce
miscellaneous				
Ginger ale	5 ounces	10 ounces	20 ounces	30 ounces
Instant coffee granules	½ ounce	1 ounce	2 ounces	3 ounces
Pineapple juice	18 ounces	36 ounces	72 ounces	108 ounces

on the beach luau shopping list: 1 to 2 days before

Ingredients	12 people	25 people	50 people	75 people
produce				
Celery	6 ounces	12 ounces	24 ounces	36 ounces
Fresh cilantro	¾ ounce	1 ounce	2¼ ounces	4½ ounces
Fresh ginger	1 ounce	2 ounces	4 ounces	6 ounces
Fresh parsley	2¼ ounces	4½ ounces	9 ounces	13½ ounces
Garlic	1 head	2 heads	3 heads	4 heads
Green onions	2 bunches	4 bunches	8 bunches	12 bunches
Jalapeño peppers	1	2	3	5
Lemon juice	1 ounce (or 1 lemon)	2 ounces (or 2 lemons)	4 ounces (or 4 lemons)	6 ounces (or 6 lemons)
Limes	3	5	10	15
Mangoes	4	8	16	24
Maui or red onions	1 pound	2 pounds	3 pounds	6 pounds
Pineapples	1 (6 ounces flesh)	1 (10 ounces flesh)	2 (20 ounces flesh)	3 (30 ounces flesh)
dairy, cheese, & deli				
Large eggs	2	4	7	11
Unsalted butter	6 ounces	12 ounces	1½ pounds	2¼ pounds
meat & seafood				
Baby-back pork spareribs	10 pounds	20 pounds	40 pounds	60 pounds
Bacon	4 ounces	8 ounces	1 pound	1½ pounds
Boneless, skinless chicken breasts	12 (6 to 8-ounce) breasts	25 (6 to 8-ounce) breasts	50 (6 to 8-ounce) breasts	75 (6 to 8-ounce) breasts
Peeled and deveined large shrimp	1¼ pounds	2½ pounds	5 pounds	7½ pounds
miscellaneous				
Orange juice	18 ounces	36 ounces	72 ounces	108 ounces

Always take a calculator when shopping for quantity recipes to quickly and easily calculate the most appropriate package sizes for your particular needs. We have listed most items in ounces so that you are not limited to size-specific packaging if shopping in bulk. When in doubt over what amount to buy, always round up—it's far better to have a little extra of an ingredient than to run out while cooking. If your eighth-grade algebra skills have gotten rusty, remember that there are 16 ounces in a pound and 8 fluid ounces in a cup. See page 73 for additional conversions.

coconut shrimp

ingredients	12 people	25 people	50 people	75 people
Unsweetened shredded coconut	3 cups	6 cups	12 cups	18 cups
All-purpose flour	3/4 cup	1 1/2 cups	3 cups	4 1/2 cups
Ginger ale	2/3 cup	1 1/4 cups	2 1/2 cups	3 3/4 cups
Baking soda	3/4 teaspoon	1 1/4 teaspoons	2 1/4 teaspoons	1 tablespoon plus 1/2 teaspoon
Salt	1/2 teaspoon	1 teaspoon	2 teaspoons	1 tablespoon
Cayenne pepper	3/4 teaspoon	1 1/2 teaspoons	1 tablespoon	1 tablespoon plus 1 1/2 teaspoons
Large eggs, lightly beaten	1	2	4	6
Vegetable or canola oil	1 quart	2 quarts	1 gallon	1 1/2 gallons
Large shrimp, peeled and deveined	1 1/4 pounds	2 1/2 pounds	5 pounds	7 1/2 pounds

(fyi) helpful hints:

• Large shrimp are often labeled as "21 to 30 count, " referring to the number of shrimp per pound.

• Save the original vegetable oil containers for easy disposal. When the used oil has cooled to room temperature, pour it back into the containers using a funnel.

do it for less time:

Use pre-peeled and deveined shrimp from the seafood or frozen section of your grocery store.

($) do it for less money:

To make your shrimp go further, supplement them with fried bananas. Slice several bananas on the diagonal, dip into the batter, dredge into the coconut, and deep-fry until golden brown. (Be sure to fry the bananas first so they don't take on the flavor of the shrimp.) Allow half a banana per guest.

directions:

1. Place the coconut in a mixing bowl.

2. In another bowl, combine the flour, ginger ale, baking soda, salt, cayenne pepper, and eggs until smooth.

3. Line up the bowl of coconut, batter, and a baking sheet lined with aluminum foil on your counter or workspace.

4. Heat the oil to 350 degrees.

5. Dip the shrimp in batter mixture, and then dredge in the coconut, pressing slightly to help coconut stick. Place the dipped shrimp on the baking sheet.

6. Fry the shrimp in small batches in the hot oil for about 3 to 5 minutes, or until golden brown. Remove with tongs and drain on paper towels.

7. Serve immediately, or keep warm in a low oven.

equipment:

• aluminum foil
• baking pans
• instant-read or candy thermometer
• large, heavy saucepan or deep fat fryer
• mixing bowls
• paper towels
• tongs

portion size: 3 shrimp

island-style chicken

ingredients	**12** people	**25** people	**50** people	**75** people
Pineapple juice, divided	2¼ cups (18 ounces)	4½ cups (36 ounces)	9 cups (72 ounces)	13½ cups (108 ounces)
Orange juice, divided	2¼ cups (18 ounces)	4½ cups (36 ounces)	9 cups (72 ounces)	13½ cups (108 ounces)
Dark brown sugar	3 cups	6 cups	12 cups	18 cups
Ketchup	3 cups	6 cups	12 cups	18 cups
Apple cider vinegar	3 cups	6 cups	12 cups	18 cups
Cornstarch	⅓ cup	¾ cup	1½ cups	2¼ cups
Boneless, skinless chicken breasts	12 (6 to 8-ounce) breasts	25 (6 to 8-ounce) breasts	50 (6 to 8-ounce) breasts	75 (6 to 8-ounce) breasts

(fyi) helpful hint:

The chicken can also be broiled or baked in a 350-degree oven.

do It ahead:

The sauce can be made a day in advance and refrigerated.

($) do it for less money:

Use 2 chicken legs or thighs per person in place of the boneless, skinless chicken breasts. Allow extra cooking time for any dark meat pieces.

directions:

1. Preheat the grill to a medium-hot fire.

2. Combine three-fourths of the pineapple juice, three-fourths of the orange juice, and all of the dark brown sugar, ketchup, and apple cider vinegar in a non-reactive saucepan. Bring to a boil over medium heat, stirring constantly, and then reduce the heat to a simmer.

3. Combine the remaining pineapple juice and orange juice in a small bowl. Stir in the cornstarch until smooth.

4. Whisk the cornstarch mixture into the hot sauce, stirring constantly until the mixture thickens and becomes smooth, about 10 minutes. (The sauce can be made up to a day in advance and refrigerated.)

5. Grill the chicken on one side for 8 to 10 minutes.

6. Turn the chicken over and baste the cooked side with the sauce. Grill until the chicken is cooked through.

7. Bring the remaining sauce to a boil if it came in contact with the raw chicken or if you would like the sauce slightly thickened. Pour the sauce over the cooked chicken and serve.

equipment:

- large non-reactive saucepans
- mixing bowls
- pastry brush
- tongs
- whisk

portion size: 1 (6 to 8-ounce) chicken breast

mango salsa

ingredients	**12**people	**25**people	**50**people	**75**people
Mangoes	4	8	16	24
Jalapeño peppers	1	2	3	5
Finely chopped Maui or red onion	½ cup	¾ cup	1½ cups	2½ cups
Minced garlic	¾ teaspoon	1½ teaspoons	1 tablespoon	2 tablespoons
Chopped fresh cilantro	¼ cup	⅓ cup	¾ cup	1½ cups
Limes, zested and juiced	3	5	10	15

equipment:

- disposable plastic gloves
- large mixing bowl
- vegetable peeler or paring knife
- wooden spoon
- zester or microplane grater

directions:

1. Peel the mangoes and remove the pits. Chop the mango flesh into ½-inch pieces and place in a mixing bowl.

2. Wearing protective gloves, use a sharp knife to remove the seeds and membranes from the jalapeños, and then dice the jalapeños. Add the jalapeños to the mangoes.

3. Add the onions, garlic, cilantro, lime juice, and lime zest to the mangoes.

4. Stir gently and refrigerate for 1 hour to allow the flavors to meld. Serve within 4 hours.

helpful hints: (fyi)

- Substitute papaya or pineapple chunks for the mango for an equally refreshing salsa.

- Wear disposable plastic gloves to peel and seed the jalapeños.

do it ahead:

The onion can be chopped and the limes can be juiced a day in advance.

do it for less time:

- Instead of making this from scratch, buy your favorite salsa and add chopped mango and fresh cilantro.

- If time is short, use bottled lime juice in place of freshly squeezed juice, or use a combination of fresh and bottled juice. If time is really precious, omit the zest and use only bottled lime juice. The lime flavor will be less intense, so adjust the amount of juice to your liking for a stronger punch.

do it for less money: ($)

Although fresh mango is preferred, frozen mango can be used. Thaw and use as the recipe directs for the fresh mango.

portion size: about 1 ounce (1 to 2 tablespoons)

hawaiian baked beans

ingredients	12 people	25 people	50 people	75 people
Bacon	4 ounces	8 ounces	1 pound	1½ pounds
Chopped Maui or red onions	2 cups	3¾ cups (1½ pounds)	7½ cups (3 pounds)	11¼ cups (4½ pounds)
Barbecue sauce	1¾ cups	3½ cups	7 cups	10½ cups
Beer	1 cup (8 ounces)	2 cups (16 ounces)	4 cups (32 ounces)	6 cups (48 ounces)
Molasses	⅓ cup	⅔ cup	1¼ cups	2 cups
Dijon mustard	2 tablespoons	¼ cup	½ cup	¾ cup
Dark brown sugar	2 tablespoons	¼ cup	½ cup	¾ cup
Worcestershire sauce	1 tablespoon	2 tablespoons	¼ cup	⅓ cup
Instant coffee granules	2 tablespoons	¼ cup	½ cup	¾ cup
Canned great Northern beans, drained	60 ounces	120 ounces	240 ounces	360 ounces

(fyi) helpful hints:

• The recipe for 12 guests can also be cooked on the stovetop in a large stockpot. Use several stockpots for larger quantities.

• Any canned white beans can be used in place of great Northern beans.

do it ahead:

These delicious beans can be made a day in advance and reheated.

($) do it for less money:

• You can substitute any sweet or red onion for the Maui onion and any strong brewed coffee for the instant coffee granules.

• To save time opening cans, look for larger sizes in club and warehouse stores.

directions:

1. Preheat the oven to 350 degrees.

2. Cook the bacon in batches in a sauté pan over medium heat until crispy. Drain the bacon on paper towels, and reserve the pan drippings. Cut the bacon into ¼-inch pieces.

3. Reheat the sauté pan containing the pan drippings. Sauté the onions in the drippings for 5 minutes, or until translucent. Place the onions in a large mixing bowl.

4. Add the bacon pieces, barbecue sauce, beer, molasses, Dijon mustard, dark brown sugar, Worcestershire sauce, and instant coffee granules. Stir until smooth.

5. Divide the beans and the barbecue sauce mixture equally among the pans. Gently stir the bean mixture to combine.

6. Bake for 1½ hours, or until slightly thickened.

equipment:

• large sauté pan
• large mixing bowl
• paper towels
• steam table pans or large roasting pans
• wooden spoon

portion size: 6 ounces

honey-barbecued pork ribs

ingredients	12 people	25 people	50 people	75 people
Baby-back pork ribs	10 pounds	20 pounds	40 pounds	60 pounds
Soy sauce	1½ cups	3 cups	6 cups	9 cups
Minced garlic	¼ cup	½ cup	1 cup	1½ cups
Minced fresh ginger	1 tablespoon	2 tablespoons	¼ cup	⅓ cup
Honey	1½ cups	3 cups	6 cups	9 cups

equipment:

- large pastry brush
- mixing bowl
- shallow roasting pans or steam table pans
- tongs
- wooden spoon

directions:

1. Place the pork ribs in the roasting pans.

2. Combine the soy sauce, garlic, ginger, and half of the honey in a mixing bowl.

3. Brush both sides of the ribs with the soy sauce mixture and marinate in the refrigerator for at least 2 hours or overnight.

4. Preheat the oven to 325 degrees.

5. Bake the ribs for 1 hour, basting every 30 minutes. Turn the ribs over, and cook for another hour, or until the meat is tender. (The ribs can be prepared up to this point a day in advance.)

6. Brush with the remaining honey, and grill or broil until browned.

helpful hint: (fyi)

When baking ribs in the oven, line the roasting pans with aluminum foil and spray with vegetable cooking spray for easy clean up, or use disposable aluminum cookie sheets available at most grocery stores.

do it ahead:

The ribs can be baked a day in advance. Before serving, brush with the extra honey and brown on the grill or under the broiler.

do it for less time:

Use pre-chopped ginger and garlic that can be found in the produce section of your grocery store.

portion size: 5 to 6 single ribs

pineapple and golden raisin rice salad

ingredients	12 people	25 people	50 people	75 people
Water	6 cups	12 cups	1½ gallons	2 gallons plus 1 quart
Long-grain white rice	1¼ pounds (3 cups)	2½ pounds (6 cups)	5 pounds (12 cups)	7½ pounds (18 cups)
Thinly sliced green onions	1½ cups	3 cups	6 cups	9 cups
Thinly sliced celery	1½ cups	3 cups	6 cups	9 cups
Chopped fresh parsley	¾ cup	1½ cups	3 cups	4½ cups
Golden raisins	1 cup	2 cups	4 cups	6 cups
Diced pineapple	⅔ cup (6 ounces flesh)	1¼ cups (10 ounces flesh)	2½ cups (20 ounces flesh)	3¾ cups (30 ounces flesh)
Extra-virgin olive oil	⅓ cup	⅔ cup	1⅓ cups	2 cups
Pineapple juice	¼ cup	½ cup	¾ cup	1¼ cups
Lemon juice	2 tablespoons	¼ cup	½ cup	¾ cup
Soy sauce	2 tablespoons	¼ cup	½ cup	¾ cup
Salt and freshly ground black pepper	to taste	to taste	to taste	to taste

do it ahead:

The salad can be made a day in advance, with the dressing added later. Toss with the dressing at least 30 minutes before serving.

do it for less time:

If you have to make very large quantities of rice and are pressed for time or short on stove-top space, order cooked rice from your local Asian restaurant and add the remaining ingredients before serving.

do it for less money:

If fresh pineapple is not available, buy canned chopped pineapple and reserve the juice. Prepare the rice using both water and the reserved juice for a sweet flavor throughout. (Be sure to measure the juice and subtract it from the water needed to cook the rice.)

directions:

1. Divide the water and rice equally among stockpots. Bring to a boil over medium heat. Reduce the heat, cover, and simmer for 25 to 35 minutes, or until the rice is tender.

2. Fluff the cooked rice with a fork, and spread the rice over baking sheets to cool.

3. Transfer the cooled rice to a large mixing bowl. Add the green onions, celery, parsley, golden raisins, and pineapple. (The salad can be made a day in advance up to this point. Cover and refrigerate until ready to toss with the dressing.)

4. Whisk together the olive oil, pineapple juice, lemon juice, and soy sauce in a separate mixing bowl. Gradually add to the rice mixture, tossing to coat.

5. Taste and season with salt and pepper. Serve chilled or at room temperature.

equipment:

- baking sheets
- large mixing bowl
- large stockpots with lids
- medium mixing bowl
- whisk
- wooden spoon

portion size: ½ cup

macadamia and white chocolate chunk cookies

ingredients	12 people (40 cookies)	25 people (75 cookies)	50 people (150 cookies)	75 people (225 cookies)
Unsalted butter, softened	1½ sticks (6 ounces)	3 sticks (12 ounces)	6 sticks (24 ounces)	9 sticks (36 ounces)
Dark brown sugar	⅔ cup, packed	1 cup plus 2 tablespoons, packed	2⅔ cups, packed	3¾ cups, packed
Granulated sugar	¼ cup	⅓ cup plus 1 tablespoon	¾ cup	1½ cups
Large eggs	1	2	4	6
Vanilla extract	¾ teaspoon	1½ teaspoons	1 tablespoon	1 tablespoon plus 1½ teaspoons
All purpose flour	1¾ cups	3¾ cups	7½ cups	11¼ cups
Baking powder	¾ teaspoon	1½ teaspoons	1 tablespoon	1 tablespoon plus 1½ teaspoons
Salt	½ teaspoon	¾ teaspoon	1½ teaspoons	2¼ teaspoons
White chocolate, chopped	6 ounces	12 ounces	24 ounces	36 ounces
Macadamia nuts, chopped	5 ounces	10 ounces	20 ounces	30 ounces

equipment:

- baking sheets
- cooling racks
- electric hand or stand mixer
- mixing bowls
- sifter
- wooden spoon

directions:

1. Preheat the oven to 350 degrees.

2. Using a mixer, cream the butter and sugars in a mixing bowl until light and fluffy. Beat in the egg and vanilla until well incorporated.

3. In a separate bowl, combine the flour, baking powder, and salt.

4. Gradually sift the flour mixture into the butter mixture, stirring constantly until combined. Stir in the white chocolate and macadamia nuts.

5. Form the cookie dough into 1-inch balls, and place the balls 1 inch apart on ungreased baking sheets. Flatten the tops of the cookie dough.

6. Bake for 10 to 14 minutes, or until slightly golden on the edges. Transfer the cookies to cooling racks. When cool, store in airtight containers for up to 2 days or freeze for up to 1 week before serving.

helpful hint: (fyi)

Unless you have a restaurant-size stand mixer, this recipe is easier to make in batches of 75 cookies. One batch of cookie dough for 75 cookies will fit into a 5-quart Kitchen Aid stand mixer.

do it ahead:

The cookies can be made two days in advance if cooled and stored in an airtight container at room temperature. They can also be frozen for up to one week and defrosted the morning of the party in an airtight container at room temperature.

do it for less time:

Instead of buying a chocolate bar and chopping it, buy the same weight in white chocolate chips. To save even more time, buy the cookies from a grocery store or ask your local bakery to make them.

do it for less money: ($)

Substitute a less-expensive nut such as walnuts or pecans for the macadamia nuts.

portion size: 2 to 3 cookies

resource guide

free invitations

- Evite (www.evite.com). The most popular free online invitation site on the web. If everyone on your list has access to email, then this site is a perfect choice. Evite allows you to track your RSVPs, which is a great feature.

- Sendomatic (www.sendomatic.com). A newer online invitation site with beautiful graphics.

purchased invitations

- Custom Paper (www.custompaper.com). Handmade papers made into lovely invitations. Save money and put your own invitations together with their pre-cut pieces.

- Dauphine Press (www.dauphinepress.com). For exquisite (if expensive) invitations, consider letterpress printing. This age-old technique presses metal type into rich papers for a gorgeous and elegant effect. Dauphine Press has numerous styles to choose from, as well as custom designs if needed. See page 19 for an example of their beautiful work.

- French Blue (www.frenchblueonline.com). Fantastic personalized invitations you order online and send out yourself. Most cards cost between $1 and $2 each.

- Invitation Box (www.invitationbox.com). If cost is no object, this site has beautiful invitations that are sure to impress. Most cards on this site come in boxes of twenty-five. A great site to get ideas to make your own.

- Vista Print (www.vistaprint.com). Hundreds of invitations to choose from. Prices are very reasonable for these customized, printed invitations.

party supplies, decorations, and favors

- 123 Party On (www.123partyon.com). A huge selection of party decorations and favors online with fast shipping. A good site to visit to get ideas.

- Amols (www.amols.com). In business since 1949, Amols offers many party supplies, decorations, and favors at discount prices.

- Favors Fantastic (www.favorsfantastic.com). A great place to buy very inexpensive frames for party favors.

- Oriental Trading Company (www.orientaltradingcompany.com or 800.875.8480). Thousands of party items, many for children. Great items like tabletop tiki torches, paper lanterns, pennants, giant parrots made out of tissue paper, toys, craft supplies, games . . . the list here is nearly endless!

• Paper Mart (www.papermart.com). Gift bags, boxes, ribbon, papers, and balloons for less.

• Party America (www.partyamerica.com). Locations in most of the central and western U.S. A great online store with fast delivery to the rest of the country.

• Party Pro (www.partypro.com). Another great site with an exhaustive list of decorations, supplies, and favors. In addition to covering every theme possible, they also carry such items as flatware, soufflé cups, trays, pitchers, doilies, bowls, and appetizer picks.

• Party Secret (www.partysecret.com). More than ten thousand items at wholesale prices.

• Party Supplies Online (www.partysuppliesonline.com). A great site for party supplies and favors.

• Plum Party (www.plumparty.com). A bit pricier than some, this site has some very cool items. Seashell and pink flamingo toothpicks, palm tree swizzle sticks, tiki platters, and coconut bowls are just some of the items in their luau section. And there are dozens more party subjects. A great site to browse and get ideas.

entertainment

• Amazon (www.amazon.com). Very large online resource for music and books.

• American Disc Jockey Association (www.adja.org or 626.844.3204). A non-profit organization with a nationwide database of licensed, professional DJs.

• ITunes (www.itunes.com). iTunes is a quick and easy site for purchasing and downloading music.

• MP3.com (www.MP3.com). One of the biggest online resources for downloadable music.

catering

• Catersource (www.catersource.com). A great magazine full of information about catering products, services, recipes, and business information.

cocktail recipes

• Barfliers (www.barfliers.com). An interesting site that not only lists recipes but also shows photos of the best pieces of barware for particular drinks. Visitors to the site can rate the cocktail recipes.

- **Bols Cocktails (www.bolscocktails.com).** A great site for cocktail recipes. You can search by name or in their categories: short drinks, long drinks, straight-up cocktails, shooters, champagne cocktails, and frozen drinks.

- **Planet Liquor (www.planetliquor.com).** Every cocktail you've ever heard of and dozens you haven't. From the classic to the silly and everything in between.

recipes and product reviews

- **Cook's Illustrated (www.cooksillustrated.com).** With both a well-indexed website, a PBS television show, and a monthly magazine that accepts no advertising, *Cook's Illustrated* is the *Consumer Reports* for the home cook. The writers deconstruct one recipe at a time to determine the very best way to, for example, roast a chicken or make osso bucco. They also do extensive testing and reviews for all sorts of cookware and other kitchen products.

- **Epicurious (www.epicurious.com).** "The world's greatest recipe collection" certainly might be. Get ideas for new dishes here and see extensive reader reviews for each recipe. They also offer product reviews by subscription.

chafing dishes, cooking equipment, serving trays, and bar supplies

- **Ace Mart (www.acemart.com).** Serving all areas of the U.S. and Canada, Acemart has twelve store locations in Texas and a huge online catalogue with more than four thousand items and competitive pricing.

- **Big Tray (www.bigtray.com).** Great prices on restaurant-grade supplies.

- **Chef's Catalog (www.chefscatalog.com).** Huge selection of products for home cooks and professional chefs alike, with full satisfaction guaranteed.

- **Cooking (www.cooking.com).** Recipes and menus, a buying guide to new and classic kitchen essentials, and full satisfaction guaranteed.

- **Costco (www.costco.com).** If you do any entertaining at all, an annual membership will save you lots of money by buying wholesale. Many store locations and a great website.

- **eBay (www.ebay.com).** You'll find a huge selection of all sorts of cookware, appliances, and serving dishes from antique to brand-new. Before bidding on any item, read the seller's feedback to see what other buyers have said about them. Find out how much the shipping will be. Also, inspect the description of the item thoroughly before buying.

- **Ekitron (www.ekitron.com).** Beautiful Japanese serving items at low prices.

- **Local area party rental companies.** Many party rental companies have annual sales where they sell items at a great discount. Call around and find out when the sales are in your area.

- **NexTag (www.nextag.com).** NexTag enables you to compare prices of products from thousands of online stores.

- **Restaurant Supply Solutions (www.restaurantsupplysolutions.com).** All items wholesale to the public. Many great bargains.

- **Smart and Final (www.smartandfinal.com).** With stores in Arizona, California, Florida, and Nevada, Smart and Final carries a nice selection of value-priced serving items.

- **Sur La Table (www.surlatable.com).** With stores in most states and a great website, it's easy to find many things you need, and even more things you didn't know you needed.

- **Surfas (www.surfasonline.com).** Known as the chef's paradise, this Los Angeles store has a large selection of serving ware and gourmet supplies. Most are available online.

- **Williams-Sonoma (www.williams-sonoma.com).** Many store locations and a beautiful website. Be sure to check out their sale items for great deals.

spices and herbs

- **American Spice (www.americanspice.com).** American Spice carries hundreds of spices, herbs, and blends.

- **Chef Shop (www.chefshop.com).** Look here for spices and herbs, as well as different kinds of delicacies. A great site to browse.

- **Cost Plus World Market (www.costplus.com).** Cost Plus carries a nice selection of low-priced spices and herbs. Many locations throughout the U.S.

- **Herb Cupboard (www.herbcupboard.com).** The Herb Cupboard carries a line of organic herbs.

- **My Spicer (www.myspicer.com).** My Spicer includes not only a great selection of spices but also oils, vinegars, a variety of dried wild mushrooms, and chile peppers.

- **Penzeys Spices (www.penzeys.com).** Penzeys has a fantastic selection of high-quality herbs, spices, and blends at low prices. You can shop online or visit one of their many stores across the U.S.

- **Vanns Spices (www.vannsspices.com).** Vanns offers some of the freshest, best-quality spices and blends in the country.

cheeses

- **Artisanal Cheese Center (www.artisanalcheese.com).** Fabulous selection of cheeses available for nation-wide shipping. The knowledgeable staff can help you find the right selection for your menu.

index

Denise Vivaldo

A seasoned food professional with 20 years of experience, Denise Vivaldo has catered more than 10,000 parties and has cooked for such guests as George H.W. Bush, Ronald Reagan, Prince Charles, Bette Midler, Suzanne Somers, Merv Griffin, Cher, Aaron Spelling, Sly Stallone, Arnold Schwarzenegger, and Maria Shriver. She began her culinary training at the Ritz Escoffier and La Varenne in Paris, and then graduated Chef de Cuisine from the California Culinary Academy in San Francisco.

In 1988, Denise founded Food Fanatics, a catering, recipe-development, and food-styling firm based in Los Angeles, California. Since that time, she has catered for such events as the Academy Awards Governor's Ball, *Sunset Magazine's* Taste of Sunset, and Hollywood wrap parties. She has also catered and styled food for countless local and nationally syndicated television shows such as *The Ellen DeGeneres Show*, *The Tonight Show* with Jay Leno, *NapaStyle* with Michael Chiarello, and *Inside Dish* with Rachel Ray.

Denise is also the author of *How to Start a Home-Based Catering Business*, which has sold more than 125,000 copies. She teaches catering classes across the country and lives with her husband in Los Angeles.

Cindie Flannigan

After 20 years of working as an art director and graphic designer, Cindie enrolled at the California Culinary Academy in San Francisco. Cooking for family and friends had always given her such joy that she decided to make a career out of food. She has been working with Food Fanatics since 2001, styling food for print and television, developing and testing recipes, and designing culinary marketing and advertising materials. Cindie is also webmaster of www.foodfanatics.com.

Terrace Publishing specializes in book packaging and publishing. They have worked with such clients as Clarkson Potter New York, Bay Books San Francisco, Hamlyn Octopus London, and Lonely Planet Australia.